Fuller in Her Own Time

WRITERS IN THEIR OWN TIME

Joel Myerson, *series editor*

FULLER
in Her Own Time

A BIOGRAPHICAL
CHRONICLE OF HER LIFE,
DRAWN FROM RECOLLECTIONS,
INTERVIEWS, AND
MEMOIRS BY FAMILY,
FRIENDS, AND
ASSOCIATES

EDITED BY

Joel Myerson

University of Iowa Press
Iowa City

University of Iowa Press, Iowa City 52242
Copyright © 2008 by the University of Iowa Press
www.uiowapress.org
Printed in the United States of America

The University of Iowa Press is a member of Green Press Initiative
and is committed to preserving natural resources.

Printed on acid-free paper

ISBN-13: 978-1-58729-691-8
ISBN-10: 1-58729-691-8
LCCN: 2008923957

08   09   10   11   12   P   5   4   3   2   1

For Greta,
of course

Contents

Contents

Contents

Introduction

> S. G. W. says How can you describe a Force?
> How can you write the life of Margaret?
> Well, the question itself is some description of her.[1]
>
> RALPH WALDO EMERSON

"MARGARET FULLER GETS HER DUE" proclaimed the headline, written a mere one hundred and forty-five years after her death.[2] What happened to Fuller between her death in a shipwreck off Fire Island, New York, in 1850 and this statement confirming the renaissance of interest in her? How did what Henry James† called the "Margaret-ghost" gain enough substance to enter American literary anthologies? And how did the way she was viewed by her contemporaries affect all of this? In many ways, the answers to these questions may be found in the present book.[3]

Thomas Carlyle,† none too modest himself, wrote after meeting Fuller: "Such a predetermination to *eat* this big universe as her oyster or her egg, and to be absolute empress of all height and glory in it that her heart could conceive, I have not before seen in any human soul." A friend, such as Ralph Waldo Emerson,† could say that Fuller "occasionally let slip, with all the innocence imaginable, some phrase betraying the presence of a rather mountainous ME." Comments like this led people like Oscar Wilde, who never met Fuller, to produce such characterizations as declaring her one "to whom Venus gave everything except beauty, and Pallas everything except wisdom."[4]

Fuller's life is a good place to start in tracing the development of both her personality and the image of her created by others. Her comment to Emerson "Who would be a goody that could be a genius" succinctly states her own feelings about conforming to the mold of conventional womanhood in early nineteenth-century America.[5] Her father educated her as if she were

The house on Cherry Street, Cambridgeport, where Margaret Fuller was born. Joel Myerson Collection of Nineteenth-Century American Literature, used by permission of the Thomas Cooper Library, University of South Carolina.

The Greene Street School in Providence, Rhode Island, where Fuller taught between 1837 and 1838. From Madeleine B. Stern, *The Life of Margaret Fuller,* 1942.

a boy, and at age fifteen she rose before five, then walked an hour and practiced on the piano an hour before eating breakfast, after which she read French and Thomas Brown's *Philosophy*. At nine-thirty, she went to school and read Greek until noon, when she went home to recite and practice until dinner at two. Then she read Italian for two hours, walked, played music or sang, and wrote in her journal. This type of education clearly did not fit Fuller for what Barbara Welter has famously called "The Cult of True Womanhood," with its "four cardinal virtues": piety, purity, submissiveness, and domesticity.[6] Fuller's piety was based more in German Romanticism than in Puritanism; her interest in purity was more aesthetic than physical; her submissiveness was nonexistent (as she wrote in 1838, "I myself am more divine than any I see"[7]); and she was more at home in a library or a meeting of the Transcendental Club than she was by the hearth of a quiet little cottage. Woman's sphere may well have been the home, but Fuller considered herself a citizen of the world. In short, Fuller wrote, "I have learned to believe that nothing, no! not perfection, is unattainable."[8]

This sense of striving for whatever she wanted came to Fuller early. The way Timothy Fuller educated his daughter meant that when the family moved to Cambridge, Massachusetts, a short distance from Harvard College, she came into contact with the best minds of her generation, and she addressed them as equals, much to their surprise and often their discomfort. She studied German literature in the original with as much enthusiasm and knowledge as any of the men who had actually studied abroad, attempting a biography of Goethe and publishing translations of Eckermann's *Conversations with Goethe* (1839) and *Günderode* (1842). She attended at least eight meetings of the Transcendental Club, the most famous grouping of the Transcendentalists,[9] edited for two years (1840–1842) their journal the *Dial*,[10] moved to New York (1844–1846) to become one of the first women journalists for a national publication when she joined the *New-York Tribune*,[11] and traveled to Europe, eventually settling in Italy in time to become a participant in the Roman Revolution of 1848.[12] Along the way, she worked in Bronson Alcott's† Temple School in Boston, taught school in Providence, Rhode Island, gave a series of Conversations on various topics in Boston, contributed to such journals as the *Western Messenger* and *Boston Quarterly Review*, wrote numerous works for the *Dial* and the *Tribune*, and published such books as *Summer on the Lakes, in 1843* (1844), an account of her travels to the midwest, *Woman in the Nineteenth Century*

1872 engraving of Fuller based on an unrecovered painting by Chappel.
Joel Myerson Collection of Nineteenth-Century American Literature. Used by
permission of the Thomas Cooper Library, University of South Carolina.

(1845), considered the first major book-length feminist call for action in America, and *Papers on Literature and Art* (1846), a two-volume compilation of her best critical work. And, while in Italy, she married an Italian count and had a child by him, though most of her friends in America were unaware of this until after she sailed for home with them in 1850.[13]

Fuller's friends wanted to memorialize her, and in 1852 the two-volume *Memoirs of Margaret Fuller Ossoli* was published, edited by William Henry Channing,† James Freeman Clarke,† and Ralph Waldo Emerson.†[14] Unfortunately, the editors presented more a picture of the Fuller they wished for the public to see than the Fuller they actually knew. The resulting portrait was of an unsensuous, intellectually aloof woman with few spiritual doubts, who pursued aesthetic pleasures wholeheartedly until she married and became fulfilled as a mother.[15] Indeed, placing "Ossoli" in the title validated Fuller's life as a married woman while it simultaneously subsumed the troublesome (to the editors) Fuller of reality. In liberally quoting from her highly edited letters and journals, the editors also provided too many awkward statements by Fuller for her detractors to use, such as "I now know all the people worth knowing in America, and I find no intellect comparable to my own."[16]

The book was in many ways an opportunity lost. The editors solicited letters by and recollections of Fuller from many people who knew her, both in America and abroad. Many of the recollections have been lost, as have a large number of letters.[17] Numerous letters first printed in the *Memoirs* that have survived demonstrate the heavy-handed editorial work involved there, as Fuller's texts were changed to reflect the vision of her held by the editors. As Robert N. Hudspeth, editor of the standard edition of Fuller's *Letters,* has explained, the editors of the *Memoirs* printed only selections from the letters, so that Fuller "sounds tiresomely serious"; erroneously depicted her as "consistent in her attitudes"; combined (without attribution) letters and published works in a way that "obliterates the rhetorical situation that prompted the writing"; presented texts out of chronological order so that the result "obscures the growth of Fuller's mind and personality"; created gaps in Fuller's life where either no materials existed or they were ignored; and reinvented Fuller's childhood from her later accounts of it rather than using her own childhood letters.[18]

But did the editors of the *Memoirs* ever stand a chance to be successful in portraying the "real" Margaret Fuller? As one of Fuller's friends later wrote,

Margaret Fuller cottage at Brook Farm, photographed in 1981 by Sterling F. Delano. Used by permission of the photographer.

"You may say many things of Margaret, but the personal magnetism is incommunicable, and died with her."[19] Other friends of hers recognized that no printed page could convey the sense of Fuller's personality, her conversational abilities, her *self*. Even her brother-in-law, poet Ellery Channing,† no true supporter of Fuller, noted, "Master of many languages, an indefatigable writer, of many experiences, is it not a formidable task to sum up all this glittering wealth, to melt it, and while warm convert it to one handsome ring." And those who were not her friends waited to see their worst suspicions confirmed. Minister Convers Francis hoped the editors had "not made the lady ridiculous," for, "I confess there is, for my taste, too profuse a manufacture of halos, crowns, regal sceptres etc.; too much jubilant glorification." Francis did not "admit that Margaret was in her own right a born queen, around whom others were to gather and worship," and even though he did agree that she was "a most worthy highly cultivated woman, full of a certain kind of energy (I say nothing of any faults;)," he asked, "but was she really divine—was she a goddess—except to her clique?"[20] And in England, Matthew Arnold ranted, "But my G–d what rot did she and the other female dogs of Boston talk about the Greek mythology! The absence

Copy of a lost daguerreotype by John Plumbe of Fuller, New York, July 1846.
Mary Caroline Crawford, *Romantic Days in Old Boston,* 1910.

of men of any culture in America, where . . . nobody knows anything worth knowing, must have made her run riot so wildly, and for many years made her unsufferable." [21] It seemed, as Fuller's friend George William Curtis† believed, that "the fate of the most scholarly accomplished American woman [is] to be known only by the tradition of her personal friends and their memoirs of her, and not in any adequate manner by her own works, for the literary remains of Margaret Fuller give no satisfactory impression of the woman herself."

Despite Curtis's warning, there have been many attempts to keep Fuller's memory and works alive by biographers and editors of her writings. Julia Ward Howe published an overly sympathetic portrait of Fuller in 1883, and Thomas Wentworth Higginson presented a balanced view of her in 1884. Higginson was the last biographer to use manuscript materials (many of which he gathered for his book) until Madeleine B. Stern's biography in 1942 and Joseph J. Deiss's account of her Roman years in 1969. Other biographers merely borrowed from earlier works or used the *Memoirs*. Indeed, when Fuller was included in nineteenth- and early-twentieth-century histories of American literature, it was generally because of the biographical, not literary, interest in her; as William Dean Howells commented in 1903, Fuller "as a literary force was spent long ago; but her tragical fate . . . has given a lasting pathos to her memory, and this is what appeals to the student of literature rather than anything she said; and she said a great many things." [22] The publication of the first volumes of Fuller's *Letters* in 1983 and Capper's biography in 1992 made it possible for today's generation to finally have a balanced portrait of Fuller. [23]

Realizing that an author whose works are out of print is an author whose works are not read, Arthur B. Fuller, with Horace Greeley's assistance, went about the task of collecting and editing his sister's works: *Woman in the Nineteenth Century, and Kindred Papers Relating to the Sphere, Condition and Duties, of Woman* (1855) included some *Tribune* essays and selections from her letters and journals; *At Home and Abroad, or Things and Thoughts in America and Europe* (1856) contained *Summer on the Lakes* and her travel letters to the *Tribune* from Europe; *Life Without and Life Within; or, Reviews, Narratives, Essays, and Poems* (1860) brought together miscellaneous journal contributions; and *Art, Literature, and the Drama* (1860) printed *Papers on Literature and Art* and Fuller's translation of *Tasso*. [24] These four titles were reprinted along with *Memoirs* as a six-vol-

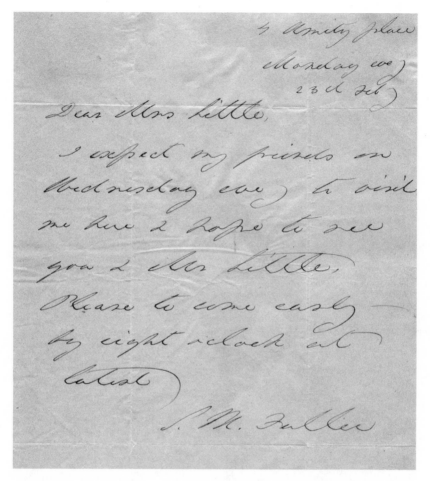

Letter from Margaret Fuller to "Mrs. Little," 23 February [no year].
Collection of Joel Myerson.

ume set of Fuller's *Works* by the Tribune Association of New York in 1869 and Roberts Brothers of Boston in 1874 (and later reprintings), but all of her writings were out of print by 1900. Even though Arthur Fuller "improved" his sister's writing by revising what he thought her ungraceful style and deleting what he considered irrelevant examples and passages, he was a model editor compared to the two men who first brought Fuller's writings before the public in the twentieth century.

Mason Wade began *The Writings of Margaret Fuller* (1941) by stating that his "book has been put together in the belief that the merit of Margaret

Painting of Margaret Fuller by Thomas Hicks, Rome, 1848. Used by permission of Constance Fuller Threinen.

Fuller's work has been obscured by the richness of her personality and the melodrama of her life," but, he then continued, "She was by no means a great writer. She wrote too much, with necessity driving her pen; she wrote too hastily, with a constitutional impatience of organization and detail; she wrote awkwardly, for conversation and not the written word was her natural medium." Even though Wade claimed that he wanted to rescue Fuller from "obscurity and neglect," it was without intending "to establish her as a great figure in American literature, for that she clearly was not, but rather as a literary journalist of no mean ability."[25] Perry Miller painted Fuller as the American Corinne, as the subtitle to his *Margaret Fuller: American Romantic* (1963) suggested. While he praised her *Tribune* articles ("Only a few of the better pieces of Edgar Allan Poe can stand beside" them), he also warned, "I insist that, in the final analysis, the publications of Margaret Fuller constitute a gallant, albeit a minor, chapter in the history of America's persisting quest for self-realization." Not only was her "'feminist' propaganda . . . actually a slight contribution to the campaign for 'women's rights,'" Fuller "may easily be dismissed as an eccentric, as no true voice of American civilization." Adding to the anti-female bias (or even downright misogyny), Miller went on: Fuller "cannot be dissociated from the hyperbolically female intellectualism of the period, the slightest invocation of which invites our laughter" and "She stood for the heart, even though so terribly endowed with brains."[26] Fortunately, more recent anthologies treat Fuller seriously as a writer and as a reformer,[27] and with the resurgence of Fuller studies in the early 1970s, it was possible to see her as worthy of being placed in the same grouping as the canonical Concord writers who were her friends and acquaintances.

Fuller in Her Own Time gives Fuller her due by presenting the differing personal reactions to her by contemporaries.[28] Surprisingly, though, there are relatively few extended recollections of Fuller, most being a sentence or two, and those very often duplicating the impressions of others. There are some obvious reasons for this: Fuller lived a relatively short life (forty years), and in only ten of those was she really in the American public's eye; many who knew her well were nonliterary women who did not leave records of their impressions; some valuable recollections were lost during the preparation of the *Memoirs;* she was not really famous in her own time, so people had no reason to comment on meeting her as they would, say, on meeting

Daguerreotype of
Giovanni Ossoli,
Margaret Fuller's husband,
1848. Used by permission
of the Houghton Library,
Harvard University.

Emerson. Then, too, their visceral reaction to this bright, assertive female led many to feel that they should not express their impressions in print. An exception was Nathaniel Hawthorne's son, Julian,† who reprinted derogatory selections from his father's journal about Fuller in 1884, which resulted in an outcry of criticism upon both father and son. This episode, says Hudspeth, "stands starkly as a sign of how deeply Fuller could disturb people who knew her; it reveals how threatening was her combination of sex and intellect." [29]

How did Fuller first appear to her contemporaries? A teenage Caroline Dall† first met Fuller at the 1841 series of Conversations and entered this description into her journal:

> Miss Fuller is lively and sarcastic in general conversation—of an under size—delicately framed—with rather sharp features, and light hair—. Her head is small—but thrown almost wholly in front of the ears—. Her forehead of a good height, her nose inclining to the Roman and her mouth, thin—and ungraceful—. Her eye is small and gray, but its flash is very vivid, and her laugh is almost childlike. [30]

Even someone who was not a friend, minister Frederic Henry Hedge,† who felt Fuller had "no pretensions to beauty" (though "she was not plain"), commented favorably on her "blond and abundant hair," her "excellent teeth," and her "sparkling, dancing, busy eyes."

Fuller had physical ailments that had an effect on how others saw her. Virtually everyone who met her commented on her spinal curvature, a type of scoliosis that got worse in life, as, for example, did George William Curtis,† who described "some affliction of the spine" that "threw her head forward in an unfortunate manner." She was also very nearsighted, so that she had "a habit of incessantly opening and closing her eyes, rather than 'winking'" (Willis†), and she used an eye-glass. Her voice was also considered too nasal by some, and the combination of all these qualities resulted in one person's reaction that she "talked in a nasal tone, and lifted up her head to shout." [31]

The main problem people had with Fuller, though, was her assertiveness. Kate Sanborn argued in 1884 that the popular impression of Fuller from age sixteen to twenty-five was as "sarcastic, supercilious, with a contemptuous benevolence for mediocrity, a strong inclination to quiz, and an overwhelming and ill-bred appreciation and expression of her own ability." [32] Fuller herself told a friend that "she was at nineteen the most intolerable girl that ever took a seat in a drawing-room" (Martineau†). Her students, though, loved her, one asking, "How and when did she ever learn about everybody that ever existed?" and another delighted because Fuller said, "we must *think* as well as *study,* and *talk* as well as *recite*" (Metcalf†, Allen†). Lydia Maria Child, a famous writer and newspaper editor, spoke for many women (and men) when she proclaimed Fuller as "a woman of the most remarkable intellect I ever met with." [33] When Frederic Henry Hedge, who knew her well, was told by Julia Ward Howe that Fuller "entertained a very good opinion of herself," he replied, "Yes, and she was entitled to it." [34]

She was also a superb conversationalist. George Holyoake remembered an evening in London with Carlyle, Fuller, and other "famous talkers," but "when Margaret Fuller took her turn they were all silenced, and—their turn came no more." [35] Her Conversations in Boston were well attended, and a major reason they were successful, according to Elizabeth Palmer Peabody,† was that she "guarded against the idea that she was to *teach* any thing," preferring instead "to be the nucleus of conversation." Some found her abrasive: Caroline Dall recalled the "cutting severity of remark to which those who attended her conversations were exposed," and occasions when she had "heard her speak to others when the tears came to my eyes, and my throat swelled at the bitterness of her words." Elizabeth Hoar† believed that Fuller was "impatient of complacency in people who thought they had claims, and stated their contrary opinion with an air," and for such people "She had no mercy"; but, Hoar added, "though not agreeable, it was just. And so her enemies were made." William Henry Channing† was blunt: "Her sincerity was terrible." At the same time, even Dall† guessed at what was often the source of Fuller's seeming outbursts: "She had been long an invalid, suffered intensely, and it seemed to me that half of her irritation was physical whenever it occurred"; and this was later confirmed by Fuller's brother, Richard,† who remembered that the Conversations produced "almost invariably torturing headaches in which her nervous agony was so great that she could not always refrain from screaming."

But it was in her one-on-one relations with people she truly cared for that Fuller excelled—more so when her feelings were returned; and when her feelings were not reciprocated, it led to awkward friendships such as that with Emerson. James Freeman Clarke† reflected on his connection to Fuller this way: "We all dated back to this or that conversation with Margaret, in which we took a complete survey of great subjects, came to some clear view of a difficult question, saw our way open before us to a higher plane of life, and were led to some definite resolution or purpose which has had a bearing on all our subsequent career." Another close friend during the 1830s, Samuel Gray Ward, recalled that at first "I was so far deterred by her formidable reputation both for scholarship and sarcasm that I did not venture to attempt any intimacy," but the following year, after they began to take walks together, "the barrier of reserve on both sides vanished." Ward found "the defensive outside, which had been unconsciously assumed as a protection by a proud and sensitive nature, placed by circumstances at great disadvantage, melted away, revealing a personality of rare gifts and solid acquirements, a noble character and unfailing intellectual sympathy." [36] Even Dall recognized that "her power and magnetic influence grew upon every one who met her more than casually." [37]

Fuller in Her Own Time, then, represents just the latest in a series of biographical studies of Fuller that rely heavily upon the words of those who knew her and were willing to record their impressions in letters and jour-

"The Death of Margaret Fuller Ossoli," a contemporary
depiction of the shipwreck. Mrs. Newton Crosland,
Memorable Women, 1854.

nals or allow them to be printed in articles or books. The result, as Ellery
Channing† sensed, is that Fuller must "be her own biographer, and like all
private persons suffer in the description." And Fuller may not have had a
problem with this, for she did once declare, "I neither rejoice nor grieve;—
for bad or for good, I acted out my character."[38]

Texts printed in this volume have generally been drawn from their earliest printed versions. In all instances, texts drawn from modern editions
that print genetic text versions of manuscript texts have been silently regu-

larized to show only the author's final level of inscription. Similarly, the author's final level of inscription is printed for all manuscript texts used in this volume, with significant revisions reported in notes. Silent emendations have been employed by the editor to provide readers of this volume with as clear and straightforward texts as possible, including, for instance, the insertion of terminal and other necessary forms of punctuation when missing in the source and the correction of obvious typographical errors. Editorial insertions in the text are enclosed within brackets. Complete bibliographical information on all manuscript and printed works cited in the headnotes to individual selections is provided in the Works Cited section at the end of the book; bibliographical information for each entry is given in an unnumbered note following the text. Throughout the introduction, a dagger (†) is used to indicate that a referenced text is printed in this volume.

The illustration on the cover of this book is a silhouette identified as being Fuller by the Concord Museum. The image is by Henry Williams, who died in 1830. The museum's records show that it was donated in 1935 by Mary Gill, the great-great-granddaughter of the sister of Margaret Fuller's father. I am grateful to the museum for bringing this to my attention and for granting permission to use it and to David Wood and Carol L. Haines for their help in confirming the attribution.

I am grateful to Charles Capper and Robert N. Hudspeth for many favors while I prepared this book. Mary Anne Ferguson, Steven Lynn, and William Rivers have supported my work at the University of South Carolina. Jessie Bray has assisted in the preparation and proofing of this book. Holly Carver has consistently supported the Writers in Their Own Time series and without her it would never have been possible. I also wish to thank Ronald A. Bosco, Ed Folsom, Leslie A. Morris, Daniel Shealy, and Constance Fuller Threinen for assistance. As usual, Greta has put up with Margaret Fuller intruding upon our lives.

Notes

1. Undated journal entry, but between 1850 and 1852, *The Journals and Miscellaneous Notebooks of Ralph Waldo Emerson,* ed. William H. Gilman, Ralph H. Orth, et al., 16 vols. (Cambridge: Harvard University Press, 1960–1982), 11:488; hereafter cited as *Journals.* "S. G. W." is Samuel Gray Ward.

2. Scott Heller, "Margaret Fuller Gets Her Due," *Chronicle of Higher Education,* 2 June 1995, A6–A7, A12.

3. A complete list of writings about Fuller may be found in these works by Joel Myerson: *Margaret Fuller: An Annotated Secondary Bibliography* (New York: Burt Franklin, 1977); "Supplement to *Margaret Fuller: An Annotated Secondary Bibliography,*" in *Studies in the American Renaissance 1984,* ed. Myerson (Charlottesville: University Press of Virginia, 1984), 331–85; and *Margaret Fuller: An Annotated Bibliography of Criticism, 1983–1995* (Westport, CT: Greenwood Press, 1998). Myerson has also published *Margaret Fuller: A Descriptive Bibliography* (Pittsburgh: University of Pittsburgh Press, 1978) and "Supplement to *Margaret Fuller: A Descriptive Bibliography,*" in *Studies in the American Renaissance 1996,* ed. Myerson (Charlottesville: University Press of Virginia, 1996), 187–240. See also Larry J. Reynolds, "Prospects for the Study of Margaret Fuller," *Resources for American Literary Study* 26, no. 2 (2000): 139–58.

4. Letter to Julia Ward Howe, 6 December 1887, *The Letters of Oscar Wilde,* ed. Rupert Hart-Davis (London: Rupert Hart-Davis, 1962), 213. Fuller seemed to be fair game for Wilde, who also reported being told when on his tour of America in 1882 "that whenever Margaret Fuller wrote an essay upon Emerson the printers had always to send out to borrow some additional capital 'I's" ("Mr. Pater's Last Volume," *Speaker* 1 [22 March 1890]: 319–20).

5. 20 October 1837, *Journals,* 5:407.

6. Barbara Welter, "The Cult of True Womanhood: 1820–1860," *American Quarterly* 18 (Spring 1966): 151–74.

7. Letter to Emerson, 1 March 1838, *The Letters of Margaret Fuller,* ed. Robert N. Hudspeth, 6 vols. (Ithaca, NY: Cornell University Press, 1983–1994), 1:327.

8. *Memoirs of Margaret Fuller Ossoli,* ed. William Henry Channing, James Freeman Clarke, and Ralph Waldo Emerson, 2 vols. (Boston: Phillips, Sampson, 1852), 1:53.

9. See Joel Myerson, "A Calendar of Transcendental Club Meetings," *American Literature* 44 (May 1972): 197–207.

10. See Joel Myerson, *The New England Transcendentalists and the Dial: A History of the Magazine and Its Contributors* (Rutherford, NJ: Fairleigh Dickinson University Press, 1980).

11. See *Margaret Fuller, Critic: Writings in the New-York Tribune, 1844–1846,* ed. Judith Mattson Bean and Joel Myerson (New York: Columbia University Press, 2000).

12. See *"These Sad But Glorious Days": Dispatches from Europe, 1846–1850,* ed. Larry J. Reynolds and Susan Belasco Smith (New Haven: Yale University Press, 1992).

13. The best biography of Fuller is Charles Capper, *Margaret Fuller: An American Romantic Life,* vol. 1, *The Private Years,* and vol. 2, *The Public Years* (New York: Oxford University Press, 1992, 2007).

14. A particularly good discussion of the editing of *Memoirs* and its ramifications is Bell Gale Chevigny, "The Long Arm of Censorship: Myth-Making in Margaret Fuller's Time and Our Own," *Signs* 2 (Winter 1976): 450–60.

15. Carlyle, no mean biographer himself, called *Memoirs* "dreadfully longwinded and

indistinct;—as if one were telling a story not in words, but in *symbolical* tunes on a bag-pipe" (19 June 1852, *New Letters of Thomas Carlyle,* ed. Alexander Carlyle, 2 vols. [London: John Lane, 1904], 2:130–31).

16. *Memoirs,* 1:234. This is also a good example of how the book distorted Fuller. The basis for this quotation comes from Emerson's journal, in which he quotes Samuel Gray Ward as reporting Fuller having said this to him (1851[?]; *Journals,* 11:498). By making it appear a direct quote from Fuller, rather than a secondhand story from Ward, Emerson heightens the sense of Fuller's egotism.

17. To be fair, they also collected reminiscences such as those by Emelyn Story†, William Hurlbert†, and others, which otherwise might not have been written down.

18. *Letters,* 1:62–65, which also discusses particular incidents of editorial tampering with Fuller's manuscripts. For another example of how individual letters in the *Memoirs* were edited to reinforce a particular view of Fuller, see Hudspeth and Joel Myerson, "Editing Margaret Fuller's Letters," *Manuscripts* 39 (Summer 1987): 242–47.

19. *Reminiscences of Ednah Dow Cheney* (Boston: Lee and Shepard, 1902), 205.

20. Francis to Theodore Parker, 3 March 1852, Gary L. Collison, "A Critical Edition of the Correspondence of Theodore Parker and Convers Francis, 1836–1859" (Ph.D. dissertation, Pennsylvania State University, 1979), 496.

21. Letter to Arthur Hugh Clough, 21 March 1853, *The Letters of Matthew Arnold,* ed. Cecil Y. Lang, 6 vols. (Charlottesville: University Press of Virginia, 1996–2000), 1:258.

22. Quoted in Claudia Stokes, *Writers in Retrospect: The Rise of American Literary History, 1875–1910* (Chapel Hill: University of North Carolina Press, 2006), 125. Stokes has an excellent discussion of how literary historians used Fuller's life to disparage critical writing by nonacademic authors as the "feminized avocation of the leisured" (124) and as an example of how unchecked reading habits (that is, a lack of a paternal critic to help and guide her) led to her later problems (see 123–37).

23. Julia Ward Howe, *Margaret Fuller (Marchesa Ossoli)* (Boston: Roberts Brothers, 1883); Thomas Wentworth Higginson, *Margaret Fuller Ossoli* (Boston: Houghton, Mifflin, 1884); Madeleine B. Stern, *The Life of Margaret Fuller* (New York: Dutton, 1942); and Joseph Jay Deiss, *The Roman Years of Margaret Fuller* (New York: Crowell, 1969).

24. *Woman* . . . was published by John P. Jewett of Boston, *At Home* . . . by Crosby, Nichols of Boston, *Life Without* and *Art* . . . by Brown, Taggard, and Chase of Boston.

25. *The Writings of Margaret Fuller,* ed. Mason Wade (New York: Viking, 1941), v–vii.

26. *Margaret Fuller: American Romantic,* ed. Perry Miller (Garden City, NY: Doubleday, 1963), xii, xvii, xxii.

27. For an extended discussion of the anthologies of Fuller's writings, see Joel Myerson, "The Canonization of Margaret Fuller," *Review* 18 (1996): 32–43.

28. An exception is the essay by Henry James†, which while about her friends the Storys, was written by one who had never met Fuller. However, her pull on him was so strong and the phrase "Margaret-ghost" so powerful (and much quoted), that it seemed an appropriate inclusion in this book.

29. *Letters,* 6:10.

30. 8 March 1841, *Selected Journals of Caroline Healey Dall, Volume I: 1838–1855,* ed. Helen R. Deese (Boston: Massachusetts Historical Society, 2006), 66.

31. Thomas Cooper, *The Life of Thomas Cooper* (London: Hodder and Stoughton, 1875), 312. Cooper met Fuller in London in 1846.

32. Kate Sanborn, "Margaret Fuller (Marchioness D'Ossoli)," in *Our Famous Women* (Hartford, CT: A. D. Worthington, 1884), 300.

33. Lydia Maria Child to Francis Shaw, 2 August 1846, *Selected Letters,* ed. Milton Meltzer and Patricia G. Holland (Amherst: University of Massachusetts Press, 1982), 229.

34. Julia Ward Howe, *Reminiscences 1818–1899* (Boston: Houghton, Mifflin, 1899), 300.

35. George Jacob Holyoake, *Sixty Years of an Agitator's Life* (London: T. Fisher Unwin, 1892).

36. Samuel Gray Ward, *Ward Family Papers* (Boston: Merrymount Press, 1900), 102.

37. Interview with Dall on 27 April 1910 by Edith Fuller, Houghton Library, Harvard University.

38. *Memoirs,* 2:277.

Chronology

1778	11 July	Timothy Fuller born
1789		Margarett Crane born (dies 1859)
1809	18 May	Timothy Fuller marries Margarett Crane
1810	23 May	Sarah Margaret Fuller born at Cambridgeport, Massachusetts
1812		Julia Adelaide Fuller (dies 1814)
1815		Eugene Fuller born (dies 1859)
1817		Timothy Fuller begins serving the first of four terms in the U. S. House of Representatives
		William Henry Fuller born (dies 1878)
1821		Attends Dr. John Park's school in Boston
1822		Arthur Buckminster Fuller born
1824		Attends Miss Prescott's Young Ladies Seminary in Groton, Massachusetts
		Richard Frederick Fuller born (dies 1869)
1825		Timothy Fuller retires from Congress to practice law
1826		Leaves Miss Prescott's school and returns to Cambridge
		James Lloyd Fuller born (dies 1891)
1828		Edward Breck Fuller born (dies 1829)

Chronology

1833		Timothy Fuller quits his law practice and moves with family to Groton
		Translates Goethe's *Torquato Tasso*
1834	27 November	Publishes first article, "In Defense of Brutus," in the *Boston Daily Advertiser & Patriot*
1835	1 October	Timothy Fuller dies from cholera
1836	17 May	Publishes poem on the death of Ralph Waldo Emerson's brother, Charles
	July	First visit to Emerson in Concord
	October	Gives private language lessons
	December	Begins teaching at Bronson Alcott's Temple School in Boston
1837	April	Resigns from Alcott's school and goes to Groton for a rest
	June	Moves to Providence, Rhode Island, as a teacher at the Green Street School
	1 September	Attends her first meeting of Transcendental Club
1838	December	Resigns from position at Green Street School and moves to Boston
1839	April	Moves with her mother and younger brothers to Jamaica Plain, near Boston
	July	Publishes Eckermann's *Conversations with Goethe*
	October	Nominated as the editor of the Transcendentalists' periodical, the *Dial*
	November	Begins the first series of Conversations for women, this one on Greek mythology
1840	July	First issue of the *Dial* is published
	November	Begins series of Conversations on the arts

1841	March–May	Gives a series of Conversations on mythology, attended by Caroline Healey Dall
	May	Visits Concord and Brook Farm
	July	Publishes "Goethe" in the *Dial*
	24 September	Ellen Kilshaw Fuller marries Ellery Channing
	November	Begins a series of Conversations on ethics
1842	March	Publishes a translation of *Günderode* (the correspondence of Fräulein Günderode with Bettine von Arnim)
		Resigns as editor of the *Dial*
	August–September	Visits the Emersons and the Hawthornes in Concord
1843	May–September	Begins the journey depicted in *Summer on the Lakes*
	July	"The Great Lawsuit" published in the *Dial*
	November	Begins a series of Conversations on education
1844	April	Concludes her final series of Conversations
	June	*Summer on the Lakes, in 1843* is published
	July	Visits the Channings, Emersons, and Hawthornes in Concord
	October	Moves to Fishkill Landing, New York, to revise "The Great Lawsuit"
		Visits women prisoners at Sing Sing prison
	November	Moves in with Horace Greeley's family in New York
	December	Starts as literary critic for the *New-York Daily Tribune*
1845	January	Meets James Nathan and falls in love
	February	*Woman in the Nineteenth Century* is published in America

	June	Nathan leaves for Europe
	September	*Woman in the Nineteenth Century* is published in England
1846	1 August	Sails for Europe with Marcus and Rebecca Spring
	8 August	Last column appears in *Tribune*
	September	*Papers on Literature and Art* is published in America and England
	Fall	Travels in England, Scotland, and France, where she meets Mazzini, Carlyle, Harriet Martineau, Wordsworth, George Sand, and Adam Mickiewicz
	24 September	First travel letter appears in the *New-York Tribune*
1847	February	Leaves France for Italy
	April–May	Travels to Rome and meets Giovanni Angelo Ossoli
	May–October	Leaves Rome and travels in northern Italy and Switzerland
	October	Begins living in Rome
1848	April?	Possibly marries Ossoli
	July	Moves to Rieti, near Rome
	5 September	Angelo Eugene Philip Ossoli born
	November	Returns to Rome
1849	February	Roman Republic proclaimed
	April–July	Siege of Rome by France begins; concludes with French invading Rome and restoring the pope to power
	May–June	Works in a hospital in Rome during the height of the Revolution

	July	Moves back to Rieti
	September	Moves with her family to Florence, where she befriends Robert and Elizabeth Barrett Browning
1850	13 February	Last dispatch is published in the *Tribune*
	17 May	Family sails on the *Elizabeth* for New York
	19 July	Fuller and her family die when the *Elizabeth* is shipwrecked off Fire Island, New York
1852	February	*Memoirs of Margaret Fuller Ossoli*, edited by William Henry Channing, James Freeman Clarke, and Ralph Waldo Emerson, published in America and England
	Spring	*Literature and Art*, a new printing of *Papers on Literature and Art*, published
1855	May	*Woman in the Nineteenth Century, and Kindred Papers Relating to the Sphere, Condition and Duties, of Woman*, edited by Arthur B. Fuller, published
1856	March	*At Home and Abroad, or Things and Thoughts in America and Europe*, edited by Arthur B. Fuller, published
1860	January	*Life Without and Life Within; or, Reviews, Narratives, Essays, and Poems*, edited by Arthur B. Fuller, published
		Art, Literature, and the Drama, a new printing of *Papers on Literature and Art*, edited by Arthur B. Fuller, published
1861	September	*Summer on the Lakes. With Autobiography* published in England
1862	11 December	Arthur Fuller dies in the Battle of Fredericksburg
1869	Fall	The Tribune Association publishes a six-volume edition of Fuller's *Works*

1874	February	Roberts Brothers publishes a six-volume edition of Fuller's *Works*
1895	October	*Margaret and Her Friends,* by Caroline Healey Dall, published
1903	June	*Love Letters of Margaret Fuller 1845–1846,* her letters to Nathan, published

[Fuller as a Schoolgirl in 1819–1820]

Oliver Wendell Holmes

Oliver Wendell Holmes (1809–1894) was, like many of Fuller's childhood friends, from a wealthy Boston Brahmin family. Although he practiced medicine (and wrote the groundbreaking *The Contagiousness of Puerperal Fever* [1843]), he is better known today as a poet ("The Chambered Nautilus") and novelist (*The Autocrat of the Breakfast-Table* [1858] and other books in the "Breakfast-Table" series).

Here, Holmes places himself in a long line of Fuller's friends and acquaintances whose first impressions of her were as someone who delighted in showing off her intellectual gifts. He also comments upon her "long, flexile neck, arching and undulating in strange sinuous movements," a physical characteristic of hers that others also noticed. Later, Fuller would report that she was "gratified to perceive" that she was "superior" to Holmes in her "training in precision of thought and clearness of utterance" (Capper, *Private Years*, 193–94).

SITTING ON THE girls' benches, conspicuous among the school-girls of unlettered origin by that look which rarely fails to betray hereditary and congenital culture, was a young person very nearly of my own age. She came with the reputation of being "smart," as we should have called it, clever as we say nowadays. This was Margaret Fuller, the only one among us who, like Jean Paul, like the Duke, like Bettina, has slipped the cable of the more distinctive name to which she was anchored, and floats on the waves of speech as Margaret. Her air to her schoolmates was marked by a certain stateliness and distance, as if she had other thoughts than theirs and was not of them. She was a great student and a great reader of what she used to call "naw-vels." I remember her so well as she appeared at school and later, that I regret that she had not been faithfully given to canvas or marble in the day of her best looks. None know her aspect who have not seen her living. Margaret, as I remember her at school and afterwards, was tall, fair complexioned, with a watery, aqua-marine lustre in her light eyes, which she used to make small, as one does who looks at the sunshine.

A remarkable point about her was that long, flexile neck, arching and undulating in strange sinuous movements, which one who loved her would compare to those of a swan, and one who loved her not to those of the ophidian [that is, snake] who tempted our common mother. Her talk was affluent, magisterial, *de haut en bas* ["from top to bottom"], some would say euphuistic, but surpassing the talk of women in breadth and audacity. Her face kindled and reddened and dilated in every feature as she spoke, and, as I once saw her in a fine storm of indignation at the supposed ill-treatment of a relative, showed itself capable of something resembling what Milton calls the viraginian aspect.

Little incidents bear telling when they recall anything of such a celebrity as Margaret. I remember being greatly awed once, in our school-days, with the maturity of one of her expressions. Some themes were brought home from the school for examination by my father, among them one of hers. I took it up with a certain emulous interest (for I fancied at that day that I too had drawn a prize, say a five-dollar one, at least, in the great intellectual life-lottery) and read the first words.

"It is a trite remark," she began.

I stopped. Alas! I did not know what *trite* meant. How could I ever judge Margaret fairly after such a crushing discovery of her superiority? I doubt if I ever did; yet O, how pleasant it would have been, at about the age, say, of threescore and ten, to rake over these ashes for cinders with her—she in a snowy cap, and I in a decent peruke! . . .

From [Oliver Wendell Holmes], "Cinders from Ashes," *Atlantic Monthly* 23 (January 1869): 115–23.

[Journal Comments on Fuller in 1836 and 1838]

Amos Bronson Alcott

Amos Bronson Alcott (1799–1888), educator, lecturer, reformer, conversationalist, poet, essayist, and father of Louisa May Alcott, was a self-taught Connecticut farmer's son. He instituted such educational reforms as light and airy classrooms, comfortable furnishings, Socratic question-and-answer discussions, allowing students to come to knowledge on their own rather than having it spoon-fed to them, and keeping journals. On the other hand, he spoke rather too candidly for the times about sexuality and religion, and he put more emphasis on the moral and spiritual growth of his charges than he did on their obtaining practical book knowledge. Like Fuller's own Conversations, Alcott's Socratic method of questioning presupposed the innate goodness of his students, and he felt his role was to bring out their abilities rather than follow the tradition of seeing them as empty vessels to be filled with knowledge.

Fuller taught Greek and Latin at Alcott's Temple School in Boston, while also serving as secretary, copying down his conversations with his children. She began in December 1836 but resigned in April 1837 because Alcott failed to pay her.

Alcott moved to Concord in 1840, visited a group in England interested in his ideas in 1842, and (with one of the Englishmen, Charles Lane) participated in the Fruitlands community in Harvard, Massachusetts, during the last half of 1843. After the failure of Fruitlands, the Alcotts moved about a good deal before permanently settling in Concord in 1857.

While Alcott considered Fuller to be "the most brilliant talker of the day," one whose "wit is ready" and "speech fluent," she did not feel the same about him. As editor of the *Dial,* she accepted his collection of "Orphic Sayings" reluctantly, mainly to please Emerson. While Fuller's friendship with and support of Alcott never wavered, her personal impressions fluctuated. After talking with Alcott in 1839, she wrote Emerson that "he appeared to me so great, that I am inclined to think he deserves your praise" (7 January 1839, *Letters,* 2:32). She did notice, though, that there was a difference between the private and public Alcott: "With me alone he is never the Messiah but one beautiful individuality and faithful soul," one who "seems really high and not merely a person of high pretensions" (31 May 1840, *Letters*, 2:135). Still, she could write Alcott in 1840, enclosing criticisms from her 1837 journal, one of which was "You are too impatient of the complex; and, not enjoying variety in unity, you become lost in abstractions, and cannot illustrate your principles" (*Memoirs*, 1:172; see June 1840, *Letters*, 2:143).

[17 DECEMBER 1836] . . . I have secured the services of Miss Fuller, a lady of high reputation, and competent to enter into the views of education, which direct the experiment in which I am now engaged. . . .

[28 March 1837] Tuesday evening I spent with Miss Fuller;—Rev Mr. Dwight also. Miss Fuller seems more inclined to take large and generous views of subjects than any woman of my acquaintance. I think her more liberal than almost any mind among us. She has more of that unspoiled integrity of being, so essential to the apprehension of truth in its unity, than any person of her sex whom I meet; and vastly more of intellectual power. Her skill in conversation is ready; few converse with greater freedom and elegance. Her range of topics seems wide; and she looks at them without narrowness or partiality. Leisure and encouragement will do much for her growth.

I am glad that some interest is felt in her behalf, by those of this metropolis, whose good word is a passport to success. She is destined, I think, to do a good work; and whether she go forth from this city, or another, on her intellectual errand, must attain her end. To her has been given, with the gift of genius, that of prudence; and when these are united, the inward cometh forth from its hidden retreats, without damage to the outward. The spark passeth harmlessly through other hearts, and doeth no hurt to the one that called it forth. When the muse holds companionship with Prudence, she shall reap her own reward; nor shall another enter into her labours, save by doing her meet honours. . . .

[April 1837] Miss M. Fuller left town this week for Groton, her paternal residence. Here she intends spending a few months, chiefly with a view of recruiting her health and fitting herself to enter the Institution at Providence under the care of Mr. Fuller, which opens in June next. She has spent the winter in this city, engaged in teaching classes in French and German, beside her engagement in my school. I have passed agreeable hours with her; and she has left I believe most favorable impressions as regards her manners and abilities. Associated as she now is to be in the enterprize of Mr F. she will have ample field for the exercise of her fine talents; and add to the reputation of the school. She takes charge of the female department, and teaches in her favorite branches. . . .

[11 March 1838] Miss F. passed the afternoon of Sunday with me, being on a short visit to this city, from Providence. Miss C. Sturgis, and my friend Wm. Russell, who gives me his society on the afternoons of Sunday, were also with me. We had pleasing conversation on worthy topics. I read passages of my "Evangele, or Apocalypse," to them, as variety.

The colloquial powers of Miss F. are of a high order. I think her the most brilliant talker of the day. Her wit is ready, and her speech fluent. Her acquirements are said to be inferior to those of no woman of her years amongst us. Add to these a mind of high order, and familiar, from childhood, with good society, and her power[?] of interesting circles of listeners are obvious.

She is engaged, at present, in translating "Goethe's Conversations with Eckerman," for the "Philosophical Miscellanies" of Mr Ripley.—She left this city a year since. While residing amongst us, she gave instruction in the Modern Languages, especially German, French, & Italian, to classes of young women. She also gave lessons in Latin, and French to the pupils of my school. She now gives four hours daily, to instruction in these languages, to the pupils of the Greene Street School in Providence—I know of no woman engaged in teaching whose compensation is so ample. In a community devoted chiefly to secular rather than intellectual benefits, $1000, per. ann. for four hours instruction daily, leaving time for personal pursuits, is ample beyond former precedent. It promises somewhat more honorable than has been awarded, heretofore, to genius and acquirement given to the interests of human culture.

I handed my Journal to Miss F. (up to the time of her visit,) for perusal. Of the women of this time, with whom I associate, she has a large share of my regard; and I deem her most likely to enter into my purposes and appreciate my privatest thoughts and feelings. As some return for the interest which she manifests in my views and position, I hand her these sheets; which, more than any other means, shall best apprize her of the intents of her friend. . . .

[27 December 1838] At eleven o.clock, I called on Miss M. Fuller, now on her way, from Providence, (having left the Greene Street School, under the charge of Mr. H Fuller) to Groton, where she intends spending the winter. She speaks with doubt as to the continuance of the institution, under the care of Mr. Fuller. I fancy that her withdrawal from the school will seal its downfall. I once had some confidence in this young man. But my confidence was, I think, misplaced, and I have ceased to correspond with him. Miss F confirms all my distrusts by facts, and experiences. There is to be no institution for Spiritual Culture as yet amongst us. We are not in earnest in this matter. Some years hence, and the thing may be a fact in the history of education amongst us.

We had fine talk on high topics. Miss Fuller is the most remarkable person of her sex, now extant, amongst us. Her powers [Alcott wrote "of apprehension", then canceled it] are great. As a converser, she is unsurpassed by any contemporary of my acquaintance. She has a high promise. Biography and Criticism are departments in literature wherein she must distinguish herself. . . . Her erudition is wide, her intellect robust, her insight sharp and deep.

Joel Myerson, "Bronson Alcott's 'Journal for 1836'," in *Studies in the American Renaissance 1978,* ed. Joel Myerson (Boston: Twayne Publishers, 1978), 88; Larry A. Carlson, "Bronson Alcott's 'Journal for 1837' (Part One)," in *Studies in the American Renaissance 1981,* ed. Joel Myerson (Boston: Twayne Publishers, 1981), 93–94, 113; Larry A. Carlson, "Bronson Alcott's 'Journal for 1838' (Part One)," in *Studies in the American Renaissance 1993,* ed. Joel Myerson (Charlottesville: University Press of Virginia, 1993), 216; Larry A. Carlson, "Bronson Alcott's 'Journal for 1838' (Part Two)," in *Studies in the American Renaissance 1994,* ed. Joel Myerson (Charlottesville: University Press of Virginia, 1994), 181.

[Epistolary Comments on Fuller in 1836, 1843, and 1850]

L I D I A N   J A C K S O N   E M E R S O N

> Lidian Jackson Emerson (1802–1892), a native of Plymouth, Massachusetts, became Ralph Waldo Emerson's second wife in 1835. Beginning in 1836, Fuller often visited and stayed with them at their house in Concord, sometimes incurring Lidian's jealousy because of Waldo's obvious desire to spend more time in conversation with her than with Lidian during these trips. Even so, Lidian attended Fuller's Conversations. Fuller thought highly of Lidian from the first, and she commented to a friend on hearing of the Emerson's engagement, "I have heard much of Miss Jackson and should think her every-way calculated to make Mr Emerson happy even on his own principle that it is not the *quantity* but the *quality* of happiness that is to be taken into consideration" (6 March 1835, *Letters*, 1:225). Lidian was far more religious (in a traditional, formal sense) than her husband, something that Fuller recognized, calling her "the sainted Lidian" and commenting to Waldo that "the thought of her holiness is very fragrant to me" (11 April 1837, 1 March 1838, *Letters*, 1:269, 328).

Lidian Jackson Emerson to Elizabeth Palmer Peabody, late July 1836

. . . Miss Fuller is with us now—and you will be glad to hear that we find real satisfaction—Miss F., Mr E[merson]. and myself—in our intercourse with each other. We like her—she likes us—I speak in this way—because you know we came together almost strangers—all to one another and the result of the experiment—as Miss F. herself said in her letter to you on the subject of a nearer acquaintance with us—was doubtful—the tendencies of all three being strong and decided—and possibly not such as could harmonize. She will be with us if not called away by her mother's ill health a week or more longer. I ought not to speak as if I had myself had much doubt that I should enjoy Miss F's society. I had heard from the best authority that she was sound at heart—and I could imagine no peculiarities of intellect or character, that could revolt me or repel my regard—if that was true of her. . . .

Lidian Jackson Emerson to Ralph Waldo Emerson, 30 January 1843

The next day Margaret F made me a long call and I had a very good time with her—but I almost fear I did what you will not like to hear in letting her read not only your last, (last written) letter . . . . But I knew it would interest Margaret so much. Both letters appeared to give her the deepest pleasure. She has such a tenderness—such a reverence for you—that I love very much to speak of you with her. It affects me as music does—when music affects me at all. . . .

Lidian Jackson Emerson to Mary Moody Emerson, 11 August 1850

. . . I feel personally bereaved in the loss of Margaret Fuller. She did me the honour and it was truly an honour to care for me somewhat. I had hoped to see much of her in the years to come. But I am very glad for her. How should I be other than glad now that first shock and dread has passed? How happy to be taken with Husband and child—to know no pang of separation to be, after a short struggle with the waters, "alive forever more." The difficulties of life, the conflict with bodily infirmities—with poverty—and perplexities of various kinds; —the *prose* of life and the decays of age all escaped. . . .

The Selected Letters of Lidian Jackson Emerson, ed. Delores Bird Carpenter (Columbia: University of Missouri Press, 1987), 49, 120, 173.

[Fuller in Providence in 1837–1838]

CHARLES T. CONGDON

Charles T. Congdon (1821–1891) attended (but did not graduate from) Brown University. He served as a journalist and newspaper editor in his hometown of New Bedford, Massachusetts, for many years, until Horace Greeley personally persuaded him to become an editorial writer on the *New-York Tribune* in 1857. He also contributed to the *Knickerbocker Magazine, North American Review,* and *Vanity Fair* and served as the New York correspondent to the *Boston Courier.* He met Fuller while working as a newspaperman in Providence, Rhode Island.

IT IS EASY to see what happened when a young person of no special natural ability and of small and fragmentary culture talked according to his own notion, as Novalis wrote. Margaret Fuller (not yet a marchioness, but a school-mistress) lived then and pursued her noble calling nobly in Providence. I saw her sometimes in company and heard her talk,—it would be hardly proper to say converse, for nobody else said much when she was in the Delphic mood. The centre of a circle of rapt and devoted admirers, she improvised not merely pamphlets, but thick octavos and quartos. Such an astonishing stream of language never came from any other woman's mouth. "She brought with her," said Mr. Emerson, "wit, anecdotes, love-stories, tragedies, oracles." She did not argue. I think she had a way of treating dissentients with a crisp contempt which was distinctly feminine. She had no taste for dialectics, as she took care to inform those who did not agree with her. She considered her own opinion to be conclusive, and a little resented any attempt to change it. Yet there was something eminently elevated in her demeanor, for it was that of a woman swaying all around her, not by fascinating manner, nor yet by personal beauty, of which she had none, but through the sheer force of a royal intellect. There were peculiarities in her ways and carriage which were not agreeable,—a fashion of moving her neck, and of looking at her shoulders as if she admired them; and her voice was not euphonious. Mr. Emerson says that personally she repelled him

[9]

upon first acquaintance; but I was so astonished and spell-bound by her eloquence, by such discourse as I had never before heard from a woman, and have never heard from a woman since, that I sat in silence, and, if my ears had been fifty instead of two, I should have found an excellent use for them. I do not mean to say that I comprehended all that she said; I had not read the philosophers and poets of Germany as she had: but simply to listen was enough, without cheap understanding. Something like this fascination must have been exercised by Coleridge over the listeners who gathered about him at Highgate, and went away charmed but puzzled,—delighted they knew not why. Was it a pleasure analogous to that of music,—a suggestion too delicate for analysis? . . .

Charles T. Congdon, *Reminiscences of a Journalist* (Boston: James R. Osgood, 1880), 118–19.

[Fuller as a Teacher in 1837–1838]

MARY WARE ALLEN

> Mary Ware Allen (1819–1897) of Northborough, Massachusetts, received
> her education at home (her father was a Unitarian minister) and in private
> schools in Brookline and Northampton, Massachusetts. She began attend-
> ing the Green Street School in Providence, Rhode Island, in December 1837,
> remaining there for less than a year. Allen married Dr. Joshua Jewett Johnson
> (1809–1884) in 1840, settling in Northborough. The couple had six children,
> the eldest of whom, Harriet Hall Johnson (1842–1929?), is the author of this
> essay and the only child to survive to adulthood. Mary Allen was strongly
> influenced by Fuller's empowering comments, such as Fuller's statement to
> the class that "we must *think* as well as *study, and talk* as well as *recite.*"

To MARGARET FULLER and her biographers the eighteen months of her employment as "Lady Superior" in the Green Street School, Providence, R.I.,
were little more than an incident in her remarkable and varied career, but
to a small group of the old scholars in that school it was a most important
epoch in their lives.

The high principles and lofty ideals of the talented woman whom they
began by fearing and ended by loving with intense devotion, inspired them
with a conscientious regard for duty and courage to meet the trials and discipline of life, which had a large share in the development of their characters; and through their mutual affection for each other and reverence for
their teacher was formed and cemented a friendship which lasted through
life, for most of the number a period of nearly sixty years.

This remarkable "school-girl friendship" appears to have crystallized
around one of their number with whom a close and intimate correspondence was maintained for all that long period, varied by occasional visits to
Providence, and receiving her friends in her own home.

Among a trunkful of old letters has recently been discovered some of the
early letters in this correspondence and also letters written by herself to her
parents while a member of the school, which give such vivid pictures of the

daily work in Miss Fuller's classes, and of her influence upon and personal relations to her pupils, that it has seemed well to reproduce them, in this centennial year of her birth, as a tribute to the woman as well as the genius and scholar.

It should be remembered that these are genuine letters, written in the freshness of youth and the exuberance of new and novel experiences, and as such give the pupil's unbiased opinion of the school and the teacher.

Mary [Allen], by and to whom these letters were written, was the eldest daughter of a country minister, himself an educator of some note and influence, with a large family and small salary, who, together with his talented and self-sacrificing wife, was always ready to make every exertion in order to give their children all educational advantages in their power.

A much beloved aunt living in Providence was most happy to give Mary a home while there, and thus make it possible for her to become for a few months a member of the school with the special object of availing herself of Miss Fuller's instructions to the utmost of her ability.

In her letters to her parents is told the story of its accomplishment. The first is dated Dec. 20, 1837:

I am delighted with the school so far. . . . Do you know, I am more deficient in history than almost anything? If you could only hear one of Miss F.'s recitations in that branch, you would say, "by all means, study history." I heard the recitation in that and in Smellie, on Tuesday, and cannot find words to express my delight and wonder. It is worth a journey to P[rovidence]. to hear Miss Fuller talk. I was very much pleased with the latter recitation, and, if I have time, I think I shall study it, for I want to be with Miss F. as much as possible. . . . I love Miss Fuller already, but I fear her. I would not for a great deal offend her in any way. She is very satirical, and I should think might be *very severe*. She formed a class in rhetoric to-day, which I have joined, and which, *with her,* I think will be made very useful and interesting. We are to recite once a week in Whateley's Rhetoric. One of the girls asked her if she should get the lesson by heart. "No," said she, "I never wish a lesson learned by *heart,* as that phrase is commonly understood. A lesson is as far as possible from being learned by heart when it is said to be, it is only learned by *body.* I wish *you* to get your lessons by *mind.*" She said she wished no one to remain in the class unless she was willing to give her mind and soul to the study, unless she was willing to communicate what was in her mind, to make the recitations social and pleasant, that we might make them very pleasant by exerting ourselves, that we should let no false modesty restrain us. She said it must not be our object to come and hear her talk.

We might think it a delightful thing to her to talk to so many interesting audi-
tors, but that was not the thing: she could not teach us so, *we* must talk and let
her understand our minds. She talked as fast as she could about half an hour.
I never heard any one who seemed to have such command of language.

Mary's next letter is dated Jan. 1, 1838, and contains a very full account
of the school in general and of the other teachers. Of Miss Fuller she says:
"Miss Fuller is as different as you can imagine. I love her, but in a different
way. I consider it a very great privilege to be under her instruction. She is
very critical and sometimes cuts us up into bits. When she cuts us all in a
lump, it is quite pleasant, for she is quite witty; but woe to the one whom
she cuts by herself! I do not know what she would say to this letter. I would
not have her see it for five dollars!"

By the time the next letter was written Mary had entered upon the full
enjoyment and appreciation of her school life, and was ready for a full account of the school exercises, and especially of Miss Fuller's share in them.
It appears wonderfully appreciative and well expressed for a country girl of
nineteen, who would be considered to have had few advantages of education or culture.

Jan. 18, 1838, she writes:—

I can never thank you and mother enough for letting me go to school here this
winter. It is *exactly* what I needed,—something to impel me forward, something
to give me a start.

Such a constant intercourse with Miss Fuller makes me feel my deficiencies.
She is very precise, and we must understand as far as we go, thoroughly. When
she first went to the school, there was a class who thought themselves ready for
Virgil, or at least thought they knew a good deal about Latin; but she found
they did not, and put them into the grammar, and they have been thirty weeks
going through it, and have just begun *Liber Primus.* I am in that class, and,
though for a short time I was sorry I began Latin, I am now very glad; for you
know I used to like it, though I did not half understand the grammar.

Now I shall want to go on with it, for she makes us understand and apply the
rules. I am studying Whateley's Rhetoric, which I like very much because we
have such pleasant conversation. The lessons are long and hard, and require
a good deal of study. In connection with that study, we write definitions of
words, which, though difficult, is very useful. The first we wrote were definitions of Logic, Rhetoric, and Philosophy, as these words were suggested by the
conversation. In another lesson something was said about Poetry. She asked us

the meaning, and, as no one could tell, she told us to write a definition. Almost all called it a "harmony of words," which she said was very incorrect.

Yesterday she gave us *her* definition, requesting us to write it in our journals; but it was so long I cannot remember more than enough to fill *half a page.* As the words "imagination" and "ideality" were used, she has given us them to define for the next time. I shall not know what to say, but I shall try, as she takes *no excuse for neglect of duty* except ill health. What is not done at one time must be at another. The study I enjoy the most is Wayland's "Moral Science." I do enjoy it exceedingly. There are not more than a dozen in the class, and we have such nice times hearing Miss Fuller talk. It is all talk, for our lessons are *very* short. She says we must *think* as well as *study,* and *talk* as well as *recite.* Then we have our poetry class, the exercises of which are diversified. We meet Mondays and Fridays, and I will try to give you a little idea of what we do. Perhaps Monday Miss F. reads us a story to paraphrase, which she has done twice since I have been here, once a long story of Ferdinand, and the other day "Romeo and Juliet," from "Stories from Shakespeare." The day she reads nothing else is done, and a week is given us to write it. If it is not done at the time, she does not like it, and finds much fault, as was the case last Monday, when not more than half brought theirs in. Then sometimes eight are chosen to read for the next time, any piece of poetry they choose, and, when nothing else takes up the time, they read.

Another exercise we have is this,—a very useful one it is. Miss F. gave us each a modern poet to find out what we could about: where born, where died, where they lived, what they wrote,—anything interesting about them.

The most modern poets were exhausted before she came to me, therefore I had Chaucer, and I have become quite interested in the old gentleman and mean to read his writings.

It was probably after one of the "cutting into bits" of which she speaks that Mary and five of her schoolmates sent Miss Fuller a "round robin,"[1] as I have been told, to which they received the following reply. The original little triangular note, yellowed with age, lies before me. It was carefully wrapped in paper, and, with a private letter from Miss Fuller, was one of Mary's most valued treasures.

To M. W. A., S. F. H., E. M., M. M., M. D. M., M. D. A.

WEDNESDAY.

My dear Girls,—I suppose you are more than half in jest, but I will answer you in earnest.

[14]

I often regret that you have not a teacher who has more heart, more health, more energy to spend upon you than I have; for truly I esteem you worthy of much more. If I were as fit to meet and use life as I was only three or four years since, I should cultivate the acquaintance of many of my scholars. I should wish to know you in your domestic relations and to help you much more and in more ways than I can now. But my duties in life are at present so many, and my health so precarious, that I dare not be *generous* lest I should thus be unable to be *just*, dare not indulge my feelings lest I should fail to discharge my duties. Since I thus act by you in so miserly a spirit, giving to each and all only what the letter of my obligation requires, let me take this opportunity to say that it is not because I do not value you and even (I use not the word lightly) love you. If I did not wish to *give* my love, some of my scholars would *gain* it by their uniformly honorable conduct and engaging manners. And you will do me justice in believing that I generally feel much more regard than I express. And, though I cannot do for you all that another might in my place, let me assure you that, if, while under my care, or after you leave me, you should feel that I can, by any counsel or words of instruction or act of kindness, benefit you where others could not, my ear and heart will always be ready to attend to your wishes.

Give my love to J. I hope I was not too rough with her this morning. Could I but teach her more confidence and self-possession, I should be satisfied with her as much as I am now interested in her.

Affectionately yours,

S. M. FULLER.

This tender and affectionate note deeply affected these warm-hearted, intelligent girls, and enlisted their affections for life, besides making them devoted to her at the time, as her most appreciative scholars, and in the later experiences of the school, her unwavering supporters.

In April, Mary writes again:—

We go on about the same at school, though we hear that it is to be broken up, on account of the heretical doctrines taught there; that is to say, because Mr. and Miss Fuller go to no particular church, and so, of course, come sometimes to ours or Mr. F.'s. One teacher is a member of Dr. ——'s church, not orthodox, and he threatens to break up the school immediately.

Perhaps it was partly owing to this condition of affairs that the next letter says:—

Miss Fuller, who is always doing something for the good of her scholars, has just commenced a Bible class, entirely independent of the school, though chiefly composed of the scholars, and devotes more than an hour a week of her precious time to us.

She has it on Thursday afternoon after school at night. We have met at her room twice, and in those two lessons have glanced over the whole of the Old Testament, which is the only part of the Bible she intends to teach.

Next time we are going to begin with the creation, and read and talk about it. She has devoted a great deal of time to the study of the Bible, though not so much, she says, as she would have liked.

She intended to make it her chief study for four years, with the best authors, but circumstances prevented after the first year, and she has a closet full of books which she will never use. I shall be sorry not to be able to study it longer with her, for she makes everything so clear and plain. You cannot tell how much I love her.

Miss Fuller was not always the severe critic and uncompromising preceptress, for in the same letter Mary says:—

We talked of having a May party on Tuesday, both scholars and teachers; but we have concluded to postpone it till we have brighter skies and softer air. Miss Fuller is going to write us a song to sing round the maypole. The worst of it is that we shall have to give up school for it, and I had rather go to school than go maying.

Soon after this a great sorrow came to Mary, and at the end of the term she left school, and came in touch with it only now and then through correspondence with former schoolmates.

One of them writes, Oct. 28, 1838:—

I cannot find words to express to you my love for dear Miss Fuller, you who know her so well can better conceive it than I describe. She is everything to me,—my teacher, my counsellor, my guide, my friend, my pillar on which I lean for support when disheartened and discouraged, and she allows me to look upon her as such. . . . I had no idea she had so much heart, but it is overflowing with affection and love.

Another, the J. to whom Miss Fuller alluded in her note, in a long letter devoted almost entirely to Miss Fuller's influence upon herself, says:—

I have thought much of late of Miss Fuller's situation. It seems to me that she will not remain long where she is; for, the better I become acquainted with the infinite capacity of her mind, the more I see of her glorious endowments. I feel that her situation is not that for which she is fitted: it seems to me that she finds not here the sympathy which her spirit craves, the minds around her do not, cannot, sympathize with hers. She cannot exercise her brightest, highest powers, for they cannot be understood; and, when she is obliged to bury, as it were, that which is most congenial to her mind, and bring it to a level with the minds around her, it must be a most irksome task, so sadly uncultivated as many of them are. . . . I do not know the motives by which she was actuated [to take the place she occupied]. I cannot conceive, perhaps, the principles by which she is guided; but . . . something within tells me that it is a noble philanthropy which actuates her; that she looks not to the present, but to the future; that she regards it, in the words of Dr. Channing, as "the noblest work on earth to act with an elevating power on a human spirit." . . . I shall ever feel it one of my greatest privileges to have been under her instruction.

That the writer just quoted was right in believing Miss Fuller would not long remain in her present situation was soon proved, for only a few weeks later came letters from each of the two girls, telling to one whom they knew would feel it as they did, of the final parting with their beloved teacher. With these touching descriptions of the last, under date of Nov. 15, 1838, the same writer gives the following interesting record of the last day, in which she had gathered all her older pupils together, a short time before she gave up her situation and left the school.

I passed the day at school yesterday. O how I wish you and Sarah could have been there. I thought before I went that it would seem very different to me from what it did when I was a scholar there; . . . but I was mistaken, for it seemed so much the same that I could hardly feel I was not a scholar still. I went again into that recitation room where we have passed together so many happy hours, and heard again from Miss Fuller's lips that never-wearying flood of goodness and eloquence. O the goodness, the tenderness of that heart! Could her pupils have been sensible of the privilege they enjoyed, what a little heaven upon earth would that place be!

In the moral science class Miss Fuller read some letters that she had requested them to write to her upon the manner in which they thought the Sabbath should be spent. She made some remarks upon them and gave her own views. She spoke of her feelings in regard to religion, and expressed in her never-to-be-forgotten tone and manner her deep interest in its truths and her desire that it might be the guide of her pupils. She then made them a most affecting request: that they would keep these letters for her sake, and that in one year from the coming Christmas they would read them and think of her, think whether they had been guided by the rules there laid down, whether they had progressed in the path of goodness, in the preparation for another and a better world. Miss Fuller spoke of our "sweet Mary" in the class, and more highly she could not have spoken of her rigid conscientiousness and her devotion to truth.

Another friend writes movingly of Miss Fuller's farewell to her scholars, thus complementing Miss Fuller's own descriptions of the same scene, and giving it from the pupil's standpoint a deeper and tenderer significance.

Under the date of Dec. 22, 1838, after speaking of a gift the members of the poetry class presented to Miss Fuller,—an elegant copy of Shakespeare and a ring,—she says:—

Wednesday, which was her last day, S. and J. went with me to see her. She talked to us beautifully in the rhetoric class, but said she should say more to us at twelve, when she wished all the oldest girls to be present. When the time came, the room was filled to overflowing. She began to speak by alluding to the circumstances under which she came here, the many difficulties she had to contend with in finding the scholars so ignorant. She spoke of her manner of teaching, so different from every other; then of her manner to us generally, that she feared it had sometimes been harsh, sometimes too ironical, but that she had never felt either towards us; that the former she had found absolutely necessary to insure obedience to her commands, and the latter she had made use of, not to wound our feelings, but to awaken in us a sense of our deficiencies, to make us feel how little we knew, comparatively, and to stimulate us to exertion. But she said she feared she had wounded many tender natures. "But for this," said she, "I humbly ask your pardon, and I can sincerely say that it was never intentional." She then spoke of what she had done for us, and how much more she had wished to do, yet she thought the time was not wasted, that it had not passed without great improvement. She then spoke of her own trials, of the disappointment of her own brilliant prospects, of her most cherished hopes, and then, oh, how beautifully, did she speak of the faith that had supported her through them all! Her eyes were filled with tears, her voice choked with emotion, and often was she obliged to stop; but she talked to us long of the blessedness of that religion which can alone support us in this sorrowing world. She said she had not introduced the subject very often, but it was on account of her own peculiar views that she had refrained from it, and, although they were everything to her, she did not wish to influence any of us. Yet, she said, her whole aim had been to inspire us with a love and respect for religion, to look upon it as the only thing on which we could lean for consolation and peace here and for happiness hereafter. You know, dear M., how the words flow from her lips, how full they are of eloquence and beauty, and you can imagine how she talked much, better than I can describe it. After once more begging our pardon for whatever in her had seemed harsh or unjust, after having expressed to us how much affection she really felt for us all, and how much she should ever feel for us, and having given us her blessing, she said, "For the last time, my girls, I say to you, you may go." No one moved, every heart was almost bursting with grief, all eyes were swollen with weeping. After a few moments had elapsed, Miss Fuller rose, went to each one, and, kissing her, said some kind word to cheer her, and then left the room. The girls soon followed, all except a few of our own little circle, the M's, J., and I. We sat there talking and weeping alternately for a long time; and is it wicked, dear M., if I compare ourselves to that little band of disciples after the crucifixion of their Master? Their sorrow was no doubt deeper, but it could not have been more sincere. Such moments are worth everything when the purest and best feelings of our nature are called forth. No words can tell how much I wished you there.

Thus the little group of girls to whom allusion was made in the beginning parted from their beloved teacher; but her words of instruction and admonition went with them and no doubt helped them to lead lives of usefulness and self-sacrifice, and gave them strength to bear the discipline of life and to be faithful unto the end.

Harriet Hall Johnson, "Margaret Fuller as Known by her Scholars," *Christian Register,* 21 April 1910, 426–29.

Note

1. It is believed that the "Round Robin" was written to vindicate a schoolmate of rare excellence and character, but so reserved and diffident that she could not always do herself justice, and so far removed in temperament from Miss Fuller that she failed to comprehend her true character, and was impatient with her apparent lack of acquirements. Her schoolmates, feeling that if Miss Fuller realized her mistake she would be too just to persist in it, took this method of calling her attention to it. The "round robin" probably does not exist, and I know of no copy. [Johnson's note]

[Fuller as a Teacher in 1838]

Evelina Metcalf

> Evelina Metcalf (1820–1883) was born in Providence, Rhode Island, and attended private schools there and in Charlestown, Massachusetts. She entered the Green Street School at age eighteen, along with her two sisters, and kept a journal between 23 April 1838 and 9 January 1839, covering eight months of Fuller's time at the school. In 1841, she married George Hunt (1811–1895), a jeweler who was passionate about entomology and botany, and she became active in various philanthropies, including the Sanity Commission during the Civil War. She died in Providence, where she had spent her entire life. Like all of Fuller's students at the Green Street School who have left records of their time there, Metcalf was much taken by her teacher, asking, "How and when did she ever learn about everybody that ever existed?"

[2 MAY 1838] Miss Fuller was quite displeased and mentioned the names of two or three who she thought had not tried nor studied their lesson at all.

She thought there were but few in school whose natural powers were not good but she wished to arouse our dormant faculties and break up the film over our mind in order that the rays of the sun might shine upon it. She wished us to know what we could do and to collect our scattered senses and not say as an answer to every question "I don't recollect" but to think and judge from our own experience if we did not know the exact words of the book.

There are some in the class who seem not to profit by Miss Fuller's kind words of reproof and advice and do little else but trifle when in the class.

I heard one of the young ladies say who did not know her lesson that we should have more time to talk if we did not know our lesson but it is the reverse for Miss F does not feel in spirits to converse after hearing a poor lesson.

After we had recited our lesson Miss Fuller told us the meaning of genius and talent and reason and understanding but I am almost afraid to try to write them and as she has promised to tell them again some time I shall leave it and try to get clearer ideas.

Miss Fuller wished us to bring her some topics on which reason and understanding can be applied and a list of men of genius and talent.

The lesson in Moral Science was very interesting being on the subject of slavery a subject that I often hear discussed at home.

Dr Wayland says domestic slavery is not the relation that exists between man and man but is a modification at least of that which exists between man and the brutes.

I have not time to write any of the conversation though I would like to.

Miss Fuller kindly offered to show the girls that stay to dinner the romantic walk that she has long been talking of. She would not tell those girls that lived on this side of the bridge because she thought they ought to know.

Six of us accompanied her and we had a very delightful walk and had I time I would write some account of it.

We were very much obliged to Miss Fuller and after school wrote her a note of thanks to which we all signed our names to show her that we were not entirely unmindful of all her kind love and treatment to us. I often think that she thinks that we are the most ungrateful beings in the world for we appear so cold and dead. . . .

[7 May 1838] After the girls had gone we had a very pleasant conversation with her until two o'clock. She described her first coming here and how much she was disappointed when she saw the great ignorance of all the girls that were placed under her care. She said she despaired at first of teaching them anything and did little else but show them their ignorance the first few weeks.

She thought their improvement had been more rapid than she could have anticipated and they had made wonderful progress in many things.

I hope she can say so of her new scholars but I fear she cannot of me. . . .

[12 December 1838] How and when did she ever learn about everybody that ever existed? I wonder if I shall know an eighth part of what she does.

Miss Fuller says she cannot be too thankful for being capable of appreciating such minds as Lord Brougham's and that next to doing a good act it is the greatest pleasure that can be enjoyed.

Miss Fuller told us a maxim which she said was worth writing down and which she believed was written by Horace. I cannot write it exactly as she told it but will try to give the meaning.

With sweetness and conciliation in your manner with firmness in your affairs.

We have today reached the end of Dr. Waylands Philosophy or at least the end of his book.

Miss Fuller says and truly that we know but very few of the Doctor's opinions.

Our lesson was very interesting and although Miss Fuller was almost sick she talked all the time as she usually does.

Much of the conversation was about the wars between different nations and the advantages and the disadvantages resulting from them.

This is the last lesson we shall have in Moral Philosophy with Miss Fuller and I never expect to find another such teacher.

Her experience has been great and she is well acquainted with human nature. She has a heart that can sympathize with all, she can rejoice with those that rejoice and weep with those that weep.

Such a heart we do not often see united with so great an intellect and blessed are those who can be taught by her even if it is a short time. Would that there were more like her in this world, how very different the state of society would be if one half the women that composed it had the high, exalted views of Miss Fuller.

May those who have been under her care show that her teachings have not been in vain and though she is no longer to be our teacher in this school let us remember that she may ever be an example for us and that we can draw moral lessons from everything around. . . .

[18 December 1838] After we had finished our lesson Miss Fuller told us some of the great advantages to be derived from History.

She says the best course to pursue in studying it is first to commence with an outline of universal History then take that of ancient Greece with its arts and literature and the character of its great men and heroes.

Then the History of Rome with its thousand interesting and useful things.

Then a general history and after that the history of England and then that of our own country.

She particularly recommended us to study the History of England from the time of its conquest by William the Conqueror.

She said it would be a constant and delightful resource to us and it was a study peculiarly adapted to females.

She said it was not to be expected that women would be good Astronomers or Geologists or Metaphysicians but they could and are expected to be good historians.

She said she had thought that at some future day she might perhaps come back to Providence and take a class in History but she supposed that not many of us would be in a situation to attend it.

If she did come I should admire to be one of her pupils.

We were pleasantly disappointed this morning again by having Miss Fuller again hear us translate but this is the last time, how sad it makes me to think and write in every class that this is the last time we shall have her with us.

How soon how much too soon the very last time of all will come but I will not dwell on it now.

Miss Fuller says we have improved a great deal in French and thinks we have no cause to be discouraged.

She says the very act of plodding and studying the lesson improves us and makes us capable of overcoming greater difficulties and those who learn languages with the greatest of facility do not always learn them best. . . .

Daniel Shealy, "Margaret Fuller and Her 'Maiden': Evelina Metcalf's 1838 School Journal," in *Studies in the American Renaissance 1996,* ed. Joel Myerson (Charlottesville: University Press of Virginia, 1996), 51–52, 56 (entries for May), and Frank Shuffelton, "Margaret Fuller at the Greene Street School: The Journal of Evelina Metcalf," in *Studies in the American Renaissance 1985,* ed. Joel Myerson (Charlottesville: University Press of Virginia, 1985), 39, 42 (entries for December).

[Fuller as a Teacher in 1838]

ANN BROWN

Ann Frances Brown (1825–after 1888) was a direct descendant of one of the founders of Providence, Rhode Island. Her journal covers the years 1836–1839, thus documenting all the time Fuller spent at the Green Street School. Brown married Darwin Hill Cooley (b. 1830), a Baptist minister, in 1857; the couple lived in Wisconsin, Illinois, and Iowa. Both were alive in 1888. Fuller called Brown and another schoolmate "lively as birds, affectionate, gentle, ambitious in good works and knowledge," with Ann the "prettiest" of the two. The "forwardness" of Ann's mind caused Fuller to take her into her "own reading class" (19 February 1838, *Letters*, 1:326).

[19 DECEMBER 1838] Miss Fuller called her class in English Poetry and when we were all seated, she talked to us so affectionately and feelingly that few could restrain their tears. I felt more sad than ever at leaving her and I never loved her so much as I did then and do now. She told us that her *brightest* hopes had been blasted; she was left without a protector and entirely dependant upon her *talents.* While in this situation, she said that she hoped she had put her trust in the Rock of Ages, which had never failed to console her, even in the darkest hour. Kindly she warned us not to place dependence upon *any* thing here below, for *she* had experienced how vain and unsatisfactory every thing is, in this state of continual change, and sorrow. When she first commenced teaching us, her health was so very bad, that she feared she must soon die; but desirous of doing what good she could while she remained on earth, she undertook to instruct us and she said she felt that she *had been* of use to us, and in this she was *very* far from being wrong. She has been so much interested in us and so anxious to do us all the good in her power, that she has devoted much more time to us than she agreed to, when she first came. And yet she feels that she has been quite deficient. She begged our pardon if she had ever hurt our feelings or been unjust to us in any manner, at the same time, assuring us that she erred *only* from judgment—She mentioned one or two individual cases where she had treated her pupils with severity that was unnecessary, but I am sure that they will *all* freely forgive her. One thing she felt sure of and that was that she had never given way to her temper, which she had tried hard to curb, and in which attempt she had not been unsuccessful. She then kissed each of us, gave us her blessing and for the last time, dismissed us. . . .

Laraine R. Fergenson, "Margaret Fuller as a Teacher in Providence: The School Journal of Ann Brown," in *Studies in the American Renaissance 1991,* ed. Joel Myerson (Charlottesville: University Press of Virginia, 1991), 111.

[Fuller as a Teacher in 1838–1839]

ANNA GALE AND OTHERS

Anna Davis Gale (1818–1851), like her best friend Mary Ware Allen, was born in Northborough, Massachusetts. She attended the Green Street School from 19 December 1837 through 7 March 1838, when she was forced to leave because of her father's financial problems. She married George Barnes (1815–1900), a farmer, in 1842. They had no children.

IN JUNE, 1837, Margaret Fuller became an assistant teacher in the Green Street School in Providence, Rhode Island. Her connection with Bronson Alcott's controversial school in Boston had been terminated in the preceding April, and, in spite of her desire to work on a projected life of Goethe, she felt the necessity of the independence which the $1,000 salary as a teacher would provide. Although she taught with reluctance, it is evident from a journal and letters written at the time that she taught well; and the fact that she was revered by many of her pupils is also made clear.

The Green Street School, which had opened in June with a dedication by Ralph Waldo Emerson, was under the direction of Mr. Hiram Fuller, who was not related to her. The building was in the architectural form of a Greek Temple, and was elegantly furnished with velvet-covered desks, a library, piano, and busts. Mr. Fuller, while not notably energetic, was an excellent disciplinarian, and he laid great stress upon the good manners of his scholars. In addition to Margaret Fuller, his assistants were Mrs. Nias and Miss Aborn. Both seem to have been competent teachers, but Miss Fuller was primarily interested in developing the originality and independence of thought of her scholars.

These glimpses, insofar as they concern her thoughts, show that she practiced what she taught. Her own originality and independence of mind were here at work. Whether the problem under discussion in class was the existence of evil, the occurrence of the millennium, the doctrine of the atonement, or the origins of piety, she wrestled with it on her own and her answer was her own. Her words on it had the aspect of self-communion.

There is thus more here than the mere content of her thought—itself of some interest—and it was doubtless this extra ingredient which, in spite of difficulties, won her the extraordinary devotion of some of her students. She was at this time under thirty.

A course in Wayland's *Moral Science* was the vehicle which she used, in large part, to disturb the preconceived ideas of her eighteen- and nineteen-year-old students, and some of the twists which she gave to Dr. Wayland's text must have seemed iconoclastic. On January 5, 1838, Anna D. Gale made the following entry in her journal:

> But the ancients formed no pure, just and sublime conceptions of a Deity, ex-cepting Socrates and his followers. Miss Fuller thought that no one ever had, or ever could exceed the views which he formed, and that if he had lived when Christ was upon the earth, he would have been glad to have owned him as one of his disciples. But those philosophers took no pains to disseminate their views amongst others—they thought the common people were incapable of un-derstanding them. Miss Fuller said that Dr. Wayland's thoughts would lay upon our minds, like a dry husk, unless they take root sufficiently deep to produce one little thought of our own, something entirely original; then we shall derive advantage from this study.

On another occasion, Anna's journal shows Margaret Fuller struggling with the conceptions of evil and reincarnation:

> The lesson today is upon the obligation we owe to God. But Miss Fuller said in the recitation room that she did not agree with Dr. Wayland. She thought that since God has created us, he is under obligation to create us capable of being happy; and that we have a claim upon the justice of God, for we cannot conceive of a God without a conscience, and therefore he could not justify himself in cre-ating a being only to be miserable. It is not necessary to bear about us this load of gratitude; there is enough left without this. Miss Fuller said that a question which had troubled many was, why God had not created us, at once, pure and holy like the angels in Heaven?—why there was evil in the world? I ventured to suggest that perhaps we were to be happier from the consciousness of having overcome temptation; but someone immediately suggested that nothing could exceed perfect happiness. I asked her what she thought angels were. She said that she supposed that they were heavenly messengers, but she could not look into angelic nature—If angels are not like unto Gods, why may we not carry this question still farther, and ask why God did not create us still more like himself. Miss Fuller said that her mind was not satisfied upon this subject; and that it

was something which could not be answered now, and its being attempted to be answered was one cause of there being so many infidels. Miss Fuller asked if we thought the world was formed to constitute our happiness. She thought it was not, for those who were the most pure and good were those who met with the most troubles and afflictions; they were the most worthy to suffer. In the course of the conversation Miss Fuller remarked that she believed the soul was progressive, though some are contented with supposing that we shall always remain in the same state. If this is true, if the soul is actually to go on progressing through the ages and ages of eternity, why may we not suppose that in the course of that endless period of time we may even surpass the angels in knowledge, power and glory, if it is possible to surpass them; and why may not this be one reason why God has created us differently. Some people believe that there is an intermediate state between this and one in which we are fixed eternally, unchangeably and forever; some believe that we have just died in some other world when we are born in this; and some believe that part of our happiness in another world will consist in having a certain number placed under our charge and care, and that to make them good and holy will be the reward of cultivating our benevolent feelings.

During her whole life, Margaret Fuller was, of course, devoted to those who, like Goethe and Emerson, were capable of original thought. This preoccupation is illustrated in the following passage:

Miss Fuller in speaking of the Bible, asked us what character in the Old Testament we thought the most interesting. Abraham, Moses, and Daniel were mentioned. Miss Fuller said she thought there was something remarkable in the character of Moses. His life was preserved in so singular a manner; he was born a slave, belonging to a persecuted nation, but was rescued from the ignorance and degradation in which they were kept, and placed amidst the splendours, luxuries, and refinements of an Egyptian court. But though surrounded by the temptations in which such a situation must necessarily have placed him, he forgot not his poor and despised people, but with the assistance of God delivered them from the hands of their cruel oppressors. His writings show that he was a man who possessed a superior mind.

The activities of the Millerites made the question of the millennium of particular concern. The teacher discussed this matter and took the occasion as well to express her views on the possibility of a new dispensation:

The subject of the millen[n]ium was introduced. Miss Fuller gave us her opinion respecting it, because she said it was so well made up. She thought there would never be a state of perfection in this world. If sin ceased to exist, virtue must. Some people have fixed the period for the commencement of the millen[n]ium within ten years from now, and some believe that all our heaven will be here; they cannot conceive of anything more beautiful than some parts of the earth, and if it were not for sin it would be perfect. Miss Fuller said she would not deny but what this might be so; but she was not so fond of pitching her tent here, she was not so much attached to this world, and she liked to think of living in some higher sphere where our minds will be more enlarged and exalted.—Dr. Wayland thought we had no reason to expect another dispensation; that in fact another would only be at variance with this. Miss Fuller said she did not see why there should not be another, if we ever should become so corrupt as to need one.

While the teacher was always willing to express her own views on any subject, there is reason to believe that she took some care not to impose her views on her students. She did not care what they thought, but she very definitely wanted them to think.

Our lesson referred to the great doctrine of atonement. Miss Fuller stated to us the two different views which were taken of it, saying that she did not wish to influence us in favour or against either, or hurt anyone's feelings. Some thought it meant reconciliation; that Jesus by his death showed us how we might be reconciled to God; that he thus testified his divine mission, by being ready to seal it with his blood. Others suppose that Jesus was offered as a sacrifice for an atonement of the sins of the world; that he bore the weights of the sins of all who lived before, and all who should live after him. And they think that none, however good their lives may appear, can enjoy happiness hereafter unless they have this belief, but this faith cannot exist without works.

Another somewhat similar entry even shows a certain amount of humility:

Miss Fuller said that she had no faith in missionaries; she thought that was not the way by which the heathen were to be converted—but far be it from her to say they did no good, or were not influenced by the highest and purest motives; she thought many of them were. But there was in this, as in everything else, much alloy. There was something affecting in it—their parting with their friends—going across the vast ocean and to a strange land to dwell among uncivilized nations, and though she had read many books upon missionaries, been interested in them and admired their characters, yet she did not think the amount of good they did was very great.

That she had scant sympathy for militant public reformers at this time is made evident by the following passage:

[29]

Miss Fuller said she did not think it was anyone's duty to go about the streets crying, and denouncing against the sins of the people, like the ancient prophets Jeremiah and Isaiah; yet there have been people, maniacs, or those who were so far carried away by the enthusiasm of their feelings as to consider this to be their duty.

Her concern for the status of women, which she was later to develop in her *Woman in the Nineteenth Century,* was also revealed in her teaching:

Milton was said to have had only one love affair and that did not amount to much. Miss Fuller said she once saw a beautiful picture of him,—he was represented as sitting at his door, with a mild look from his blind eyes, his hair parted in front and hanging in curls, as was the fashion in those times, whilst his two daughters sat near him, one reading, the other writing. But she said she did not take so much pleasure in it as she should if she did not know that they did not understand what they were doing, for he would not allow his daughters to be instructed.

Over and over again Miss Fuller emphasized the importance of reflective and independent thought.

Miss Fuller remarked that in reading the Bible we must exercise our intellectual faculties; we must not hastily glance over passages, but we must reflect upon them and study into their meaning. Miss Fuller said she once heard of an old lady who was accustomed to have the Bible read aloud to her every day, and she said it was the most uninteresting book she ever heard—One of the young ladies remarked that she had heard people say they had read through the Bible, hard words and all. Such reading is of no use, it is worse than a mere waste of time, for it is accustoming us to read without attention.

Her life-long distaste for hypocrisy and cant is evident in her remarks on charity:

We then had some pleasant conversation respecting the various motives which influence people in performing their acts of charity. Miss Fuller thought it was unnecessary to use all those phrases and epithets which some think indispensibly requisite—in obtaining God's blessing for their virtuous deeds. She thought its influence bad, and tended to harden the heart, to deaden the feelings by making them so common, and that we could perform no good action without being influenced by a love of God, or I should have said, no benevolent action; and God will reward every action performed from good and pure motives, "even a cup of cold water given in his name." But, given in his name, does not imply using his name; but given in his spirit, to be actuated by the same benevolent feeling which he, who repeated those words, showed throughout his life.

Margaret Fuller was far from an irreligious person, and the following long passage discloses her conviction that genuine piety was a natural attribute of man:

Miss Fuller said that Religion consisted of two parts,—Piety and Morality. Piety was the law, Morality the practice. She defined "transcendent" to be a comparative term signifying "beyond what we can conceive." Miss Fuller said that some people dwelt upon the blessing of existence as being a cause of great gratitude to God, but she thought that this of itself, independent of everything else, was not a blessing; and it was only rendered one by God's placing before us the power of rendering ourselves eternally happy; for it would have been better for us not to have existed than to exist only to be eternally miserable. God sacrifices nothing in creating us; He only calls into exercise his omnipotent power, and we reasonably suppose that it would naturally be his employment to create beings and worlds for happiness. Dr. Wayland compares the difference between us and God to that between a servant and his master. Miss Fuller showed us that the difference was still greater; for a servant might do more than was required of him and by a thousand little offices of kindness oblige his master to feel as though he had incurred a debt which he could not repay with money. Not so with us; we can never do more than our duty. We were led to speak of the various idols which people have, such as Money, Fame and Power. Beauty was mentioned, but Miss Fuller thought we could not love Beauty too well if we looked up through Nature to Nature's God. The possession of it could not injure us, if we were contented with simply being beautiful. Speaking of gratitude to God Miss F. asked us if we thought it was a natural impulse of our nature. If she had asked me in particular I should unhesitatingly have answered that it was. She then asked us if we could think of any particular instance in our lives—if ever anything had occurred so particularly agreeable and pleasant that our first thought was to fall upon our knees and thank God; or whether we should do thus only because we have been taught to do so. She then referred us to little children. If you give them anything new they do not stop and thank you, but you must tell them to do it over and over again. This I have seen done too often to doubt its truth, and I concluded that my opinion was going to be proved entirely wrong, though for once I did not like to give it up. But Miss Fuller said that she had never been taught to feel this gratitude, and there had been instances in her life when she thought this feeling sprung up spontaneously. She thought we naturally possessed such a feeling, but it was destroyed by being drilled into us when children. Children think they are born to be happy,—that everybody is to contribute to their happiness—and it is hard for them to think it otherwise; but it is a lesson that they learn the first time they are shut up in a closet. Miss Fuller said that we are apt to make a wrong estimate of happiness. We see those who are young, rich and beautiful, and we think they must be the happiest; but it is not so. The balance of happiness is more equal than we imagine. We cannot judge of the happiness of others.

Biographers have made little mention of Miss Fuller's sense of humor, but the following passage in Anna's journal is evidence that Margaret on occasion could be facetious:

Miss Landon was a poetess who caused us some amusement. Her poetry is not very valuable. It is very sentimental, being mostly about broken hearts, forlorn lovers, and those who have been disappointed in their love. One of the young ladies asked if Miss Landon's heart had been broken. Miss F. said she did not know; that if it had it was probably mended. Some broken hearts get mended again, fastened together by putty or something, whilst others always remain broken. Miss F. said if we read her poetry we must sigh over it, or we should be much behindhand; for many ladies read it, and wept over it. It would introduce us to many ladies with swanlike necks; more ladies with swanlike necks than were in this school. Miss Landon is now about twenty-eight.

Many people have left records of Margaret Fuller's sarcasm, and it was much in evidence when her students were ill-prepared. One example occurred during a visit to the school by her mother:

One circumstance occurred yesterday of some importance which I forgot to mention. It was an introduction to Mrs. Fuller, Miss Fuller's own mother, though I could scarcely believe it possible she appeared so young. She spent the whole morning in the school and I saw her while in the poetry class. This reminds me of some things Miss Fuller said in that class and which I would fain remember—We finished giving an account of our various poets which was very badly done—and Miss Fuller said that with few exceptions we had taken but very little pains to obtain information concerning them. She pitied us if we had not one amongst our acquaintance who could assist us; she did not know what she should do in such a case, but at all events she should do some thing; she did not know but what she should pull her hair. She said we might perhaps advertise it in the paper. She told us of someone who took a light in his hand, very early one morning, I think before darkness had disappeared, and went about the street as if searching for something. Being asked what he was looking for,

he answered, "An honest man." So we might take our light and go into different streets, and on being asked what we were looking for, answer "A literary
gentleman, who can give me some information respecting the most celebrated
poets," and she thought we should be directed to several—She knew there
were many such gentlemen in Providence for she read it in their countenance
when she met them in the streets. However she would give us some account
of them herself the next time we met; and after that we might go out with our
lights.

Upon another occasion, Anna recorded in her journal an example of her
teacher's directness:

Miss Fuller returned my paraphrase, saying it was wrote [*sic*] without lines—
and she did not like to take the trouble to read anything so crooked, and likewise there was some mistakes in spelling—but they seemed to be owing to
heedlessness—and might be corrected by care and attention.

After Anna Gale had left the school and returned to her home in Northboro, Massachusetts, she received a letter from Mary W. Allen, who was
still at the Green Street School. This disclosed a similar facet of their
teacher's nature.

Today we had an unpleasant ending to the week, for we had in our poetry class
some close questioning from Miss Fuller—questions on general subjects which
we were not able to answer. You know what a faculty she has for making us feel
our deficiencies.

The degree of devotion which Miss Fuller inspired in her scholars is disclosed in the letters Anna continued to receive from her schoolmates. Her
closest friend and roommate, Mary W. Allen, wrote as follows:

Miss Fuller is as dear as ever—says she would rather have you back, than to
have three new scholars—I think she is less satirical than she was last term, and
I love her more than words can tell. She is so funny—she makes me laugh half
the time—We had a glorious time Wednesday—for we recite in Wayland now
on that day, and also in Rhetoric as formerly—We spent an hour in reciting each
lesson, & in Wayland we did not recite half the lesson—not more than three
pages—I enjoyed that day finely. Our Rhetoric is much more interesting than it
was last term . . . I have just finished a horrid job—*writing a paraphrase.* I have
just finished it and I feel free—It is Twelfth Night—I have written it without
copying it—and if Miss F. don't like it, I shan't do it again.

Another classmate, Juliet Graves, earlier in the year had been subjected to an attack of Miss Fuller's sarcasm and singled out in class for her faults. This was done in such a manner that several of the girls felt impelled to write a round-robin letter of remonstrance to the teacher in their school-mate's behalf. It is surprising to find Juliet thereafter exhibiting unmistak-able signs of hero-worship:

I am seated in school but it seems not pleasant as usual here. I hardly know whether it is the absence of the sun's bright beams or of Miss Fuller's shining light which causes me to feel less happy than usual. It is a mixture of both I suppose—Miss Fuller has been absent the last two days but it seems a month al-most since I have seen her. She has gone to New Bedford to attend the interest-ing services at the new church there. She has not been well for some time—she exerts herself often far beyond her strength for our improvement and I fear we do not repay her as we ought. No we cannot—it is beyond our power to repay her for all that she does—We must ever remain under obligations to her that we cannot repay. I feel that I love her every day more and more. She is ever true to our best interests—untiring in her exertions—never weary. I hope that her visit will be the means of doing her much good and restore her to us better able to perform her duties.

On another occasion, she wrote to Anna a letter filled with more encomiums:

But I cannot leave without mentioning Miss Fuller. I have never known her truly, fully until now. I thought I knew her long since but find that I did not, and perhaps I do not know her fully now, for every day that I have been with her has discovered to my mind something which I knew not that she possessed before. O the deep love of her heart! the power that she has of controlling her feelings, so as to exercise always the patience, the forebearance, the kindness that she does. She has a great deal to try her—not only from impatient, careless, thought-less scholars, but from her own feeble health, being obliged to exert herself far beyond her strength, and now too she has a heavy grief pressing upon her—she has lately heard of the dangerous illness of her only sister, one whom she has long been hoping would assist her to discharge her arduous duties. She fears that she cannot recover. At times this presses upon her with such force, that it seems as if her heart would break, and yet she sees the necessity of controlling her feelings for the sake of those around her. She puts forth the effort, and her grief is hidden in her heart. She wears a smiling countenance and speaks in cheerful tones. I look upon her with wonder sometimes when I see how every other feeling is swallowed up in duty and then I think of myself, and ask myself if her example shall not have the power of forming within me new principles of action—of guiding me to that spirit, on whom she leans for support.

Louisa Hunt, a friend of Anna's from Northboro, had entered the school after the latter had left. Her first letter showed her early impressions:

I like the school very much, the teachers—the room—and all connected with it. Mr. Fuller I do not yet feel acquainted with—Miss Fuller I am rather in fear of, although I like her very much, a great deal better than I thought I should.

Five months later this girl, who was originally "rather in fear of" Miss Fuller, had lost that feeling:

I have only one thing to regret and that is, having Miss Fuller leave. I do love her very dearly, and shall miss her nearly as much out of school as in, for I have seen more of her this term than before. She often speaks of you and seldom does so without expressing great regret that you could not have staid here another term.

The rapid decline of the Green Street School now began, in part because of the departure of Margaret Fuller. On February 13, 1839, Louisa Hunt wrote:

I suppose you know from Mary that I have left Mr. Fuller's school (it is six weeks since) partly on account of the distance—and partly because Miss Fuller left it—and I could not bear to conform to a new teacher. I now continue the same studies with Miss Ames every morning—and continue my French with Mrs. Nias—I go to her twice a week.

Three months later, on May 23, 1839, Louisa wrote:

I have not seen Mr. Fuller since you wrote me. It is feared he will be obliged to give up his school—for there has been an orthodox one established in Aborn street lately—and it is thought it will affect him very materially—but I hope not—it would be too bad to be obliged to give up that room to them—the whole of that beautiful building.

On that same day Juliet Graves also wrote Anna:

But it is now much changed. Miss Fuller is no longer there, and many of the scholars have left. Mr. Fuller of late I have heard has been much discouraged. . . .

From Edward A. Hoyt and Loriman S. Brigham, "Glimpses of Margaret Fuller: The Green Street School and Florence," *New England Quarterly* 29 (March 1956): 87–98. Gale's complete school journal is published in Paula Kopacz, "The School Journal of Hannah (Anna) Gale," in *Studies in the American Renaissance 1996,* ed. Joel Myerson (Charlottesville: University Press of Virginia, 1996), 67–113.

[Fuller's Conversations in 1839 and 1840]

Elizabeth Palmer Peabody

Elizabeth Palmer Peabody (1804–1894) was an educational and social reformer who assisted Bronson Alcott in the Temple School, contributed articles to and published the *Dial,* operated a bookstore and circulating library in
Boston, and helped begin the kindergarten movement in America. Peabody
had heard Fuller spoken of as a "wonderful child" as early as 1822, but the
two did not meet until 1827 or 1828, when Peabody was "impressed strongly
with her perfect good nature," her eyes that "overflowed with fun," and her
"intellect sharp as a diamond." Still, Peabody later admitted to Emerson
when he was collecting material for the *Memoirs,* she did not count herself
among Fuller's "intimate friends," as Fuller "decidedly wished" she should
not (1851[?], Emerson, *Journals,* 11:482). Fuller liked Peabody and supported
her educational ideas but disagreed with Peabody's conservative views of the
role of women in society. She also had problems (as did many others) with
Peabody's prose style: "I never saw any thing like her for impossibility of being clear and accurate in a brief space" (18 April 1842, *Letters,* 3:60).

   No doubt Peabody heard herself referred to when Fuller commented that
"women were capable of intellectual improvement, and therefore designed
by God for it." Her reports of Fuller's Conversations are especially interesting
because they describe some of the major themes that Fuller would later develop in her writings, especially, *Woman in the Nineteenth Century,* with such
comments as "the man and the woman had each every faculty and element
of mind—but that they were combined in different proportions. . . . [One
participant] asked if she thought that there was any quality in the masculine
or in the feminine mind that did not belong to the other. Margaret said no—
she did not. . . . Because if all admitted it, it would follow of course that we
should hear no more of repressing or subduing faculties because they were
not fit for women to cultivate." Peabody's account of Fuller's Conversations is
valuable as a report of one attended by women only, whereas Caroline Dall's
account (below) documents a series at which men were admitted; and the
men tended to dominate, both because of their own proclivities and because
they often did not feel that women were worth listening to.

MISS FULLER IN HER introductory conversation enlarged upon the topics which she touched in her letter to Mrs. Ripley. She spoke of the education of our grandmothers as healthy though confined, and said that in what was called the improved education of the present day the boundaries had been enlarged but not filled up faithfully—and consequently superficialness, unhealthiness, and pedantry had been introduced—This perhaps was a necessary effect—temporarily,—of the transition—and did not prove that an attempt at enlargement was not legitimate. She believed that enlargement not only lawful in itself—but inevitable. In our country women had grown to be in situations which gave them a great deal of leisure—even discharging all their domestic duties—all the duties involved in the cultivation of the affections as their especial province—they had more leisure on the whole than the men of our country. This leisure must be employed in some way—to employ it intellectually was on all accounts the best way—for women were capable of intellectual improvement, and therefore designed by God for it.

But the attempts at intellectual cultivation involved these evils of unhealthiness of mind—pedantry—superficialness.

The question is, why is it so? Is it that there is too much intellectual cultivation or not enough? Let us examine. Women now are taught all that men are. Is it so? Or is it not that they run over superficially even *more* studies—without being really taught any thing. Thus when they come to the business of life and the application of knowledge they find that they are *inferior*—and all their studies have not given them that practical good sense and mother wisdom and wit which grew up with our grandmothers at the spinning wheel. Is not the difference between [two or three words lost] education of women and that of men this. Men are called on from a very early period to *reproduce* all that they learn. First their college exercises—their political duties—the exercises of professional study—the very first action of life in any direction—calls upon them for *reproduction* of what they have learnt. This is what is most neglected in the education of women—they learn without any attempt to reproduce. The little reproduction to which they are called seems mainly for the purposes of idle display. It is to supply this deficiency that these conversations have been planned. Miss Fuller guarded against the idea that she was to *teach* any thing. She merely meant to be the nucleus of conversation. She had had some experience in conducting such a conversation,—and she proposed to be *one*

[38]

to give her own best thoughts on any subject that was named, as a means of calling out the thoughts of others. She thought it would be a good plan to take up subjects on which we knew words—and had impressions, and vague irregular notions, and compel ourselves to define those words, to turn these impressions into thoughts, and to systematise these thoughts. We should probably have to go through some mortification in finding how much less we knew than we thought—and on the other hand we should probably find ourselves encouraged by seeing how much and how rapidly we should gain by making a simple and clear effort for expression.

These were Miss Fuller's most important thoughts. They were expressed with much illustration—and many more ideas were mingled with them—and all was expressed with the most captivating address and grace—and the most beautiful modesty. The position in which she placed herself with respect to the rest was entirely ladylike and companionable. She said all that she intended, to express the earnest purpose with which she came, and expected all who shared her purpose to come—and with great tact indicated all things she thought might spoil the meeting. . . .

. . . The question was then started as to the degree in which this element [Genius] should act in the true culture of a human being. This Miss F. said was the great question. How far—how predominatingly should Genius be cultivated or rather allowed free play. The question was also started whether genius produced happiness—on the whole. Miss F. admitted that if genius was to be judged by its quantity rather than its *quality,* Genius might as well be left out. (As I did not hear this conversation I can do no Justice to details and the answers to these questions.) Bacchus was mentioned. Miss F. said he signified to her mind the Earth's answer to the Sun—he was the *warm side* of Genius as Apollo was the *light* of Genius. . . .

Miss Fuller began the eighth conversation by reading her statement— viz. "I accept the Trinity of Beautiful, Good, and True, as the best statement I know of the Absolute. Of their absolute existence we can only say. It is—for the Finite vainly questions the Infinite with why or how. When the Finite says 'Are you there?' it is answered 'yes.' When the Finite says 'let me draw nearer and look more closely,' it is not denied—but when it says 'Give me thy secret' the answer is 'Not unless you become myself. Be me, else you shall not know me.' And all further questioning is but the impatient longing of a love which would fain drink now to thirst no more, and relieves its feverish restlessness by means only so far availing as they serve to fill up the interval of separation, not make it be forgotten. Since then, this existence cannot be scrutinized by us, limited existences, how are we to define Beauty. The word implies a thought, what are the limitations of the thought? In reference to us there are conditions, limitations ascertainable. How shall we limit that perception of the Infinite which calls up in our minds the term Beauty? I suppose best by its mode of action as distinguishable from the other constituents of Divine law. When divine law operates toward us in any perfect manifestation, Good implies the design, Truth the organic relation, Beauty the result. We answer to this threefold appeal, with the intellect to the true, with the affection to the good,—to the Beautiful with that result of both, which we call soul. From this response in the human soul, I infer that in the divine Soul True and Good are enfolded in the Beautiful, that but for us or for secondary existences like us they would never manifest themselves separately, that there would be no Good, no True, no Beautiful even, for all would be comprehended in the circle of Beauty. Thus I perceived a seemed truth in what some present have felt, that we injured Beauty by attempting to bound it in the same way as truth or good.—That it is the result of which truth and good are the constituents."

I also found my thought expressed, where it was said that Beauty integrates the whole. Truth and good are as absolute as Beauty, but in the whole they are in Beauty, not beauty in them.

Proportion, adaptation of means to an end, are indispensable conditions of Beauty. But in the operation of Beauty the means are the best, the aim perfection not convenience. When the aim is temporary, the most admirable proportion of parts to a whole, of means to an end, produces no beauty. The useful is sometimes spoken of as beautiful, only because it suggests the possibility of beauty, when the same just use of means shall be applied to an infinite aim.

The work of Utility speaks of human living, the work of Beauty of divine life. Every work of Beauty is a distinct passage in the universal harmony. I prefer the word harmony to unity, because unity is the "I am," harmony the "being" of the Absolute. In unity it pauses self enfolded. In harmony it multiplies and feels itself living. Beauty is thus, or nothing. We need not the word Beauty if not to express one in many. Else would the word Unity suffice to our thought. But these words we use are most of all inadequate to such themes. The best language is that of Nature in which God writes. Next best, the fine arts, especially Music which most of any disarms the senses, and gives Beauty free passage to the soul. Last and worst, this arbitrary language, degraded too by being much used for the low purposes of the prose day. It is sufficient for my purpose in our meetings that Beauty be recognised as a principle, as absolute, immutable, not to be affected by our affections.

More than this I myself do not know. As much as this I demand of every person with whom I would really converse, secure that meeting on this ground our intercourse will not be that of vanity, weakness, idleness, but the reciprocal encouragement of beings who acknowledging a common standard, aid each other in seeking ground on which to plant its staff. To me the highest watch word, that which best rouses from every slumber or prolonged repast is this beauty which in its apparition of Duty "preserves the stars from wrong" and through whom "the most ancient heavens are fresh and strong."

Caroline Sturgis remarked of the word *Good* as used in this piece that it was not so good a word as Love. This gave rise to the question what is *Good*. And the answer that it was *the action* of absolute Love. Maryann Jackson asked if Good and right were not synonymous? It seemed to be settled that *right* had relation to the perception of the intellect, rather than to the *Love* of the Soul.

The question was started whether nature or the fine arts were calculated to give more pleasure to the uncultivated— "the savages of our New-England towns" as Miss Fuller called them. Miss Fuller thought their sensibility to nature *very small*. Expressed how it had disappointed her when she went to live in the country. Remarks were made on country people's never walking, and never sympathising with the walkers from the cities. On the other hand the peculiar characteristics of mountainous people and people whose towns lay high, and of sailors. A work of the fine arts Miss Fuller said addressed human sympathy. *A man did it.* It spoke of obstacles overcome. Thus works of the fine arts seemed often to cheer people in sorrow. They spoke of man's power. Grief prostrated—this proof of man's divinity lifted us up. Etc.

Of music as a language Miss F. spoke with enthusiasm. Its power to excite thought—especially Beethoven's. She spoke of music as a mere expression of thought and feeling. Something consecrated from all lower ends than beauty—the singing voice *sacred*—the lyre and other instruments set apart for this high communion of Soul with Soul the sense of awe that one worthy to touch this consecrated instrument would cherish. (It was very beautiful but I cannot remember it)

Wisdom was spoken of—but no good thing was said about it. It was spoken of as something higher than prudence but as combining always the idea of execution. Maryann Jackson asked if it was *Genius in action,* but this did not seem to be allowed. It was proposed to see the relations that the mythology placed Minerva and Apollo in—as illustrations of this subject.

Dr [William Ellery] *Channing* said yesterday—when I told him about the above conversation, that Wisdom was, in the first place, the insight and appreciation of the highest good of man—the supreme end of the human being—(This idea was a direct one) and secondly, it was the appreciation and use of all circumstances as bearing upon it. This Idea of the highest good was not in proportion to the Genius of a man—but in proportion to his fidelity to principle—and we often see it in those who are utterly incapable of understanding the workings of the nature, and of representing them—which is Genius. Genius has moral indifferency. It even delights in Evil because it can make so vivid a representation of it. The best men have excelled in their delineations of evil rather than good. Witness Satan in Milton—and Dante's Inferno. It is the highest effort of Genius to embody Good in vivid forms. This has never been done so as to satisfy us. Genius sees the Ideal of every thing—Give it a passion or any element—it sees its pure and perfect operation and represents it.

Miss Fuller's 16th conversation took place a week ago—and I do not know whether I can remember much of it. The articles read were on woman and the first one was very good indeed, and described a beautiful woman, quite an ideal. The subject of the conversation was woman—but I can remember little of it. There seemed to be a general agreement that women were not systematically enough cultivated, and that they feared to trust their own thoughts on the subject lest they should be wounded in heart. Some one suggested that it was the frivolous women and not men who objected to woman's culture. Another thought men feared for the loss of what was peculiarly feminine in women. Mrs [Samuel?] Hoar of Concord who was present, thought that men desired that women should have knowledge, courage, reason, all those things which are called masculine qualities, provided they do not interfere with gentleness, docility, and other charming traits. That it was the absence of the latter, not the presence of the former which was deprecated by men. Miss Fuller asked what was the distinction of feminine and masculine when applied to character and mind. That there was such a distinction was evident or we should not say 'a masculine woman,' etc. Ellen Hooper thought women were instinctive—they had spontaneously what men have by study reflection and induction. Another remarked that this had been said to be the distinction of poets among men. Another said that this would confirm Coleridge's remark that every man of great poetical genius had something feminine in his face.

Miss Fuller thought that the man and the woman had each every faculty and element of mind—but that they were combined in different proportions. That this was proved by the praise implied in the expressions "a courageous woman—a thoughtful woman—a reasonable woman." And on the other hand by the praise which we bestowed on men who to courage—intellect etc. added tenderness etc. etc. Could there be such a woman as Napoleon? was asked. Queen Elizabeth, Catherine II and Lady Macbeth were spoken of. Maryann Jackson asked if there could be such a man as Corinne. Miss F thought Tasso was such a man, and characterised him in a wonderful manner. I wish I could remember it. Ellen suggested that the ideal woman of a fine man would perhaps give us light. Miss Fuller said we had these in literature, and proposed we should seek them out. She characterised Dante admirably, and then sketched Beatrice.

Miss Fuller's 17th conversation began with reading the articles upon the intellectual differences between men and women. The first made the difference to consist in the fineness and delicacy of organization—the greater openness to impressions—etc. Margaret remarked that this made no essential difference—it was only more or less. Ellen Hooper asked if the difference of organization were not essential—if it did not begin in the mind—and if this was not the author's idea? Margaret looked again and thought it was—but still said that she did not find that the author made any quality belong to the one mind that did not belong to the other. Ellen asked if she thought that there was any quality in the masculine or in the feminine mind that did not belong to the other. Margaret said no—she did not—and therefore she wished to see if the others fully admitted this. Because if all admitted it, it would follow of course that we should hear no more of repressing or subduing faculties because they were not fit for women to cultivate. She desired that whatever faculty we felt to be moving within us, that we should consider a principle of our perfection, and cultivate it accordingly. And not excuse ourselves from any duty on the ground that we had not the intellectual powers for it; that it was not for women to do, *on an intellectual ground.* Some farther remarks were made on the point of the want of objectiveness of woman, as the cause of her not giving herself to the fine arts. It was also attributed to her want of isolation. The physical inconveniences of sculpture, architecture and even of painting were adverted to. But why not music and poetry? Miss Fuller said it had troubled her to think there was no great musical composer among women. It is true that at the period of life when men gave themselves to their pursuit most women became mothers— but there were some women who never married. I suggested that these too often spent the rest of their lives in mourning over this fact—and society spoke so uniformly of woman as more respectable for being married—that it was long before she entirely despaired. This caused some lively talk all round—and Margaret averred that there came a time however when every one *must give up.* I might have answered that then it was but too common for youth to be past—and the mind to have wedded itself to that mediocrity, which is too commonly the result of disappointed hope, especially if hopes are not the highest.

The second piece that was read spoke of the subtlety of woman's mind. Miss Fuller summed it up after she had finished it, with the words. Woman more pervasive. Man more prominent. While speaking of this piece the question came up whether Brutus' great action could have been performed by a woman. It was decided that if there were no doubt about the duty in Brutus' case there could be none about the duty being obligatory on a woman who had the same general office; else the moral nature could not be the same in man and woman. A great deal of talk arose here—and Margaret repelled the sentimentalism that took away woman's moral power of performing stern duty. In answer to one thing she said that as soon as we began to calculate our condition and to make allowances for it, we sank into the depths of sentimentalism. And again. Nothing I hate to hear of so much as *woman's lot.* I wish I never could hear that word *lot.* Something must be wrong where there is a universal lamentation. Youth ought not to be mourned—for it ought to be replaced with something better. . . .

I asked Miss Fuller if she did not think there was an illusion also in the

[44]

idea that women of genius suffered so out of proportion to women who were ordinary. Supposing we had the history of the latter should we not find that *small faculties* involved evil and suffering such as we were apt to forget. Was not Mr Emerson's expression, the "tragedy of *limitation*" true to experience. There might be something in that, Miss Fuller thought— but she declared the belief that if women *wanted to have a good time* as the *first thing,* they must ignore their higher faculties. Thought and feeling brought exquisite pleasures—pleasures *worth* infinite sacrifices—but they inevitably brought sufferings. The Idea of Perfection in a world of Imperfection must expose the one who had it to pain. But this pain was of value—it quickened thought and feeling to deeper and higher discoveries. The young soul true to itself, desired—*demanded* in its unfoldings the *Universe*—it wanted to reform society—to know every thing—to beautify every thing and to have a perfect friend. It could not in this world have or do any of this. This it soon began to see—and then it yielded and sunk, and assimilated itself to what was—called the imperfect Perfect—till it lost the idea of perfection—narrowed its desire till it believed its small circle was the universe. *Or*—it remained faithful to itself—suffered all the pains of deprivation—and disappointment—again and again—and for the forever of this world—but abandoned never those innate immortal truths by which all things were made unsatisfactory. Yet it did not mourn and weep forever—it triumphed—it accepted the limitation and the imperfect friend as they were, and never doubting that the first duty is to preserve a trust in the Ideal, waited—enjoyed what there is, and trusted that it *may* be what it is not. Then all the signatures of the future and immortal will be appreciated; then that which limits and corrupts it, will not limit or corrupt us. Then suffering itself becomes the pledge of immortality—that word on every lip, but whose *meaning* is the rarest thought in minds. (These were some of her best thoughts—but imperfectly given, for they came out in conversation, not in one long speech.) She said besides that she did not love *pain*—nor should it ever be *coaxed*—but always triumphed over. Yet it must be acknowledged and accepted and allowed to act so as to be met by thought and feeling. Those who had not suffered had not *lived as yet.* The happiness that was worth any thing was not that which arose out of ignorance of evil—or of shuffling it aside or turning the back on it—but out of looking it in the face-accepting it—suffering it—yet feeling it was *finite* before the infinite Soul. Much more was said. . . .

FULLER IN HER OWN TIME

Nancy Craig Simmons, "Margaret Fuller's Boston Conversations: The 1839–1840 Series," in *Studies in the American Renaissance 1994,* ed. Joel Myerson (Charlottesville: University Press of Virginia, 1994), 203–204, 206, 212–16, 218. Dashes in the manuscript, used to show punctuation at the end of a sentence (always indicated in Simmons's edition by an em-space after the dash), have been changed to periods.

[Epistolary and Journal Comments on Fuller in 1839, 1841, and 1842]

Nathaniel Hawthorne

Nathaniel Hawthorne (1804–1864) has a reputation as a solitary, gloomy fiction writer of such works as *The Scarlet Letter*, but, as these comments on Fuller show, he also had a sense of humor. Hawthorne's future wife, Sophia Peabody, was a friend of Fuller's and attended her Conversations, and her sister, Elizabeth Palmer Peabody, had been a champion of both Fuller and Hawthorne for many years. Before Peabody's marriage to Hawthorne, Fuller wrote her, "I think there will be great happiness, for if ever I saw a man who combined delicate tenderness to understand the heart of a woman, with quiet depth and manliness enough to satisfy her, it is Mr Hawthorne" (4 June 1842, *Letters*, 3:66). Hawthorne was drawn into Fuller's orbit as well by her visits to Concord while he was residing there; indeed, she sometimes stayed at the Hawthornes' house, the Old Manse, when she visited the town. When Fuller read his story "The Gentle Boy" (published anonymously), she felt it "marked by so much grace and delicacy of feeling" that she thought the author "a lady" ([ca. 1834?], *Letters*, 1:198). Later, she reviewed positively his *Twice-Told Tales* for the *Dial* and *Mosses from an Old Manse* for the *New-York Tribune;* while praising both for their "studies of familiar life," Fuller was nevertheless concerned about the "mere imaginative pieces," which lacked invention and characterization. They seem to have had a good relationship, though Hawthorne did not appreciate what he thought was Fuller's personal and intellectual aggressiveness, and especially her arguments for women's rights. In short, there is nothing in these early descriptions of Fuller that would explain the later comments Hawthorne made in Rome about her (see below).

His jest while at Brook Farm at the "transcendental heifer, belonging to Miss Margaret Fuller," who was "very fractious," and who might, "in these traits of character," resemble "her mistress," are often taken out of context to suggest his dislike for Fuller, but as the comments from his notebooks show, he and Fuller also agreed about many things, including how childhood experiences can influence adult actions. Nevertheless, as the Hawthornes became more concerned about the radicalism of Transcendentalism, they were less enthusiastic about Fuller; and when "The Great Lawsuit" was published, Sophia wrote that if Fuller "were married truly, she would no longer be troubled about the rights of women" (Hawthorne, *Hawthorne and His Wife*, 1:257). Many nineteenth-century and early-twentieth-century critics assumed that the character of Zenobia in *The Blithedale Romance* (1852) was Hawthorne's fictional depiction of Fuller, but all the evidence indicates that Hawthorne drew upon her and many other women for this fictional portrait.

Nathaniel Hawthorne to Sophia Peabody, 5 December 1839

I was invited to dine at Mr. [George] Bancroft's, yesterday, with Miss Margaret Fuller; but Providence had given me some business to do; for which I was very thankful. When my Dove and Sophie Hawthorne can go with me, I shall not be afraid to accept invitations to meet literary lions and lionesses; because I shall then put the above-said redoubtable little personage in the front of the battle. . . .

Nathaniel Hawthorne to Sophia Peabody, 13 April 1841

. . . I went to see our cows [at Brook Farm] foddered, yesterday afternoon. We have eight of our own; and the number is now increased by a transcendental heifer, belonging to Miss Margaret Fuller. She is very fractious, I believe, and apt to kick over the milk pail. Thou knowest best, whether, in these traits of character, she resembles her mistress. . . .

Belovedest, Miss Fuller's cow hooks the other cows, and has made herself ruler of the herd, and behaves in a very tyrannical manner. . . .

Nathaniel Hawthorne to Sophia Peabody, 16 April 1841

Belovedest, the herd have rebelled against the usurpation of Miss Fuller's cow; and whenever they are turned out of the barn, she is compelled to take refuge under our protection. So much did she impede thy husband's labors, by keeping close to him, that he found it necessary to give her two or three gentle pats with a shovel; but still she preferred to trust herself to my tender mercies, rather than venture among the horns of the herd. She is not an amiable cow; but she has a very intelligent face, and seems to be of a reflective cast of character. I doubt not that she will soon perceive the expediency of being on good terms with the rest of the sisterhood. . . .

Journal Entry of 22 August 1842

After leaving the book at Mr. Emerson's, I returned through the woods, and entering Sleepy Hollow, I perceived a lady reclining near the path which bends along its verge. It was Margaret herself. She had been there the whole afternoon, meditating or reading; for she had a book in her hand, with some strange title, which I did not understand and have forgotten. She said that nobody had broken her solitude, and was just giving utterance to a theory that no inhabitant of Concord ever visited Sleepy Hollow, when we saw a whole group of people entering the sacred precincts. Most of them followed a path that led them remote from us; but an old man passed near us, and smiled to see Margaret lying on the ground, and me sitting by her side. He made some remark about the beauty of the afternoon, and withdrew himself into the shadow of the wood. Then we talked about Autumn—and about the pleasures of getting lost in the woods—and about the crows, whose voices Margaret had heard—and about the experiences of early childhood, whose influence remains upon the character after the collection of them has passed away—and about the sight of mountains from a distance, and the view from their summits—and about other matters of high and low philosophy. In the midst of our talk, we heard footsteps above us, on the high bank; and while the intruder was still hidden among the trees, he called to Margaret, of whom he had gotten a glimpse. Then he emerged from the green shade; and, behold, it was Mr. Emerson, who, in spite of his clerical consecration, had found no better way of spending the Sabbath than to ramble among the woods. He appeared to have had a pleasant time; for he said that there were Muses in the woods to-day, and whispers to be heard in the breezes. It being now nearly six o'clock, we separated, Mr. Emerson and Margaret towards his house, and I towards mine, where my little wife was very busy getting tea.

Nathaniel Hawthorne, *The Letters, 1813–1843,* ed. Thomas Woodson et al. (Columbus: Ohio State University Press, 1984), 382, 526–28, 531; *The American Notebooks,* ed. Claude M. Simpson (Columbus: Ohio State University Press, 1972), 342–43. Fuller's reviews are in the *Dial* 3 (July 1842): 130–31 (from which the quotations are taken) and *New-York Daily Tribune,* 22 June 1846, 1; reprinted in *Papers on Literature and Art,* 2:143–46.

[Epistolary Comments on Fuller in 1839, 1841, and 1850]

Elizabeth Hoar

> Elizabeth Sherman Hoar (1814–1878), friend and neighbor of the Emerson family, had been engaged to Waldo's brother Charles. When he died in 1836, only a year after their betrothal, the Emerson family all treated Elizabeth Hoar as their sister. Hoar and Henry David Thoreau were close friends, and she and Fuller also became close during the latter's many visits to Concord and when Hoar attended Fuller's Conversations. Fuller complimented her "justness of perception," and called her a "rare being; she is one not only pure and of noble intent, but of real refinement *both* of character and intellect" ([8?] March, 1 July 1842, *Letters*, 3:48, 76). In 1849, she may have assisted Eliza Rotch Farrar in establishing a fund that would pay Fuller three hundred dollars a year after she returned to America. Here, Hoar echoes the comments of many that, upon first meeting Fuller, her wit appears to be "ridicule or disregard of the sufferings they bring to you," but that is not, in fact, the case. Hoar's comment that Fuller's "friends were a necklace of diamonds about her neck" became a popular one for biographers to quote as a means of suggesting how Fuller collected rather than cherished friends.

Elizabeth Hoar to Hannah L. Chappell, 3 April 1839

Both your letters found me at Mr. Emerson's, but I waited until I came home, to answer them. Miss Fuller has been there for a week past, and I have not yet learned the art of self-regulation so far as to be able to do anything when she is near. I see so few people who are anything but pictures or furniture, to me, that the stimulus of such a person is great and overpowering for the time. And indeed, if I saw all the people whom I think of as desirable, and if I *could* help myself, I do not think I should abate any of my interest in her. Her wit, her insight into characters,—such that she seems to read them aloud to you as if they were printed books, her wide range of thought and cultivation,—the rapidity with which she appropriates all knowledge, joined with habits of severe mental discipline (so rare in women, and in literary men not technically 'men of science'); her passionate love of all beauty, her sympathy with all noble effort; then her energy of character and the regal manner in which she takes possession of society wherever she is, and creates her own circumstances; and—these things keep me full of admiration—not astonished,—but pleased admiration—and, as genius does always (*vide* R. W. E. on 'Genius'), inspire me with new life, new confidence in my own power, new desires to fulfill 'the possible' in myself. You would, perhaps, have an impression of levity, of want of tenderness, from her *superficial* manner. The mean hindrances of life, the mistakes, the tedium, which eat into your soul, and will take no form to you but the tragic, she takes up with her defying wit and sets them down in comic groups and they cease to be 'respectabilities.' You feel at first as if this included ridicule or disregard of the sufferings they bring to you: but not so. Her heart is helpfully sympathizing with all striving souls. And she has overcome so much extreme physical and mental pain, and such disappointments of external fortune, that she has a right to play as she will with these arrows of fate. She is a high-minded and generous servant of Duty, and a Christian (not a *traditional* Christian, not made one by *authority*) in her idea of life. But this is all catalogue; you cannot write down Genius, and I write it more because I am thinking about her than from any hope of doing her justice. Only her presence can give you the meaning of the name Margaret Fuller, and this not once or twice, but as various occasions bring out the many sides. And her power of bringing out Mr. Emerson has doubled my enjoyment of that blessing to be in one house and room with him." . . .

Elizabeth Hoar to Mary Moody Emerson, 23 April 1839

. . . Miss Fuller, whose visit [to Concord] was a great and very agreeable excitement to me—I staid at Waldo's [R. W. Emerson's] while she was there, and we occupied the same room, so that I saw her a great deal, and with increasing admiration of her powers & acquirements, as well as respect for her character.[1] . . . I had double enjoyment in being near Waldo, through her power of making him talk,—He is a ray of white light, and she is a prism—If not so pure and calm, yet she has all the elements of the ray in her varied being.—She knows so many beautiful people, that her friends are like a diamond chain about her neck and she surrounds herself with an atmosphere of beautiful associations. . . . I can see points of attack, of possible repulsion, for she is far from making the impression of a symmetrical beautiful whole yet I think the spell of so much wit and so much will would be too strong for all these. . . .

Elizabeth Hoar to Ralph Waldo Emerson, [20 March? or May? 1841]

I have so often spoken coldly and doubtingly when we talked of Margaret that I must tell you now how true I feel her to be, how noble, how loving—It seems my poverty and coldness of nature that was slow to conceive and inadequate to comprehend a soul so rich, so warm, so devoted. These days have melted me into her being, and there has not been a moment of withdrawal or hesitation and if absence should ever bring them again the want of faith in her will be my own narrowness and indolence. . . .

Elizabeth Hoar to [Hannah L. Chappell?], [July 1850?]

Her friends were a necklace of diamonds about her neck. The confidences given her were their best, and she held them to them; the honor of the conversations was the high tone of sincerity and culture from so many consenting individuals, and Margaret was the keystone of the whole. She was, perhaps, impatient of complacency in people who thought they had claims, and stated their contrary opinion with an air. For such she had no mercy. But, though not agreeable, it was just. And so her enemies were made.

Elizabeth Maxfield-Miller, "Elizabeth of Concord: Selected Letters of Elizabeth Sherman Hoar (1814–1878) to the Emersons, Family, and the Emerson Circle (Parts Two-Three)," in *Studies in the American Renaissance 1985–1986,* ed. Joel Myerson (Charlottesville: University Press of Virginia, 1985–1986), 153, 119 (letters of 23 April 1839 and 1841); Thomas Wentworth Higginson, *Margaret Fuller Ossoli* (Boston: Houghton, Mifflin, 1884), 64–65, 119 (letters of 3 April 1839 and 1850, the latter dated and Chappell identified as the probable recipient in Maxfield-Miller, "Elizabeth . . . [Part Three]," 167).

Note

1. Deleted here is this passage substantially repeated from Hoar's letter to Chappell of 3 April 1839: "Her wit . . . and faith.", with these two significant revisions: "and in literary men not technically 'men of science')" is not present, and "She is a high-minded and generous servant of Duty, and a Christian (not a *traditional* Christian, not made one by *authority*) in her idea of life." is changed to "She is a high-minded and generous servant of Duty and a Christian in endeavour and faith."

[Journal Comments on Fuller in 1840]

THEODORE PARKER

Theodore Parker (1810–1860), a self-educated farmer's son, was a Harvard Divinity School graduate and member of the Transcendental Club, whose South Boston Sermon on "The Transient and Permanent in Christianity" (1841) created more controversy than Emerson's "Divinity School Address" (1838). Parker contributed to the *Dial* and, as minister in West Roxbury (1837–1846), was a frequent visitor to Brook Farm. In 1846, he organized his own congregation in Boston and preached to large crowds at the Boston Melodeon. Fuller and Parker first met in 1837, but their conversation was interrupted before she "could get to Spinoza" (11 April 1837, *Letters*, 1:269). Parker admired Fuller's ability to converse, saying, "she smites and kindles, with all the force, irregularity and matchless beauty of lightning" (Grodzins, *Parker*, 111). Fuller later reviewed favorably three of Parker's sermons in the *New-York Tribune*.

According to Caroline Dall (see next entry), Fuller and Parker "alike required a sort of personal submission before new-comers could be admitted to a cordial understanding"; and, it seemed to Dall, that "Parker hates Margaret, and I never can understand why, unless it be that in their *faults*, they resemble each other." Unfortunately, like Hawthorne, Parker did not like intellectually aggressive women, complaining of Fuller's "Macedonian-phalanx march" (Capper, *Private Years*, 319). Moreover, Parker was interested in theology, not aesthetics, and practical reform, not theorizing about it, and he differed with Fuller in both areas, even though their personal relations were cordial.

[3 AUGUST 1840] . . . Saw Miss *Fuller*, but did not get much. I seldom get much from her. Is it my fault? No doubt. This much, she said some good things about the influence of Christianity at this day. Read me some beautiful poetry, which will shine upon the Dial. . . .

[7 September 1840] But what shall I say of Miss F.? I grieve to say what I *must* say. I have latterly seen in her deportment indications of that same *violence* and *unregenerate passion* so strongly naked on her face. I did not think Religion had softened a spirit naturally so austere; nor that charity had tempered a character so selfish and tyrannical by birth. I did not dream those silken cords had joined her so softly to the sky. But I did dream that considerations of Prudence, suggestions of the Understanding, not a little experience of the world, and a very subtle understanding with considerable insight into first principles—had done the work as well as such agents could effect it. Now I see my mistake. Nor that alone but my old Rule—to which in her case I was making a conjectural exception—that Religion alone can regenerate a spirit at first ill-born, holds good. I need not mention particulars to prove these statements. It is enough that I find the worst suggestions of Mr Alcott confirmed, and I am filled with grief at the discovery. After wandering some 30 years in the Saharas and Siberias; the Englands and Egypts of life finding a sad mingling of Earth and Heaven,—to see one of vast gifts of intellect, great and diversified culture in elegant letters and the arts—of deep experience, in the detail of life, one tried by suffering mind and body),—to see a woman giving way to petty jealousies, contemptible lust of power, and falling into freaks of passion, it is ludicrous first, and then it is melancholy. It is not for me to forgive anything. Thank God I have no occasion, but it is for me to pity and to mourn. It is for me to show others the only salvation for themselves. "My Soul come not thou in her secrets: to her assembly mine honour be not thou united."[1]

Carol Elizabeth Johnston, "The Journals of Theodore Parker: July–December 1840" (Ph.D. dissertation, University of South Carolina, 1980), 33, 60–61; transcribed from the manuscript "Journals of Theodore Parker" at the Andover Theological Library, Harvard Divinity School, Harvard University.

Note

1. The quotation at the end of Parker's text is from Genesis 49:6: "O my soul, come not thou into their secret; unto their assembly, mine honor, be not thou united: for in their anger they slew a man, and in their self-will they digged down a wall."

[Fuller's Conversations in 1841]

CAROLINE HEALEY DALL

Caroline Wells Healey Dall (1822–1912), author, editor, lecturer, and reformer, recorded more personal recollections of Fuller than did anyone except the editors of the *Memoirs*. She was born into a wealthy Boston family whose father attended Emerson's lectures. With the help of Elizabeth Palmer Peabody, she attended Fuller's 1841 Conversations; ironically, given her many comments on Fuller, these were their only face-to-face encounters (Dall is not even mentioned in Fuller's published letters). Her father's financial difficulties forced her to go to Washington, D.C., in 1842 to teach school. She married Charles Henry Appleton Dall (1816–1886), a Unitarian minister, with whom she had two children. He was not a successful minister, and in 1855 he left to be a missionary in Calcutta, where he stayed, except for rare visits home, the rest of his life. In her many publications, Dall continually referred to Fuller's intellectual greatness, support for women's rights, and place as a seminal figure in American culture (see, for example, her extended comments in *Historical Pictures Retouched* [1860]).

Although Dall commented after the first meeting of the class that "I think I never enjoyed an evening so much," and that she found Fuller "more agreeable—*modest*—than I anticipated" (1 March 1841, Dall, *Selected Journals*, 63–64), she felt, from the beginning, an outsider at the Conversations. The teenager was generally ignored, seemed too intrusive when she did participate, and—even worse—felt "it was very evident to me that Margaret did not like me." Later, after reading *Papers on Literature and Art* (1846), Dall concluded that Fuller "can discourse, but she cannot converse," though her "flow of language and power of association is very great" (18 September 1846, Dall, *Selected Journals*, 224). In 1860, the Fuller family contacted Dall about writing a biography of Fuller, but she declined, saying she was unqualified because Fuller had never "loved" her (Myerson, "Mrs. Dall Edits Miss Fuller," 194).

Dall's book covers the Conversations on mythology held between 1 March and 6 May 1841. She made "abstracts" of each Conversation the next day, omitting whatever was "not worth recording" and "anything that I could not understand" (Dall, *Margaret and Her Friends*, 11). In early 1895, she pulled

together and revised these notes, wrote to surviving members of the class for
their recollections, and raised a subscription fund to subsidize publication.
Margaret and Her Friends was published in mid-October 1895 in a printing
of 600 copies; a second printing of 280 copies was done in April 1897. There
were few reviews, and the ones that did appear treated the book as an oddity.
To the *Atlantic Monthly*'s reviewer, it was a "bit of driftwood from that far-off
Utopia of Transcendentalism" (see Myerson, "Mrs. Dall Edits Miss Fuller").

The Conversations Dall attended were open to men and women, unlike the
ones reported on by Peabody, where only women took part. Unfortunately,
the men tended to dominate, as when Dall complains that Emerson "pursued his own train of thought" and "seemed to forget that we had come together to pursue Margaret's." (Emerson did apologize to Fuller: "The young
people wished to know what possessed me to tease you with so much prose,
and becloud the fine conversation?" (14 March 1841, *Letters*, 2:384–85).

[MARCH 8, 1841] MARGARET recapitulated the statements she made last
week. By thus giving to each fabled Deity its place in the scheme of Mythology, she did not mean to ignore the enfolding ideas, the one thought developed in all—as in Rhea, Bacchus, Pan. She would only imply that each
personification was individual, served a particular purpose, and was wor-
shipped in a particular way.

Before proceeding to talk about Ceres, she wished to remind us of the
mischief of wandering from our subject. She hoped the ground she offered
would be accepted *at least to talk about!* Certainly no one could deny that
a mythos was the last and best growth of a national mind, and that in this
case the characteristics of the Greek mind were best gathered from this
creation.

Ceres, Persephone, and Isis, as well as Rhea, Diana, and so on, seem to
be only modifications of one enfolding idea,—a goddess accepted by all nations, and not peculiar to Greece. The pilgrimages of the more prominent
of these goddesses, Ceres and Isis, seem to indicate the life which loses
what is dear in childhood, to seek in weary pain for what after all can be
but half regained. Ceres regained her daughter, but only for half the year.
Isis found her husband, but dismembered. This era in Mythology seems
to mark the progress of a people from an unconscious to a conscious state.
Persephone's periodical exile shows the impossibility of resuming an un-

consciousness from which we have been once aroused, the need thought has, having once felt the influence of the Seasons, to retire into itself.

CHARLES WHEELER reminded Margaret that she had said that the predominant goddesses, without reference to Greece, enfolded only one idea, that of the female Will or Genius,—*the bounteous giver*. He had asked her if she could sustain herself by etymological facts, and she replied that her knowledge of the Greek was not critical enough. Since then he had inquired into the origin of the proper names of the Greek deities, and found that it confirmed her impression. The names of Rhea, Tellus, Isis, and Diana were resolvable into one, and the difference in their etymology was only a common and permissible change in the position of the letters of which they are composed, or a mere provincial dialectic change. Diana is the same as Dione, also one of the names of Juno.

E[LIZABETH]. P[ALMER]. P[EABODY]. asked if Homer ever confounded the last two?

MARGARET thought not. Homer was purely objective. He knew little and cared less about the primitive creation of the myths.

R. W. EMERSON thought it would be very difficult to detect this secret. Jupiter, for instance, might have been a man who was the exponent of Will to his race.

MARGARET said, "No; they could have deduced him just as easily from Nature herself, or from a single exhibition of will power."

R. W. EMERSON said that a man like Napoleon would easily have suggested it. "What a God-send is a Napoleon!" exclaimed CHARLES WHEELER; "let us pray for scores of such, that a new and superior mythos may arise for us!" Is it malicious to suspect a subtle irony turned against the sacred person of R. W. E. in this speech?

MARGARET retorted indignantly that if they came, *we* should do nothing better than write memoirs of their hats, coats, and swords, as we had done already, without thinking of any lesson they might teach. She could not see why we were not content to take the beautiful Greek mythi as they were, without troubling ourselves about those which might arise for us!

R. W. E. acknowledged that the Greeks had a quicker perception of the beautiful than we. Their genius lay in the material expression of it. If we knew the real meaning of the names of their Deities, the story would take to flight. We should have only the working of abstract ideas as we might adjust them for ourselves.

[57]

FULLER IN HER OWN TIME

MARGARET said that a fable was more than a mere word. It was a word of the purest kind rather, the passing of thought into form. R. W. E. had made no allowance for time or space or climate, and there was a want of truth in that. The age of the Greeks was the age of Poetry; ours was the age of Analysis. *We* could not create a Mythology.

EMERSON asked, "Why not? We had still better material."

MARGARET said, irrelevantly as it seemed to me, that Carlyle had attempted to deduce new principles from present history, and that was the reason he did not *respect* the *respectable*.

EMERSON said Carlyle was unfortunate in his figures, but we might have mythology as beautiful as the Greek.

MARGARET thought each age of the world had its own work to do. The transition of thought into form marked the Greek period. It was most easily done through fable, on account of their intense perception of beauty.

EMERSON pursued his own train of thought. He seemed to forget that we had come together to pursue Margaret's. He said it was impossible that men or events should *stand out* in a population of twenty millions as they could from a population of a single million, to which the whole population of the ancient world could hardly have amounted. As Hercules stood to Greece, no modern man could ever stand in relation to his own world.

MARGARET thought Hercules and Jupiter quite different creations. The first might have been a deified life. The second could not.

CHARLES WHEELER said that R. W. E.'s view carried no historical obligation of belief with it. We could not deny the heroic origin of the Greek demigods, but the highest dynasty was the exponent of translated thought.

SOPHIA RIPLEY asked if the life of an individual fitly interwoven with her experience was not as fine a Poem as the story of Ceres, her wanderings and her tears? Did not Margaret know such lives?

R. W. E. thought every man had probably met his Jupiter, Juno, Minerva, Venus, or Ceres in society!

MARGARET was sure she never had!

R. W. E. explained: "Not in the world, but each on his own platform."

WILLIAM STORY objected. The life of an individual was not universal. (!)

SOPHIA RIPLEY repeated, "The inner life."

WILLIAM STORY claimed to be an individual, and did not think individual experience could ever meet all minds,—like the story of Ceres, for example.

[58]

SOPHIA said all experience was universal.

I said nothing, but held this colloquy with myself. Thought is the best of human nature; its fulness urges expression: its need of being met, not only by *one* other but by every other, *craves* it. This craving is the acknowledgment of the universal experience. What is *purely* individual is perishable. *Identity* is to be separated from individuality for this cause.

MARGARET said the element of beauty would be wanting to our creations. A fine emotion glowed through features which seem to fall like a soft veil over the soul, while it could scarce do more than animate those that were obtuse and coarse in every outline. (!)

"Then," said WILLIAM STORY, and my heart thanked the *preux chevalier,*—"then something is wanting in the emotion itself."

WILLIAM WHITE said, stupidly, that sunlight could not fall with equal charm on rocks and the green grass. (!)

I asked if the rock could not give what it did not receive? Flung back by rugged points and relieved by dark shadows, was not the sunlight itself transfigured?

STORY said every face had its own beauty. No act that was natural could be ungraceful.

EMERSON said that we all did sundry graceful acts, in our caps and tunics, which we never could do again, which we never wanted to do again.

MARGARET said, at last we had touched the point. We could not restore the childhood of the world, but could we not admire this simple plastic period, and gather from it some notion of the Greek genius?

R. W. E. thought this legitimate. He would have it that we could not determine the origin of a mythos, but we might fulfil Miss Fuller's intention.

MARGARET said history reconciled us to life, by showing that man had redeemed himself. Genius needed that encouragement.

Not Genius, SOPHIA RIPLEY thought; common natures needed it, but Genius was self-supported.

MARGARET said it might be the consolation of Genius.

MRS. RUSSELL asked why Miss Fuller found so much fault with the present.

MARGARET *had* no fault to find with it. She took facts as they were. Every age did something toward fulfilling the cycle of mind. The work of the Greeks was not ours.

SOPHIA RIPLEY asked if the mythology had been a prophecy of the Greek mind to itself, or if the nation had experienced life in any wide or deep sense.

MARGARET seemed a little out of patience, and no wonder! She said it did not matter which. The question was, what could *we find* in the mythi, and what did the Greeks mean that we should find there. Coleridge once said that certain people were continually saying of Shakespeare, that he did not mean to impart certain spiritual meanings to some of his sketches of life and character; but if Shakespeare did not mean it his Genius did: so if the Greeks meant not this or that, the Greek genius meant it.

In relation to the progress of the ages, JAMES F. CLARKE said that the story of Persephone concealed in the bowels of the earth for half the year seemed to him to indicate something of their comparative states. Persephone was the seed which must return to earth before it could fructify. Thought must retire into itself before it can be regenerate.

MARGARET was pleased with this, more especially as in the story of the Goddess it is eating the pomegranate, whose seed is longest in germinating, which dooms her to the realm of Pluto.

GEORGE RIPLEY remarked that we saw this need of withdrawal in the slothful ages when mind seemed to be imbibing energy for future action. The world sometimes forsook a quest and returned to it. We had forsaken Beauty, but we might return to it.

Certainly, MARGARET assented. A perfect mind would detect all beauty in the hearth-rug at her feet: the meanest part of creation contained the whole; but the labor we were now at to appreciate the Greek proved conclusively that *we* were not Greek. A simple plastic nature would take it all in with delight, without doubt or question.

Or rather, amended EMERSON, would take it up and go forward with it.

It makes no difference, said MARGARET for we live in a circle.

I did not think it pleasant to track and retrack the same arc, and preferred to go forward with R. W. E., so I asked if there was to be no *higher* poetry.

MARGARET acknowledged that there was something beyond the aspiration of the Egyptian or the poetry of the Greek.

GEORGE RIPLEY thought we had not lost all reverence for these abstract forces. The Eleusinian mysteries might be forgotten, but not Ceres. We did not worship in ignorance. The mysteries led back to the Infinite. The processes of vegetation were actually heart-rending!

Here, *I* thought, was a basis for my higher poetry.

GEORGE RIPLEY acknowledged that it was so. He seemed to be more conscious of the movement of the world than any of our party. He said we must not measure creation by Boston and Washington, as we were too apt to do. There was still France, Germany, and Prussia,—perhaps Russia! The work of this generation was not religious nor poetic; still, there was a tendency to go back to both. There were to be ultraisms, but also, he hoped, consistent development.

CHARLES WHEELER then related the story of Isis, of her hovering in the form of a swallow round the tree in which the sarcophagus of Osiris had been enclosed by Typhon; of her being allowed to fell the tree; of the odor emitted by the royal maidens whom she touched, which revealed her Divinity to the Queen; of the second loss of the body, as she returned home, and its final dismemberment.

There was little success in spiritualizing more of this story than the pilgrimage, and R. W. E. seemed to feel this; for when MARGARET had remarked that even a divine force must become as the birds of the air to compass its ends, and that it was in the carelessness of conscious success that the second loss occurred, he said that it was impossible to detect an inner sense in all these stories.

MARGARET replied, that she had not attempted that, but she could see it in all the prominent points.

CHARLES WHEELER said that the varieties of anecdote proved that the stories were not all authentic. It was an ancient custom to strike off medals in honor of certain acts of the Gods. To these graven pictures the common people gave their own vulgar interpretations, as they did also to the bas-reliefs on their temples and monuments.

E. P. P. said this accounted for many of the stories transmitted by Homer. When sculpture and architecture had lost their meaning, his inventive genius was only the more stimulated to find one.

CHARLES WHEELER asked what Margaret would make of the story that the tears of Isis frightened children to death?

There was a general laugh, but MARGARET said coolly, that children always shrank from a baffled hope.

Some one contrasted Persephone with her mother.

MARGARET assented to whatever was said, and added that she had been particularly struck with it in an engraving she had recently seen, in which Ceres stood with lifted eyes, full-eyed, matronly, bounteous, ready to give all to all, while Persephone, dejected and thoughtful, sat meditating; and the idea was strengthened by her discovering that Persephone was the same as Ariadne the deserted. I could only guess at the remark by Margaret's comment. It seemed to imply baffled hope for Persephone.

The Eleusinian mysteries were now alluded to. Although it has been said that only moral precepts were inculcated through these, WHEELER urged that a whole school of Continental authors now acknowledged that the higher doctrines of philosophy were taught.

R. W. E. added, that as initiation became more easy such instruction must have degenerated into a mere matter of form, and many of the *un*initiated surpass the initiated in wisdom.

MARGARET admitted this. Socrates was one of the uninitiated. The crowd seldom felt the full force of beauty in Art or Literature. To prove it, it was only necessary to walk once through the Hall of Sculpture at the Athenæum, and catch the remarks of any half-dozen on Michael Angelo's "Day and Night." He would be fortunate who heard a single observer comment on its power.

MRS. RUSSELL asked why the images of the sun and moon were introduced into these mysterious celebrations.

MARGARET asked impatiently why they had always been invoked by every child who could string two rhymes together.

I said that if Ceres was the simple *agricultural* productive energy, of course the sun was her first minister, its genial influence being as manifest as the energy itself.

In regard to the etymology of the proper names, it seemed reasonable to me that this energy should have gained attributes as it did names. Any nation devoted to the chase would learn to call the lunar deity Diana; any devoted to the cultivation of grain would project her as Ceres. The reproductive powers of flocks and herds would suggest Rhea or Juno, and philosophy or art would invoke Persephone.

When we were talking about beauty, J. F. C. quoted Goethe, and said that the spirit sometimes made a mistake and clothed itself in the wrong garment. . . .

Caroline Dall, *Margaret and Her Friends* (Boston: Roberts Brothers, 1895), 40–59. In the headnote, Dall's comment that "Margaret did not like me" comes from a letter to Thomas Wentworth Higginson (copy), 29 May 1908, Houghton Library, Harvard University.

[Fuller in New York in 1844–1846]

HORACE GREELEY

MY FIRST ACQUAINTANCE with Margaret Fuller was made through the pages of "The Dial." The lofty range and rare ability of that work, and its un-American richness of culture and ripeness of thought, naturally filled the 'fit audience, though few,' with a high estimate of those who were known as its conductors and principal writers. Yet I do not now remember that any article, which strongly impressed me, was recognized as from the pen of its female editor, prior to the appearance of "The Great Lawsuit," afterwards matured into the volume more distinctively, yet not quite accurately, entitled "Woman in the Nineteenth Century." I think this can hardly have failed to make a deep impression on the mind of every thoughtful reader, as the production of an original, vigorous, and earnest mind. "Summer on the Lakes," which appeared some time after that essay, though before its expansion into a book, struck me as less ambitious in its aim, but more graceful and delicate in its execution; and as one of the clearest and most graphic delineations, ever given, of the Great Lakes, of the Prairies, and of the receding barbarism, and the rapidly advancing, but rude, repulsive semi-civilization, which were contending with most unequal forces for the possession of those rich lands. I still consider "Summer on the Lakes" unequalled, especially in its pictures of the Prairies and of the sunnier aspects of Pioneer life.

Yet, it was the suggestion of Mrs. Greeley,—who had spent some weeks of successive seasons in or near Boston, and who had there made the personal acquaintance of Miss Fuller, and formed a very high estimate and warm attachment for her,—that induced me, in the autumn of 1844, to offer her terms, which were accepted, for her assistance in the literary department of the Tribune. A home in my family was included in the stipulation. I was myself barely acquainted with her, when she thus came to reside with us, and I did not fully appreciate her nobler qualities for some months afterward. Though we were members of the same household, we scarcely met save at breakfast; and my time and thoughts were absorbed in duties and cares, which left me little leisure or inclination for the amenities of social intercourse. Fortune seemed to delight in placing us two in relations of friendly antagonism,—or rather, to develop all possible contrasts in our ideas and social habits. She was naturally inclined to luxury and a good appearance before the world. My pride, if I had any, delighted in bare walls and rugged fare. She was addicted to strong tea and coffee, both which I rejected and contemned, even in the most homoeopathic dilutions: while, my general health being sound, and hers sadly impaired, I could not fail to find in her dietetic habits the causes of her almost habitual illness; and once, while we were still barely acquainted, when she came to the breakfast-table with a very severe headache, I was tempted to attribute it to her strong potations of the Chinese leaf the night before. She told me quite frankly that she "declined being lectured on the food or beverage she saw fit to take;" which was but reasonable in one who had arrived at her maturity of intellect and fixedness of habits. So the subject was thenceforth tacitly avoided between us; but, though words were suppressed, looks and involuntary gestures could not so well be; and an utter divergency of views on this and kindred themes created a perceptible distance between us.

Her earlier contributions to the Tribune were not her best, and I did not at first prize her aid so highly as I afterwards learned to do. She wrote always freshly, vigorously, but not always clearly; for her full and intimate acquaintance with continental literature, especially German, seemed to have marred her felicity and readiness of expression in her mother tongue. While I never met another woman who conversed more freely or lucidly, the attempt to commit her thoughts to paper seemed to induce a singular embarrassment and hesitation. She could write only when in the vein; and this needed often to be waited for through several days, while the occasion sometimes required an immediate utterance. The new book must be reviewed before other journals had thoroughly dissected and discussed it, else the ablest critique would command no general attention, and perhaps be, by the greater number, unread. That the writer should wait the flow of inspiration, or at least the recurrence of elasticity of spirits and relative health of body, will not seem unreasonable to the general reader; but to the inveterate hack-horse of the daily press, accustomed to write at any time, on any subject, and with a rapidity limited only by the physical ability to form the requisite pen-strokes, the notion of waiting for a brighter day, or a happier frame of mind, appears fantastic and absurd. He would as soon think of waiting for a change in the moon. Hence, while I realized that her contributions evinced rare intellectual wealth and force, I did not value them as I should have done had they been written more fluently and promptly. They often seemed to make their appearance "a day after the fair."

One other point of tacit antagonism between us may as well be noted. Margaret was always a most earnest, devoted champion of the Emancipation of Women, from their past and present condition of inferiority, to an independence on Men. She demanded for them the fullest recognition of Social and Political Equality with the rougher sex; the freest access to all stations, professions, employments, which are open to any. To this demand I heartily acceded. It seemed to me, however, that her clear perceptions of abstract right were often overborne, in practice, by the influence of education and habit; that while she demanded absolute equality for Woman, she exacted a deference and courtesy from men to women, *as* women, which was entirely inconsistent with that requirement. In my view, the equalizing theory can be enforced only by ignoring the habitual discrimination of men and women, as forming separate *classes,* and regarding all alike as simply *persons,*—as human beings. So long as a lady shall deem herself in need of some gentleman's arm to conduct her properly out of a dining or ball-room,—so long as she shall consider it dangerous or unbecoming to walk half a mile alone by night,—I cannot see how the "Woman's Rights" theory is ever to be anything more than a logically defensible abstraction. In this view Margaret did not at all concur, and the diversity was the incitement to much perfectly good-natured, but nevertheless sharpish sparring between us. Whenever she said or did anything implying the usual demand of Woman on the courtesy and protection of Manhood, I was apt, before complying, to look her in the face and exclaim with marked emphasis,—quoting from her "Woman in the Nineteenth Century,"—"LET THEM BE SEA-CAPTAINS IF THEY WILL!" Of course, this was given and received as raillery, but it did not tend to ripen our intimacy or quicken my esteem into admiration. Though no unkind word ever passed between us, nor any approach to one, yet we two dwelt for months under the same roof, as scarcely more than acquaintances, meeting once a day at a common board, and having certain business relations with each other. Personally, I regarded her rather as my wife's cherished friend than as my own, possessing many lofty qualities and some prominent weaknesses, and a good deal spoiled by the unmeasured flattery of her little circle of inordinate admirers. For myself, burning no incense on any human shrine, I half-consciously resolved to "keep my eye-beam clear," and escape the fascination which she seemed to exert over the eminent and cultivated persons, mainly women, who came to our out-of-the-way dwelling to visit her, and who seemed generally to regard her with a strangely Oriental adoration.

But as time wore on, and I became inevitably better and better acquainted with her, I found myself drawn, almost irresistibly, into the general current. I found that her faults and weaknesses were all superficial and ob-vious to the most casual, if undazzled, observer. They rather dwindled than expanded upon a fuller knowledge; or rather, took on new and brighter as-pects in the light of her radiant and lofty soul. I learned to know her as a most fearless and unselfish champion of Truth and Human Good at all hazards, ready to be their standard-bearer through danger and obloquy, and, if need be, their martyr. I think few have more keenly appreciated the material goods of life,—Rank, Riches, Power, Luxury, Enjoyment; but I know none who would have more cheerfully surrendered them all, if the well-being of our Race could thereby have been promoted. I have never met another in whom the inspiring hope of Immortality was so strengthened into profoundest conviction. She did not *believe* in our future and unend-ing existence,—she *knew* it, and lived ever in the broad glare of its morning twilight. With a limited income and liberal wants, she was yet generous beyond the bounds of reason. Had the gold of California been all her own, she would have disbursed nine tenths of it in eager and well-directed ef-forts to stay, or at least diminish, the flood of human misery. And it is but fair to state, that the liberality she evinced was fully paralleled by the lib-erality she experienced at the hands of others. Had she needed thousands, and made her wants known, she had friends who would have cheerfully supplied her. I think few persons, in their pecuniary dealings, have experi-enced and evinced more of the better qualities of human nature than Mar-garet Fuller. She seemed to inspire those who approached her with that generosity which was a part of her nature.

Of her writings I do not purpose to speak critically. I think most of her contributions to the Tribune, while she remained with us, were character-ized by a directness, terseness, and practicality, which are wanting in some of her earlier productions. Good judges have confirmed my own opinion, that, while her essays in the Dial are more elaborate and ambitious, her reviews in the Tribune are far better adapted to win the favor and sway the judgment of the great majority of readers. But, one characteristic of her writings I feel bound to commend,—their absolute truthfulness. She never asked how this would sound, nor whether that would do, nor what would be the effect of saying anything; but simply, "Is it the truth? Is it such as the public should know?" And if her judgment answered, "Yes," she uttered it; no matter what turmoil it might excite, nor what odium it might draw down on her own head. Perfect conscientiousness was an unfailing characteristic of her literary efforts. Even the severest of her critiques,—that on Longfellow's Poems,—for which an impulse in personal pique has been alleged, I happen with certainty to know had no such origin. When I first handed her the book to review, she excused herself, assigning the wide divergence of her views of Poetry from those of the author and his school, as her reason. She thus induced me to attempt the task of reviewing it myself. But day after day sped by, and I could find no hour that was not absolutely required for the performance of some duty that *would not* be put off, nor turned over to another. At length I carried the book back to her in utter despair of ever finding an hour in which even to look through it; and, at my renewed and earnest request, she reluctantly undertook its discussion. The statement of these facts is but an act of justice to her memory.

Profoundly religious,—though her creed was, at once, very broad and very short, with a genuine love for inferiors in social position, whom she was habitually studying, by her counsel and teachings, to elevate and improve,—she won the confidence and affection of those who attracted her, by unbounded sympathy and trust. She probably knew the cherished secrets of more hearts than any one else, because she freely imparted her own. With a full share both of intellectual and of family pride, she preëminently recognized and responded to the essential brotherhood of all human kind, and needed but to know that a fellow-being required her counsel or assistance, to render her, not merely willing, but eager to impart it. Loving ease, luxury, and the world's good opinion, she stood ready to renounce them all, at the call of pity or of duty. I think no one, not radically averse to the whole system of domestic servitude, would have treated servants, of whatever class, with such uniform and thoughtful consideration,—a regard which wholly merged their factitious condition in their antecedent and permanent humanity. I think few servants ever lived weeks with her, who were not dignified and lastingly benefited by her influence and her counsels. They might be at first repelled, by what seemed her too stately manner and exacting disposition, but they soon learned to esteem and love her.

I have known few women, and scarcely another maiden, who had the heart and the courage to speak with such frank compassion, in mixed circles, of the most degraded and outcast portion of the sex. The contemplation of their treatment, especially by the guilty authors of their ruin, moved her to a calm and mournful indignation, which she did not attempt to suppress nor control. Others were willing to pity and deplore; Margaret was more inclined to vindicate and to redeem. She did not hesitate to avow that on meeting some of these abused, unhappy sisters, she had been surprised to find them scarcely fallen morally below the ordinary standard of Womanhood,—realizing and loathing their debasement; anxious to escape it; and only repelled by the sad consciousness that for them sympathy and society remained only so long as they should persist in the ways of pollution. Those who have read her "Woman," may remember some daring comparisons therein suggested between these Pariahs of society and large classes of their respectable sisters; and that was no fitful expression,—no sudden outbreak,—but impelled by her most deliberate convictions. I think, if she had been born to large fortune, a house of refuge for all female outcasts desiring to return to the ways of Virtue, would have been one of her most cherished and first realized conceptions.

Her love of children was one of her most prominent characteristics. The pleasure she enjoyed in their society was fully counterpoised by that she imparted. To them she was never lofty, nor reserved, nor mystical; for no one had ever a more perfect faculty for entering into their sports, their feelings, their enjoyments. She could narrate almost any story in language level to their capacities, and in a manner calculated to bring out their hearty and often boisterously expressed delight. She possessed marvellous powers of observation and imitation or mimicry; and, had she been attracted to the stage, would have been the first actress America has produced, whether in tragedy or comedy. Her faculty of mimicking was not needed to commend her to the hearts of children, but it had its effect in increasing the fascinations of her genial nature and heartfelt joy in their society. To amuse and instruct them was an achievement for which she would readily forego any personal object; and her intuitive perception of the toys, games, stories, rhymes, &c., best adapted to arrest and enchain their attention, was unsurpassed. Between her and my only child, then living, who was eight months old when she came to us, and something over two years when she sailed for Europe, tendrils of affection gradually intertwined themselves, which I trust Death has not severed, but rather multiplied and strengthened. She became his teacher, playmate, and monitor; and he requited her with a prodigality of love and admiration.

I shall not soon forget their meeting in my office, after some weeks' separation, just before she left us forever. His mother had brought him in from the country and left him asleep on my sofa, while she was absent making purchases, and he had rolled off and hurt himself in the fall, waking with the shock in a phrensy of anger, just before Margaret, hearing of his arrival, rushed into the office to find him. I was vainly attempting to soothe him as she entered; but he was running from one end to the other of the office, crying passionately, and refusing to be pacified. She hastened to him, in perfect confidence that her endearments would calm the current of his feelings,—that the sound of her well-remembered voice would banish all thought of his pain,—and that another moment would see him restored to gentleness; but, half-wakened, he did not heed her, and probably did not even realize who it was that caught him repeatedly in her arms and tenderly insisted that he should restrain himself. At last she desisted in despair; and, with the bitter tears streaming down her face, observed:—"Pickie, many friends have treated me unkindly, but no one had ever the power to cut me to the heart, as you have!" Being thus let alone, he soon came to himself, and their mutual delight in the meeting was rather heightened by the momentary estrangement.

They had one more meeting; their last on earth! "Aunty Margaret" was to embark for Europe on a certain day, and "Pickie" was brought into the city to bid her farewell. They met this time also at my office, and together we thence repaired to the ferry-boat, on which she was returning to her residence in Brooklyn to complete her preparations for the voyage. There they took a tender and affecting leave of each other. But soon his mother called at the office, on her way to the departing ship, and we were easily persuaded to accompany her thither, and say farewell once more, to the manifest satisfaction of both Margaret and the youngest of her devoted friends. Thus they parted, never to meet again in time. She sent him messages and presents repeatedly from Europe; and he, when somewhat older, dictated a letter in return, which was joyfully received and acknowledged. When the mother of our great-souled friend spent some days with us nearly two years afterward, "Pickie" talked to her often and lovingly of "Aunty Margaret," proposing that they two should "take a boat and go over and see her,"—for, to his infantile conception, the low coast of Long Island, visible just across the East River, was that Europe to which she had sailed, and where she was unaccountably detained so long. Alas! a far longer and more adventurous journey was required to reunite those loving souls! The 12th of July, 1849, saw him stricken down, from health to death, by the relentless cholera; and my letter, announcing that calamity, drew from her a burst of passionate

[70]

sorrow, such as hardly any bereavement but the loss of a very near relative could have impelled. Another year had just ended, when a calamity,
equally sudden, bereft a wide circle of her likewise, with her husband and
infant son. Little did I fear, when I bade her a confident Good-by, on the
deck of her outward-bound ship, that the sea would close over her earthly
remains, ere we should meet again; far less that the light of my eyes and the
cynosure of my hopes, who then bade her a tenderer and sadder farewell,
would precede her on the dim pathway to that "Father's house," whence
is no returning! Ah, well! God is above all, and gracious alike in what he
conceals and what he discloses;—benignant and bounteous, as well when
he reclaims as when he bestows. In a few years, at farthest, our loved and
lost ones will welcome us to their home. . . .

Memoirs of Margaret Fuller Ossoli, ed. William Henry Channing, James Freeman Clarke,
and Ralph Waldo Emerson, 2 vols. (Boston: Phillips, Sampson, 1852), 2:152–63.

"The Literati of New York City" (1846)

Edgar Allan Poe

> Edgar Allan Poe (1809–1849), journalist, short story writer, and poet, was a regular critic of what he perceived as the excesses of Transcendentalism and its adherents. He met Fuller in New York during one of the literary salons hosted by Anne Charlotte Lynch, where, according to one observer, he bested her in conversation: "The Raven has perched upon the casque [that is, helmet] of Pallas, and pulled all the feathers out of her cap" (Thomas and Jackson, *Poe Log*, 616). They reviewed each other's works favorably, with Fuller generally praising *Tales* and *The Raven and Other Poems*, and Poe calling *Woman in the Nineteenth Century* "nervous, forcible, thoughtful, suggestive, [and] brilliant." They probably fell out when Fuller and Lynch tried to intercede on behalf of two women vying for Poe's attention by asking Poe to return letters one of them had written, resulting in him calling them "Busybodies!" (Miller, *Poe's Helen Remembers*, 21). Poe may also have been miffed when Fuller failed to mention him in her survey of "American Literature" in *Papers on Literature and Art* (1846). After his death, Fuller wrote, "I did not know him, though I saw and talked with him often, but he always seemed to me shrouded in an assumed character" (6 December 1849, *Letters*, 5:289).

. . . WHAT POET, in especial, but must feel at least the better portion of himself more fairly represented in even his commonest sonnet (earnestly written) than in his most elaborate or most intimate personalities?

I put all this as a general proposition, to which Miss Fuller affords a marked exception—to this extent, that her personal character and her printed book are merely one and the same thing. We get access to her soul as directly from the one as from the other—no *more* readily from this than from that—easily from either. Her acts are bookish, and her books are less thoughts than acts. Her literary and her conversational manner are identical. Here is a passage from her "Summer on the Lakes:"—

> "The rapids enchanted me far beyond what I expected; they are so swift that they cease to *seem* so—you can think only of their *beauty*. The fountain beyond

the Moss islands I discovered for myself, and thought it for some time an *accidental* beauty which it would not do to *leave,* lest I might never see it again. After I found it *permanent,* I returned many times to watch the play of its crest. In the little waterfall beyond, Nature seems, as she often does, to have made a *study* for some larger design. She delights in this—a sketch within a sketch—a dream within a *dream.* Wherever we see it, the lines of the great buttress in the fragment of stone, the hues of the waterfall, copied in the flowers that star its bordering mosses, we are *delighted;* for all the lineaments become *fluent,* and we mould the scene in congenial thought with its *genius.*"

Now all this is precisely as Miss Fuller would *speak* it. She is perpetually saying just such things in just such words. To get the *conversational* woman in the mind's eye, all that is needed is to imagine her reciting the paragraph just quoted: but first let us have the *personal* woman. She is of the medium height; nothing remarkable about the figure; a profusion of lustrous light hair; eyes a bluish gray, full of fire; capacious forehead; the mouth when in repose indicates profound sensibility, capacity for affection, for love—when moved by a slight smile, it becomes even beautiful in the intensity of this expression; but the upper lip, as if impelled by the action of involuntary muscles, habitually uplifts itself, conveying the impression of a sneer. Imagine, now, a person of this description looking you at one moment earnestly in the face, at the next seeming to look only within her own spirit or at the wall; moving nervously every now and then in her chair; speaking in a high key, but musically, deliberately, (not hurriedly or loudly,) with a delicious distinctness of enunciation—speaking, I say, the paragraph in question, and emphasizing the words which I have italicized, not by impulsion of the breath, (as is usual,) but by drawing them out as long as possible, nearly closing her eyes the while—imagine all this, and we have both the woman and the authoress before us.

From Edgar Allan Poe, "The Literati of New York City.—No. IV. Sarah Margaret Fuller," *Godey's Magazine and Lady's Book* 33 (August 1846): 72–75. Poe's comment on *Woman* in the headnote also comes from this essay.

[Fuller at the Italian School, London, in 1846]

C. S. H.

The Italian Gratuitous School was opened at 5 Greville Street, Hatton Garden, London, on 10 November 1841. The driving force behind the school was Italian patriot and friend of Fuller's, Giuseppe Mazzini. A contemporary account of the school describes it this way: "There was not much outward grandeur: two mean rooms, with a few chairs for the more distinguished visitors, and forms [that is, long, thin benches without backs] for the rest, with no ornaments, except a few maps hung on the walls, and a bust of Dante over the fire-place. And yet there was not wanting the true grandeur of earnestness, of faith, and gratitude" (Linton, "Italian School," 147). Approximately sixty boys attended the school, which was supported mainly by donations from Italians. Fuller favorably describes this occasion thus: "The whole evening gave a true and deep pleasure, though tinged with sadness. We saw a planting of the Kingdom of Heaven, though now no larger than a grain of mustard-seed, and though, perhaps, none of those who watch the spot may live to see the birds singing in its branches" (*Dispatches from Europe*, 100).

MISS FULLER (the authoress of *Woman in the Nineteenth Century,* the best work on the subject which has yet appeared,) kindly consented to the request that she would say a few words to the meeting [on 10 November 1846]. Miss Fuller had no expectation that she would be thus solicited, but expression is an easy matter when, as in this lady's case, trains of excellent thought stream uninterruptedly through the mind, and no vanity or littleness of feeling disturbs the serene calmness of the pure spirit. Accordingly, in simple truthful tones, rendered pathetic by the heartfelt sympathy she evidently had in the object of the meeting, Miss Fuller began by saying that she knew not how usual it might be in this country for women to address assemblies, like the present, but that in her country—America—it was extremely common, and that she had often herself spoken in schools to large numbers, but that she had never done so with more pleasure than on the present occasion, for it had long been a favourite idea with her that there

[74]

should be an international moral exchange, we should accept from each its own peculiar excellence. In the Germans we perceive simplicity, unwearied industry, and extensive mental culture. The English are distinguished for mechanical skill and a certain spirit of honour; whilst Italy, herself so fair, has bestowed on the rest of the world, beyond any other country, save ancient Greece, those arts which, pourtraying the beautiful and the graceful, awaken the love of the beautiful and the good, and thus refine the human soul. To the poet and the artist, Italy must ever be most dear; nor can anyone, capable of thought on the subject, be indifferent to the emancipation of this fair land from present degradation.

The speaker then proceeded to say how much satisfaction she had had in observing the neatness of the writing of the pupils, and the excellence of their drawing, and added, that habits of order and neatness and the contemplation and copy of elegant form had a use beyond the mere accomplishment: such habits induced a moral state of mind, and the life would become through these habits more pure, and orderly, and excellent.

Miss Fuller suggested to the pupils that they should communicate to their companions and younger relatives the knowledge which they received in the school; and she exemplified the possibility of the young doing much for education, by an instance which fell under her own notice. She heard that there was a child who had an extraordinary love of teaching; going to see her, she found her busy with children, all of whom she had washed and made neat before beginning lessons, and she was now employing them all with slates and books, in the nicest manner. This child was placed by the wealthy persons whom her conduct interested in school, where she herself could receive a good education, though without breaking up her own little school, which would have been a pity.

To the friends of the institution, she would say, as she has often said, to those persons in America who had asked her in what way she would advise them to attempt to do good, for it was so difficult to know when money was well bestowed, that no one could possibly do wrong by giving *time* and *exertions* for the inculcation of good instruction: and that, possibly, friends might help materially by teaching in this school. . . .

In concluding, Miss Fuller said, "I do not know that I have anything more to say, except, 'Heaven bless you.'" The burst of applause which followed these words was, doubtless, the heartfelt echo of the same wish on the part of the audience towards the noble and pure-hearted speaker, whose lofty and poetic mind and infinite charity (in St. Paul's sense of the word) render her an object of affectionate admiration. . . .

From C. S. H., "Italian School, Greville St.," *People's Journal* 4 (16 January 1847): appendix, 5–6.

[Epistolary Comments on Fuller in 1846 and 1852]

Thomas Carlyle

Thomas Carlyle (1795–1881), Scottish essayist and biographer, maintained a lifelong friendship and correspondence with Emerson, though it grew strained in later years as Carlyle became more critical of what he considered the Transcendentalists' impractical idealism. Fuller had studied Carlyle's writings since 1832, especially those on German literature; she also reviewed his works favorably in the *Dial* and the *New-York Tribune*. For his part, he enjoyed reading *Papers on Literature and Art* ("the undeniable utterances . . . of a true heroic mind"). Emerson had sent Fuller's translation of Eckermann's *Conversations with Goethe* to Carlyle in 1839, so it was natural Emerson would alert him that Fuller was coming in 1846 to London, where Carlyle and his wife, Jane Welsh Carlyle (1801–1866), lived. Fuller's visit in October was an interesting one. She thoroughly enjoyed meeting one of her idols, though she did complain that "To interrupt him is a physical impossibility" (16 November 1846, *Letters*, 4:248). Although Fuller also liked Jane ("full of grace, sweetness, and talent" [*Letters*, 4:248]), she apparently disliked Fuller, and when she wrote to a friend, Geraldine Jewsbury, about the visit, she received this response: "I loathe her heartily from your description." Jewsbury had "no patience with theoretical profligacy," believing it "does the heart and soul more harm than a course of blackguardism!" To her, Fuller "must be, and cannot help but be, a hypocrite, if she be tempted to death to live 'a free and easy life', and yet keeps herself straitlaced up in practice to keep in with Emerson & Co.! . . . And then those doctrines from an irredeemably ugly, uninteresting woman are really 'damnable' " (19 October 1846, *Letters to Jane Carlyle*, 215). Thomas was milder, telling his brother that Fuller was "a strange *lilting* lean old-maid, not nearly such a bore as I expected" and writing his sister that Fuller was "rather a good woman," but "I remember I *was* somewhat hard upon her and certain crotchets of hers" (8 October 1846, *Collected Letters*, 21:72; 25 March 1847, *New Letters*, 2:32).

Thomas Carlyle to Ralph Waldo Emerson, 18 December 1846

Miss Fuller came duly as you announced; was welcomed for your sake and her own. A high-soaring, clear, enthusiast soul; in whose speech there is much of all that one wants to find in speech. A sharp subtle intellect too; and less of that shoreless Asiastic dreaminess than I have sometimes met with in her writings. We liked one another very well, I think, and the Springs too were favourites. But, on the whole, it could not be concealed, least of all from the sharp female intellect, that this Carlyle was a dreadfully heterodox, not to say a dreadfully savage fellow, at heart; believing no syllable of all that Gospel of Fraternity, Benevolence, and *new* Heaven-on-Earth, preached forth by all manner of "advanced" creatures from George Sand to Elihu Burritt, in these days; that in fact the said Carlyle not only disbelieved all that, but treated it as poisonous cant,—*sweetness* of sugar-of-lead,—a detestable *phosphorescence* from the dead body of a Christianity, that would not admit itself to be dead, and lie buried with all its unspeakable putrescences, as a venerable dead one ought! Surely detestable enough.—To all which Margaret listened with much good nature; tho' of course with sad reflexions not a few.—She is coming back to us, she promises. Her dialect is very vernacular,—extremely exotic in the London climate. If she do not gravitate too irresistibly towards that class of New-Era people (which includes whatsoever we have of prurient, esurient, morbid, flimsy, and in fact pitiable and unprofitable, and is at a sad discount among men of sense), she may get into good tracks of inquiry and connexion here, and be very useful to herself and others. . . .

Thomas Carlyle to Ralph Waldo Emerson, 7 May 1852

Poor Margaret, that is a strange tragedy that history of hers; and has many traits of the Heroic in it, tho' it is wild as the prophecy of a sybil. Such a predetermination to *eat* this big universe as her oyster or her egg, and to be absolute empress of all height and glory in it that her heart could conceive, I have not before seen in any human soul. Her "mountain *me*" indeed:—but her courage too is high and clear, her chivalrous nobleness indeed is great; her veracity, in its deepest sense, *à toute épreuve*. . . .

The Correspondence of Emerson and Carlyle, ed. Joseph Slater (New York: Columbia University Press, 1964), 410, 478, which also prints Carlyle's comments on *Papers on Literature and Art* (2 March 1847, 418).

[Fuller in Italy in 1847]

GEORGE PALMER PUTNAM

George Palmer Putnam (1814–1872) spent his whole life working in the pub-lishing world. In 1840, he founded the firm of Wiley and Putnam, settling with his new wife, Victorine Haven (1824–1891), in England in 1841, where he served as the firm's English agent until 1847. Wiley and Putnam had pub-lished Fuller's *Papers on Literature and Art* in 1846. In 1853, he founded *Put-nam's Monthly Magazine* and in 1866 he began the firm of G. P. Putnam & Son, which survives today.

The Putnams and Fuller briefly traveled together, and her account of the steamer incident described below is in *Dispatches from Europe*, 130–31. Putnam's story of Fuller's first meeting with Ossoli should be compared to Emelyn Story's account. Closer to the actual time of the incident, he had written how he had found Fuller "in tribulation, she having lost her party in the crowd" (Putnam, "Foreign Correspondence," 156). Putnam also wrote about this incident to a friend in New York, Evert A. Duyckinck (who had helped obtain *Papers on Literature and Art* for Wiley and Putnam). In his di-ary, Duyckinck summarized Putnam's letter as being about Fuller's "loss by day among thirty thousand people in St Peters," adding that within "the pre-cincts of the sanctuary it is said she received very singular suggestions from the young men of Rome which may afford instructive notes to a future edition of *Woman in the Nineteenth Century*" (Yannella and Yannella, "Duyckinck's Diary," 225).

IT SO HAPPENED that our party in Genoa, Leghorn, Naples, and Rome, was a good deal with that of Miss Fuller. Between Leghorn and Civita Vec-chia our steamer, an English one, was run down in the night by a French steamer. As they were going in opposite directions, at the rate of twelve miles an hour, such a shock in the dead of night, knocking us out of our berths, was not fitted to soothe an anxious spirit. The first impulse was to rush on deck to see if we were actually sinking. Fortunately the bow of the Frenchman had merely smashed one of our paddle-boxes, and the wheel itself, but had not injured the hull; so I jumped down to the ladies' cabin, to re-assure my wife and the other ladies. The door was opened by Miss Fuller in her night-dress. Instead of hysterical fright, as I expected, my hurried report that there would be time to dress before we went to the bottom, was met by Miss Fuller by the remark that seemed to me superhuman in its quiet calmness: "Oh, we—had not—made up our minds, that it was— worth while—to be at all—alarmed!" Verily woman—American woman, at least—is wonderful for her cool philosophy and strong nerved stoicism in great danger!

The narration in the memoirs of Miss Fuller of her first meeting with her future husband, the Marquis d'Ossoli, is not accurate. Her party had been attending some of the services of Holy Week in St. Peter's—ours had heard the miserère in the Sistine Chapel. As we came away from the Chapel, and met the throng from the great church on the steps, Miss Fuller stepped out quickly to overtake us, saying she had lost her friends; and as it was nearly dark, she seemed quite bewildered—more alarmed, indeed, than when we were really in danger of being drowned in the Mediterranean. She had taken the arm of a young gentleman in the crowd, who had politely offered to escort her home, or to a cab; but on joining us, she took leave of him, as we thought, rather ungraciously. She certainly did not give her address to him, but left him in the crowd, and we ourselves took her to her lodgings. How and when they met again, we do not know. But this was the first time the Marquis had seen her, and he left her in the confusion, without knowing who she was or where she lived.

From [George Palmer Putnam], "Leaves from a Publishers Letter-Book—I," *Putnam's Magazine*, n.s. 4 (October 1869): 467–74, substantially reprinted in *A Memoir of George Palmer Putnam* (New York: Putnam's, 1903), 1:143–46. His account in "Foreign Correspondence" refers to Fuller as "Miss * * * *," a reference to her signature of "*" in the *New-York Tribune*.

[Fuller in Rome in 1847–1849]

EMELYN STORY

As soon as she heard of our arrival [in Rome, November 1847] she stretched forth a friendly, cordial hand and greeted us most warmly—she gave us great assistance in our search for convenient lodgings, and we were soon happily established near her. Our intercourse was henceforth most frequent and intimate and knew not cloud nor coldness. Daily we were much together, and daily felt more sensible of the worth and value of our friend. To me she seemed so unlike what I had known her in America that I continually said to her "how have I misjudged you—you are not at all such a person as I took you to be in America." To this she replied, "I am not the same person, I am in many respects another. My life has new channels now and how thankful I am that I have been able to come out into larger interests—but partly, you did not know me at home in the true light."

I did not know her much personally, when in Boston, but through her friends,—who were mine also—I learned to think of her as a person on intellectual stilts, with a large share of arrogance and little sweetness of

[81]

temper. How unlike to this was she now,—so delicate, so simple, confiding—and affectionate,—with a true womanly heart and soul,—sensitive and generous, and what was to me a still greater surprise, possessed with broad charity that she could cover with its mantle the faults and defects of those about her.

We soon became acquainted with the young Marquis Ossoli, and met him frequently at Margaret's rooms. He appeared to be of a reserved and gentle nature, with quiet gentlemanlike manners, and there was something melancholy in the expression of his face which makes one desire to know more of him. In figure he was tall and of slender frame, dark eyes and hair and we judged that he was about thirty years of age, possibly younger. Margaret spoke of him most frankly to us and soon told us the history of her acquaintance with him which as nearly as I can recall was as follows:—

She went to hear vespers—the evening soon after her first coming to Rome [spring 1847]—at St. Peter's. She proposed to her companions, Mr and Mrs Spring, that some place should be designated where after the services they should meet, she being inclined, as was her custom always in St. Peter's, to wander alone among the different chapels. When at length she saw that the crowd was dispersing, she returned to the place assigned but could not find her party. In some perplexity she wandered about, with her glass carefully examining each group. Presently a young man of gentlemanlike address came up to her, and begged if she were seeking any one that he might be permitted to assist her. And together they continued the search through all parts of the church. At last it became evident, beyond a doubt, that her party could no longer be there, and, as it was then quite late, the crowd all gone, they went out into the piazza to find a carriage in which she might go home. In the piazza in front of St. Peter's generally may be found many carriages, but owing to the delay they had made, there were then none. And Margaret was compelled to walk with her stranger friend all the long distance between the Vatican and the Corso. At this time she had little command of the language for conversational purposes and their words were few, but enough to create in each a desire for further knowledge and acquaintance. At her door, they parted and Margaret, finding her friends already at home, related the adventure.[1]

After her return from Naples they met and he became her constant visitor and as in those days Margaret watched with zeal and intense interest the tide of political events, his mind was also turned in the direction of Liberty and better government. Whether or not Ossoli, unassisted, would have been able to emancipate himself from the influence of his family and early education, both eminently conservative and narrow, may be a question but that he did throw off the shackles is true and that he gave the cause of liberty his warm espousal is most certain.—Margaret had known Mazzini in London, had partaken of his schemes for the future of his country and was watching with great interest the current events, as well as taking every pains to inform herself in regard to action of all parties, with a view to write a history of the Period. Ossoli brought her every intelligence that might be of interest to her, and busied himself in learning the views of both parties that she might be able to view the matter impartially. Here, I may say, that in the estimation of most of those who were in Italy at this time the loss of Margaret's history and notes is a great and irreparable one. No one could have possessed so many avenues of direct information from both sides—while she was the friend and correspondent of Mazzini and knew the springs of action of his party,—through her husband's family and connections she knew the other view. So that whatever might be the value of her deductions, her facts could not have been otherwise than of highest value in this age of incorrect report and perverted statement. Together Margaret and Ossoli went to the meetings of either side—to her he carried all the flying reports of the day—such as he had heard in the café, or through his friends.

Not long after our coming to Rome, the old Marquis Ossoli died and as Angelo was his youngest son and only unmarried one, the care of his father during his last illness fell upon him. A few hasty moments of these days of anxiety he went to pass with Margaret, who tried to console him in his deep affliction. When at length his Father died, he told Margaret that he loved her and must marry her or be miserable. She still refused to look upon him as a Lover, and insisted that it was not fitting, that it was best he should marry a younger woman—that she would be his friend but not his wife. In this way it rested for some time during which we saw Ossoli pale, dejected and unhappy. He was always with her but in a sort of hopeless, desperate manner attending her, until at length he convinced her of his love and she married him.[2]

Shortly after this we went to Naples and she, in course of some months, to Aquila and Rieti. During this summer we heard from her often by letter and wrote to urge her to join us in our villa at Sorrento. During this summer she wrote constantly upon her history of the Italian movement for which she had collected material during the winter.[3] We did not again meet until the following spring, March 1849, when we went from Florence back to Rome.

She was at that time living on the Piazza Barberini. We proposed at once that she should come to live with us but as we could not find rooms significant in number for our party she kept for a while her own rooms. Again we were with her in most familiar every day intercourse, and as at this time a change of government had taken place,—the Pope having gone to Molo di Gaeta—we watched with her the great movements of the day. Ossoli was now actively interested; he was holding the office of captain of a regiment of the *Guardia Civica* and most enthusiastically looking forward to the success of the new measures.

At this time, during the spring of 49, Mazzini came to Rome. He went at once to see Margaret and at her rooms met Ossoli. After this interview with Mazzini it was quite evident that they had lost something of the faith and hopeful certainty with which they had regarded the issue, for Mazzini had discovered the want of singleness of purpose in the leaders. Still zealously Margaret and Ossoli aided in every way the progress of events, and when it was certain that the French had landed forces at Civita Vecchia and would attack Rome, Ossoli took station with his men on the walls of the Vatican, where he remained faithfully to the end of the attack. Margaret had, at the same time, the entire charge of one of the hospitals, and was the assistant of the Princess Belgioioso, in charge of *"dei Pellegrini,"* where, during the first day, they received seventy wounded men, French and Romans.

Night and day, Margaret was occupied, and, with the princess, so ordered and disposed the hospitals, that their conduct was truly admirable. All the work was skilfully divided, so that there was no confusion or hurry, and, from the chaotic condition in which these places had been left by the priests,—who previously had charge of them,—they brought them to a perfect state of regularity and discipline. Of money they had very little, and they were obliged to give their own time and thoughts, in its place. From the Americans in Rome, they raised a subscription for the aid of the wounded of either party; but, besides this, they had scarcely any means to use. I have walked through the wards with Margaret, and seen how comforting was her presence to the poor suffering men. "How long will the Signora stay?" "When will the Signora come again?" they eagerly asked. For each one's peculiar tastes she had a care: to one she carried books; to another she told the news of the day; and listened to another's oft-repeated

tale of wrongs, as the best sympathy she could give. They raised themselves up on their elbows, to get[4] the last glimpse of her as she was going
away. There were some of the poor sturdy fellows of Garibaldi's regiment
there, and to them she listened, as with delight they spoke of their Chief, of
his courage and skill for he seemed to have won the hearts of his men in a
remarkable manner.

One thing I may as well say in this connection, it happened that some
time before the coming of the French, while Margaret was travelling in the
country quite by herself, as she perhaps was returning from a visit to her
child who was out at nurse in the country, that she rested for an hour or
two at a little wayside *Osteria*. While there she was startled by the *Padrone*,
who with great alarm rushed into the room and said "We are quite lost,
here is the Legion Garibaldi, and these men always pillage, and if we do not
give all up to them without pay they will kill us." Margaret looked out upon
the road and saw that it was quite true, that the legion was coming thither
with all speed. For a moment she said that she felt uncomfortably, such
was the exaggerated account of the conduct of the men, that she thought
it quite possible that they would take her horses and so leave her without
the means of proceeding upon her journey. They came and she had determined to offer them a lunch at her own expence, having faith that gentleness and courtesy was the best protection from injury. Accordingly as soon
as they arrived and came boisterously into the *Osteria*, she rose and said
to the *Padrone*, "Give these good men wine and bread on my account, for
after their ride they must need the refreshment." Immediately the noise and
confusion subsided and with respectful bows to her they seated themselves
and partook of the lunch, giving her an account of their journey. When she
was ready to go and her vettura was at the door they waited upon her, took
her down the steps, and assisted her in with much gentleness and respect
of manner, and she drove off wondering how men with such natures could
have the reputation they had.

And so far as we could gather, except in this instance, their conduct was
of a most disorderly kind. Again in another instance she showed how great
was her power over rude men.

This was once when two men (contadini) being in a violent quarrel, had
rushed upon each other with knives. Margaret was called by the women bystanders, as the Signora who could most influence the men—She went directly up to the men—whose rage was truly awful to behold—and stepping

between them commanded them to separate. They parted, but with such a look of deadly revenge, that Margaret saw her work was but half accomplished. She sought them out separately, talked with them, urging forgiveness, but it was long before she could see any change of purpose in them and it was only after repeated conversations with them that she brought about the thing that she desired and saw them meet as friends.

After this her reputation as peacemaker was large and the women in the neighborhood came to her with long tales of trouble, urging her intervention. I have never known anything more extraordinary than this influence of hers over the passion and violence of the Italian character. Repeated instances come to my mind when a look from her has had more power to quiet excitement than the arguments and reasonings that could be brought to bear upon the subject. Something quite superior and apart from them who thought her and yet knew her as the gentle tender judge of their vices.

I may also mention here, that Margaret's charities, according to her means, were larger than those of any other whom I ever knew. At one time, in Rome, while she lived upon the simplest, slenderest fare, spending only some ten or twelve cents a day for her dinner, she lent, unsolicited, her last fifty dollars to an artist, who was then in need. That it would ever be returned to her, she did not know; but the doubt did not restrain the hand from giving. In this instance, it was soon repaid her; but her charities were not always towards the most deserving. Repeated instances of the false pretences, under which demands for charity are made, were known to her after she had given to unworthy objects; but no experience of this sort ever checked her kindly impulse to give, and being once deceived taught her no lesson of distrust. She ever listened with ready ear to all who came to her in any form of distress. Indeed, to use the language of another friend, "the prevalent impression at Rome, among all who knew her, was, that she was a mild saint and a ministering angel."[5]

I have in order to bring in these instances of her influence on those about her, deviated somewhat from my track,—we return to the life she led in Rome during the attack of the French and her charge of the hospitals where she spent daily some seven or eight hours, often, the entire night.

Her feeble frame was a good deal shaken by so uncommon a demand upon her strength, while at the same time the anxiety of her mind was intense. I well remember how exhausted and weary she was, how pale and agitated she returned to us after her days and nights watching—how eagerly she asked for news of Ossoli, and how seldom we had any to give her, for he was unable to send her a word for two or three days at a time.—Letters from the country there were none for the communication between Rieti and Rome was cut off.

After one such day she called me to her bedside and said that I must consent for her sake to keep the secret she was about to confide—Then she told me where her child was, when it was born; and gave me certain papers and parchment documents, which I was to keep, and, in the event of her death I was to take the boy to her Mother in America and confide him to her care and that of her friend Caroline Tappan.

The papers thus given me I had perfect liberty to read, but after she had told me her story I desired no confirmation of this fact, beyond what her words had given me. One or two of the papers she opened and we together read them. One was written on parchment in Latin, and was a certificate given by the Priest who married them saying that Angelo Eugene Ossoli was the legal [three words illegible] heir of whatever title and fortune should come to his Father. To this was affixed his seal with those of the other witnesses, and the Ossoli crest was drawn in full upon the paper. There was also a book in which Margaret had written the history of her acquaintance and marriage with Ossoli, and the birth of her child. In giving that to me she said "If I do not survive to tell this myself to my family, this book will be to them invaluable. Therefore keep it for them. If I live it is of no use, for my word will be all that they will ask." I took the papers and locked them up, never feeling any desire to look into them and never did, and as she gave them to me, I returned them to her, when I left Rome for Switzerland. After this she often spoke to me of the necessity there had been and still existed for her keeping her marriage a secret. At the time I argued in favor of her making it public but subsequent events have shown me the wisdom of her decision—The explanation she gave me of the secret marriage was this. They were married soon after I think but am not positive the death of the old Marquis Ossoli. The estate he had left was undivided and the two brothers attached to the Papal household were to be the executors. This property was not large, but when fairly divided would bring to each a little property, an income sufficient with economy for life in Rome. Every one knows, that Law is subject to ecclesiastical influence in Rome, and that marriage with a Protestant would be destructive to all prospects of favorable administration. Beside being of another Religious Faith there was in this case the additional crime of having married a Liberal, one who had publicly interested herself in favor of radical views—taking the two together there was good reason to suppose that if it were known, Ossoli must be a beggar and a banished man under the existing government but waiting a little while then there was a chance (a fair one too) of an honorable post under the new form of government which everybody anticipated. Leaving Rome at that time was leaving the field wherein they might hope to work much good and where they felt that they were needed. Ossoli's brothers had long before begun to look jealously upon him, knowing of his acquaintance with Margaret they feared the influence she might exert over his mind in favor of Liberal sentiments and had not hesitated to threaten the Papal displeasure. Ossoli's education had been such that it certainly argues an uncommon character that he remained so firm and single in his political views and was indifferent to the pecuniary advantages which his former position offered.

For many years the Ossoli family have been high in favor and in office in Rome and he had the same vista for his own future had he chosen to follow their lead. The Pope left for Mole di Gaeta and then came a suspension of all Legal procedure,—so that the estate never was divided before we left Italy. I do not know that it has ever been.

Ossoli had the feeling that while his own sister and family could not know of his marriage, no others ought to know of it and from day to day they hoped on for the favorable change which should enable them to declare it.

Their child was born and for his sake in order to defend him, as Margaret said, from the stings of poverty, they were patient waiters for the restored Law of the Land. Margaret felt that in this bold way she would, at any cost to herself, gladly preserve for her child from something of its [the world's] frigidity and although it was a severe trial (as her letters to us attest) she resolved to wait and hope and keep her secret. At the time when she took me into her confidence she was so full of anxiety and dread of some shock, from which she might not recover, that it was absolutely necessary to make it known to *some* friend. She was living with us at the time, and she gave it to me. Most sacredly, but timidly, did I keep her secret, for all the while I was tormented with desire to be of active service to her while I was incapacitated from any action by the position in which I was placed.

Ossoli's position [during the siege of Rome] was one of considerable danger, he being in one of the most exposed places and as Margaret saw his wounded and dying comrades she felt that another shot might take him from her or bring him to her care in the hospital.

Eagerly she watched as the carts came up with their suffering loads, aware that her worst fears might be confirmed. No argument of ours could persuade Ossoli to leave his post to take food or rest. Sometimes we went to him and carried a concealed basket of provisions, but he always shared it with so many of his fellows that his own portion must have been almost nothing. Haggard, worn, and pale, he walked over the [Vatican] grounds with us pointing out now here, now there, where some poor fellow's blood sprinkled the wall. Margaret was with us and for a few moments they could have an anxious talk about their child whose health was in some peril, news having arrived that the small pox had broken out in the house in which they had left him at Rieti.

To get to him or to send to him was quite impossible and for days they were in complete ignorance about him. After waiting upon the post office with the anxiety that a mother only can know at length a letter came but it only relieved her from her present anxiety with regard to the boy's health to give her another cause of uneasiness. The nurse declared that unless means were immediately found for sending her in advance payment, a certain sum of money, she would altogether abandon the child. It seemed at first impossible to send money, the road was insecure, the bearer of any parcel was likely to be seized by one party or the other and treated as a spy. But happily after much consideration, it was sent to the address of a physician who had charge to look after the child and I think did reach its destination, and for a while answered the purpose of keeping the wretched nurse faithful to her charge.

I have heard it suggested by someone that Ossoli had married Margaret under the impression of her having a large Fortune.[6]

That this is utterly false I can declare, since to my own knowledge he was in the habit even from their first acquaintance of making for her what the Italians term, little economies, and was in Margaret's unreserved confidence as to the feeble state of her purse.

Again, I have heard it said that he was a person entirely without education—I can only say that his education was equal to that of most Roman gentlemen, not thorough but such as suited him for his rank and position. He had been from his youth under the care of a Priest who taught him as a tutor. He knew not much of foreign languages, read French a little and was a good-deal interested in Italian history.

Many of our countrymen who saw him could discover little in him but that was rather because he was not quickly interested in others, than that he lacked interesting points.

He was always reserved, and when with Margaret preferred always to hear her talk even when she spoke a language he did not know than to talk himself or hear any one else. His manner toward Margaret was devoted and lover-like to a striking degree. He cared not how trivial was the service if he might perform it for her—I remember to have seen him one morning after they had been married nearly two years, set off on an errand to get the handle of her parasol mended with as much genuine knightly zeal as if the charge had been a much weightier one. As he took it he said "how sweet it is to do little things for you, never attend to such yourself, always leave them to me for my pleasure." When she was ill he nursed and watched over with the tenderness of woman. When she said to him, "how have you learned to be so good a nurse," he said "my Father was ill and I tended upon him." No service was too trivial, no sacrifice too great for him—He never wished her to give up any pleasure because he could not share it, but if she were interested, he would go with her to any house, leave her and call again to take her home. Such tender unselfish love I have rarely before seen. It made green her days and gave her an expression of peace and serenity which before was a stranger to her face.

"No companion in nature was ever so much to me as is Ossoli," does not this show that his soul was deep and full of emotion, for who that knew Margaret would believe that any other companion would have been agreeable to her in her communion with nature. What a beautiful picture is that of their return to Rome, after a day spent on the Campagna! . . .

Emelyn Story, [Margaret Fuller in Rome], 1851–1852, from "The Private Marriage," at the Boston Public Library. Story prepared this account for use in *Memoirs,* and parts of it do appear there, with significant stylistic revisions and some revisions of substantive matters (2:281–93).

Notes

1. The manuscript has a pasted-on slip with a comment written in William Henry Channing's hand: "This chance meeting at Vespers service in St Peters prepared the way

for many interviews; and it was before Margaret's departure for Venice, Milan & Como, that Ossoli first offered his hand and was refused. Mrs Story continues", which was printed in *Memoirs*.

2. This paragraph is not printed in *Memoirs*.

3. The manuscript reads: "winter [followed by cancelled "; & during this [word?] in September her child was born.—"]". This does not appear in *Memoirs*.

4. "faithfully to the end . . . their elbows, to get" is not present in the manuscript and is inserted from *Memoirs*, 2:285–86.

5. This paragraph is not present in the manuscript and is inserted from *Memoirs*, 2:288–89.

6. This paragraph and the remaining paragraphs were not printed in *Memoirs*.

[Fuller in Rome in 1849]

FREDERICK WILLIAM GALE

> Frederick William Gale (1816–1854) graduated from Harvard University in 1836 and later worked as an attorney in St. Louis and then Worcester, Massachusetts.

BY A PECULIAR COINCIDENCE, Anna [Gale]'s brother, Frederick W. Gale, who had graduated with honors from Harvard in 1836, and had visited her at the Green Street School happened to be living in Florence, Italy, in December of 1849. He was a well-educated man, who had not been particularly impressed in the past by Margaret Fuller or her writings. By means of the entries in his journal and his letters, we have glimpses of her through a man's eyes near the close of her life. On December 10, 1849, he wrote in his journal:

> Studied till 2 P.M. In eve at Doney's and saw Mr. Sumner again, and the husband of the quondam Miss Fuller, the Marquis of Ossoli, a Roman who is obliged to fly from the Roman States on account of the part he took in favor of the recent republic.

On the next day Gale wrote to his sister, Anna, saying:

> But there is also one of your old friends here—you can't guess who! Well, it is the quondam Margaret Fuller—now transformed, by marriage, into no less a personage than the *Marchioness of Ossoli*. Her husband is more than ten years younger than herself, I am told. He is a Roman Marquis, was married to her in private 2 years ago, and they have a son of 15 months. He rebelled against the government of the Pope, and was obliged to fly from the Papal States, and is now here with his wife and child, reduced to poverty, and all are depending upon her pen for a subsistence. What a strange story, is it not? Now that the scornful, manhating Margaret of 40 has got a husband, really no old maid need despair, while there is life in her body!

Five days later, on December 15, 1849, he noted in his journal a description of Margaret herself:

In the eve to Mozier's house, where I met a large company—mostly artists— among them *Geo. P. Marsh* (was not introduced) and *Madame Ossioli* [*sic*] and the young *Marquis d'Ossioli,* her spouse. I found her much older and uglier than I had anticipated. There are wrinkles and lines in her face, old enough for 60! Her husband is handsome and hardly looks 30. She appeared sad and depressed to me—bent in body and in fact an old woman before her time. The political events in Italy in which she had embarked, as it were, by her marriage with the Marquis—a rebel against the Pope and Officer in the service of the Republicans, have probably contributed to this result. But I heard nothing like that tone of scorn and contempt which I expected in her conversation. I talked a good deal with her, and chiefly about the sad manner in which the progressive movements of the recent struggles have been managed.

On December 18 Gale had a further conversation with Madame Ossoli, and then, on December 29, his description of a party for members of the American colony indicates that even he had succumbed to a degree to the charm of Margaret Fuller.

In eve to Mozier's—met a large party of Americans—had a fine supper in which cold turkey, duck, maryonaise [*sic*], champagne and whisky punch played a prominent part—and the transcendental ex-editress of the Dial devoted her- self with unmistakeable ardor to them all not even declining that vulgar, but comforting beverage—so unfashionable for Boston blues, *the whisky punch.* I danced two cotillions with her and found her none the worse for the liquor— but merry and agreeable. Her spouse says nothing. The ladies left before 2, but a party of gentlemen told stories and renewed the potations somewhat later.

From Edward A. Hoyt and Loriman S. Brigham, "Glimpses of Margaret Fuller: The Green Street School and Florence," *New England Quarterly* 29 (March 1956): 87–98.

[Fuller in Florence in 1850]

WILLIAM HENRY HURLBERT

> William Henry Hurlbert (1827–1895) was born in Charleston, South Carolina,
> as "Hurlbut" but changed his name. He graduated from Harvard University
> in 1847 and from the Harvard Divinity School in 1849, after which he spent
> two years studying in Europe. Hurlbert was variously a newspaper reporter,
> writer, drama critic, abolitionist, and playwright. One who was at divinity
> school with him wrote that while in Italy, Hurlbert was not only "blessed by
> the Pope, but by the society of the Countess Ossoli whom he admires very
> much" (Higginson, *Letters and Journals,* 29). Hurlbert's account was one of
> the many solicited for *Memoirs of Margaret Fuller Ossoli* by the editors.

I PASSED ABOUT six weeks in the city of Florence, during the months of
March and April, 1850. During the whole of that time Madame Ossoli was
residing in a house at the corner of the Via della Misericordia and the Piazza Santa Maria Novella. This house is one of those large, well built modern houses that show strangely in the streets of the stately Tuscan city.
But if her rooms were less characteristically Italian, they were the more
comfortable, and, though small, had a quiet, home-like air. Her windows
opened upon a fine view of the beautiful Piazza; for such was their position,
that while the card-board façade of the church of Sta. Maria Novella could
only be seen at an angle, the exquisite Campanile rose fair and full against
the sky. She enjoyed this most graceful tower very much, and, I think, preferred it even to Giotto's noble work. Its quiet religious grace was grateful
to her spirit, which seemed to be yearning for peace from the cares that had
so vexed and heated the world about her for a year past.

I saw her frequently at these rooms, where, surrounded by her books
and papers, she used to devote her mornings to her literary labors. Once
or twice I called in the morning, and found her quite immersed in manuscripts and journals. Her evenings were passed usually in the society of her
friends, at her own rooms, or at theirs. With the pleasant circle of Americans, then living in Florence, she was on the best terms, and though she
seemed always to bring with her her own most intimate society, and never

to be quite free from the company of busy thoughts, and the cares to which her life had introduced her, she was always cheerful, and her remarkable powers of conversation subserved on all occasions the kindliest, purposes of good-will in social intercourse.

The friends with whom she seemed to be on the terms of most sympathy, were an Italian lady, the Marchesa Arconati Visconti,[1]—the exquisite sweetness of whose voice interpreted, even to those who knew her only as a transient acquaintance, the harmony of her nature,—and some English residents in Florence, among whom I need only name Mr. and Mrs. Browning, to satisfy the most anxious friends of Madame Ossoli that the last months of her Italian life were cheered by all the light that communion with gifted and noble natures could afford.

The Marchesa Arconati used to persuade Madame Ossoli to occasional excursions with her into the environs of Florence, and she passed some days of the beautiful spring weather at the villa of that lady.

Her delight in nature seemed to be a source of great comfort and strength to her. I shall not easily forget the account she gave me, on the evening of one delicious Sunday in April, of a walk which she had taken with her husband in the afternoon of that day, to the hill of San Miniato. The amethystine beauty of the Apennines,—the cypress trees that sentinel the way up to the ancient and deserted church,—the church itself, standing high and lonely on its hill, begirt with the vine-clad, crumbling walls of Michel Angelo,—the repose of the dome-crowned city in the vale below,—seemed to have wrought their impression with peculiar force upon her mind that afternoon. On their way home, they had entered the conventual church that stands half way up the hill, just as the vesper service was beginning, and she spoke of the simple spirit of devotion that filled the place, and of the gentle wonder with which, to use her own words, the "peasant women turned their glances, the soft dark glances of the Tuscan peasant's eyes," upon the strangers, with a singular enthusiasm. She was in the habit of taking such walks with her husband, and she never returned from one of them, I believe, without some new impression of beauty and of lasting truth. While her judgment, intense in its sincerity, tested, like an *aqua regia*,[2] the value of all facts that came within her notice, her sympathies seemed, by an instinctive and unerring action, to transmute all her experiences instantly into permanent treasures.

The economy of the house in which she lived afforded me occasions for observing the decisive power, both of control and of consolation, which she could exert over others. Her maid,—an impetuous girl of Rieti, a town which rivals Tivoli as a hot-bed of homicide,—was constantly involved in disputes with a young Jewess, who occupied the floor above Madame Ossoli. On one occasion, this Jewess offered the maid a deliberate and unprovoked insult. The girl of Rieti, snatching up a knife, ran up stairs to revenge herself after her national fashion. The porter's little daughter followed her and, running into Madame Ossoli's rooms, besought her interference. Madame Ossoli reached the apartment of the Jewess, just in time to interpose between that beetle-browed lady and her infuriated assailant. Those who know the insane license of spirit which distinguishes the Roman mountaineers, will understand that this was a position of no slight hazard. The Jewess aggravated the danger of the offence by the obstinate maliciousness of her aspect and words. Such, however, was Madame Ossoli's entire self-possession and forbearance, that she was able to hold her ground, and to remonstrate with this difficult pair of antagonists so effectually, as to bring the maid to penitent tears, and the Jewess to a confession of her injustice, and a promise of future good behavior.

The porter of the house, who lived in a dark cavernous hole on the first floor, was slowly dying of a consumption, the sufferings of which were imbittered by the chill dampness of his abode. His hollow voice and hacking cough, however, could not veil the grateful accent with which he uttered any allusion to Madame Ossoli. He was so close a prisoner to his narrow, windowless chamber, that when I inquired for Madame Ossoli he was often obliged to call his little daughter, before he could tell me whether Madame was at home, or not; and he always tempered the official uniformity of the question with some word of tenderness. Indeed, he rarely pronounced her name; sufficiently indicating to the child whom it was that I was seeking, by the affectionate epithet he used, *"Lita! e la cara Signora in casa?"*

The composure and force of Madame Ossoli's character would, indeed, have given her a strong influence for good over any person with whom she was brought into contact; but this influence must have been even extraordinary over the impulsive and ill-disciplined children of passion and of sorrow, among whom she was thrown in Italy.

Her husband related to me once, with a most reverent enthusiasm, some stories of the good she had done in Rieti, during her residence there. The Spanish troops were quartered in that town, and the dissipated habits of the officers, as well as the excesses of the soldiery, kept the place in a constant irritation. Though overwhelmed with cares and anxieties, Madame Ossoli found time and collectedness of mind enough to interest herself in the distresses of the townspeople, and to pour the soothing oil of a wise sympathy upon their wounded and indignant feelings. On one occasion, as the Marchese told me, she undoubtedly saved the lives of a family in Rieti, by inducing them to pass over in silence an insult offered to one of them by an intoxicated Spanish soldier,—and, on another, she interfered between two brothers, maddened by passion, and threatening to stain the family hearth with the guilt of fratricide.[3]

Such incidents, and the calm tenor of Madame Ossoli's confident hopes,—the assured faith and unshaken bravery, with which she met and turned aside the complicated troubles, rising sometimes into absolute perils, of their last year in Italy,—seemed to have inspired her husband with a feeling of respect for her, amounting to reverence. This feeling, modifying the manifest tenderness with which he hung upon her every word and look, and sought to anticipate her simplest wishes, was luminously visible in the air and manner of his affectionate devotion to her.

The frank and simple recognition of his wife's singular nobleness, which he always displayed, was the best evidence that his own nature was of a fine and noble strain. And those who knew him best, are, I believe, unanimous in testifying that his character did in no respect belie the evidence borne by his manly and truthful countenance, to its warmth and its sincerity. He seemed quite absorbed in his wife and child. I cannot remember ever to have found Madame Ossoli alone, on those evenings when she remained at home. Her husband was always with her. The picture of their room rises clearly on my memory. A small square room, sparingly, yet sufficiently furnished, with polished floor and frescoed ceiling,—and, drawn up closely before the cheerful fire, an oval table, on which stood a monkish lamp of brass, with depending chains that support quaint classic cups for the olive oil. There, seated beside his wife, I was sure to find the Marchese, reading from some patriotic book, and dressed in the dark brown, red-corded coat of the Guardia Civica, which it was his melancholy pleasure to wear at home. So long as the conversation could be carried on in Italian, he used to remain, though he rarely joined in it to any considerable degree; but if a number of English and American visitors came in, he used to take his leave and go to the Café d'Italia, being very unwilling, as Madame Ossoli told me, to impose any seeming restraint, by his presence, upon her friends, with whom he was unable to converse. For the same reason, he rarely remained with her at the houses of her English or American friends, though he always accompanied her thither, and returned to escort her home.

I conversed with him so little that I can hardly venture to make any remarks on the impression which I received from his conversation, with regard to the character of his mind. Notwithstanding his general reserve and curtness of speech, on two or three occasions he showed himself to possess quite a quick and vivid fancy, and even a certain share of humor. I have heard him tell stories remarkably well. One tale, especially, which related to a dream he had in early life, about a treasure concealed in his father's house, which was thrice repeated, and made so strong an impression on his mind as to induce him to batter a certain panel in the library almost to pieces, in vain, but which received something like a confirmation from the fact, that a Roman attorney, who rented that and other rooms from the family, after his father's death, grew suddenly and unaccountably rich,—I remember as being told with great felicity and vivacity of expression.

His recollections of the trouble and the dangers through which he had passed with his wife seemed to be overpoweringly painful. On one occasion, he began to tell me a story of their stay in the mountains: He had gone out to walk, and had unconsciously crossed the Neapolitan frontier. Suddenly meeting with a party of the Neapolitan *gendarmerie,* he was called to account for his trespass, and being unable to produce any papers testifying to his loyalty, or the legality of his existence, he was carried off, despite his protestations, and lodged for the night in a miserable guard-house, whence he was taken, next morning, to the headquarters of the officer commanding in the neighborhood. Here, matters might have gone badly with him, but for the accident that he had upon his person a business letter directed to himself as the Marchese Ossoli. A certain abbé, the regimental chaplain, having once spent some time in Rome, recognized the name as that of an officer in the Pope's Guardia Nobile,[4] whereupon, the Neapolitan officers not only ordered him to be released, but sent him back, with many apologies, in a carriage, and under an armed escort, to the Roman territory. When he reached this part of his story, and came to his meeting with Madame Ossoli, the remembrance of her terrible distress during the period of his detention so overcame him, that he was quite unable to go on.

Towards their child he manifested an overflowing tenderness, and most affectionate care.

Notwithstanding the intense contempt and hatred which Signore Ossoli, in common with all the Italian liberals, cherished towards the ecclesiastical body, he seemed to be a very devout Catholic. He used to attend regularly the vesper service, in some of the older and quieter churches of Florence; and, though I presume Madame Ossoli never accepted in any degree the Roman Catholic forms of faith, she frequently accompanied him on these occasions. And I know that she enjoyed the devotional influences of the church ritual, as performed in the cathedral, and at Santa Croce, especially during the Easter-week.

Though condemned by her somewhat uncertain position at Florence,[5] as well as by the state of things in Tuscany at that time, to a comparative inaction, Madame Ossoli never seemed to lose in the least the warmth of her interest in the affairs of Italy, nor did she bate one jot of heart or hope for the future of that country. She was much depressed, however, I think, by the apparent apathy and prostration of the Liberals in Tuscany; and the presence of the Austrian troops in Florence was as painful and annoying to her, as it could have been to any Florentine patriot. When it was understood that Prince Lichtenstein had requested the Grand Duke to order a general illumination in honor of the anniversary of the battle of Novara, Madame Ossoli, I recollect, was more moved, than I remember on any other occasion to have seen her. And she used to speak very regretfully of the change which had come over the spirit of Florence, since her former residence there. Then all was gayety and hope. Bodies of artisans, gathering recruits as they passed along, used to form themselves into choral bands, as they returned from their work at the close of the day, and filled the air with the chants of liberty. Now, all was a sombre and desolate silence.

Her own various cares so occupied Madame Ossoli that she seemed to be very much withdrawn from the world of art. During the whole time of my stay in Florence, I do not think she once visited either of the Grand Ducal Galleries, and the only studio in which she seemed to feel any very strong interest, was that of Mademoiselle Favand, a lady whose independence of character, self-reliance, and courageous genius, could hardly have failed to attract her congenial sympathies.

But among all my remembrances of Madame Ossoli, there are none more beautiful or more enduring than those which recall to me another person, a young stranger, alone and in feeble health, who found, in her society, her sympathy, and her counsels, a constant atmosphere of comfort and of peace. Every morning, wild-flowers, freshly gathered, were laid upon her table by the grateful hands of this young man; every evening, beside her seat in her little room, his mild, pure face was to be seen, bright with a quiet happiness, that must have bound his heart by no weak ties to her with whose fate his own was so closely to be linked.

And the recollection of such benign and holy influences breathed upon the human hearts of those who came within her sphere, will not, I trust, be valueless to those friends, in whose love her memory is enshrined with more immortal honors than the world can give or take away.

Memoirs of Margaret Fuller Ossoli, ed. William Henry Channing, James Freeman Clarke, and Ralph Waldo Emerson, 2 vols. (Boston: Phillips, Sampson, 1852), 2:320–30, where Hurlbert is incorrectly identified as "Hurlbut."

Notes

1. Just before I left Florence, Madame Ossoli showed me a small marble figure of a child, playing among flowers or vine leaves, which, she said, was a portrait of the child of Madame Arconati, presented to her by that lady. I mention this circumstance, because I have understood that a figure answering this description was recovered from the wreck of the *Elizabeth.* [Hurlbert's note]

2. "Aqua regia" is a mixture of acids that can dissolve gold.

3. The circumstances of this story, perhaps, deserve to be recorded. The brothers were two young men, the sons and the chief supports of Madame Ossoli's landlord at Rieti. They were both married,—the younger one to a beautiful girl, who had brought him no dowry, and who, in the opinion of her husband's family, had not shown a proper disposition to bear her share of the domestic burdens and duties. The bickerings and disputes which resulted from this state of affairs, on one unlucky day, took the form of an open and violent quarrel. The younger son, who was absent from home when the conflict began, returned to find it at its height, and was received by his wife with passionate tears, and by his relations with sharp recriminations. His brother, especially, took it upon himself to up-braid him, in the name of all his family, for bringing into their home-circle such a firebrand of discord. Charges and counter charges followed in rapid succession, and hasty words soon led to blows. From blows the appeal to the knife was swiftly made, and when Madame Ossoli, attracted by the unusual clamor, entered upon the scene of action, she found that blood had been already drawn, and that the younger brother was only restrained from fol-lowing up the first assault by the united force of all the females, who hung about him, while the older brother, grasping a heavy billet of wood, and pale with rage, stood awaiting his

antagonist. Passing through the group of weeping and terrified women, Madame Ossoli made her way up to the younger brother and, laying her hand upon his shoulder, asked him to put down his weapon and listen to her. It was in vain that he attempted to ignore her presence. Before the spell of her calm, firm, well-known voice, his fury melted away. She spoke to him again, and besought him to show himself a man, and to master his foolish and wicked rage. With a sudden impulse, he flung his knife upon the ground, turned to Madame Ossoli, clasped and kissed her hand, and then running towards his brother, the two met in a fraternal embrace, which brought the threatened tragedy to a joyful termination. [Hurlbert's note]

4. It will be understood, that this officer was the Marchese's older brother, who still adheres to the Papal cause. [Hurlbert's note]

5. She believed herself to be, and I suppose really was, under the surveillance of the police during her residence in Florence. [Hurlbert's note]

[Fuller's Death in 1850]

WILLIAM HENRY CHANNING

William Henry Channing (1810–1884), nephew of the well-known Unitarian preacher William Ellery Channing and cousin of William Ellery Channing the Younger, is immortalized as the "evil time's sole patriot" in Emerson's "Ode" inscribed to him. The Harvard College and Divinity School graduate preached in Cincinnati, Ohio (1838–1841), coedited the Transcendentalist journal in the midwest, the *Western Messenger* (1839-1841), contributed to the *Dial*, and edited the reform journal the *Present* (1843–1844). Channing was also a frequent visitor to the Brook Farm community. In 1842, he moved to New York, where Fuller often saw him after she moved there.

Although Channing and Fuller became good friends by 1838, they had not been attracted to each other when they had first met a decade earlier, for in 1833 James Freeman Clarke asked Channing, "Is it that you feel her defects to be similar to your own, and she not being on the right way would exercise a bad influence on the growth of your mind?" (Capper, *Private Years*, 321). But as they negotiated their personal and professional journeys together, their correspondence was a warm one. Fuller told Channing that his "influence on me, in whatever shape it comes, has always been purifying, ennobling, and of late it has been so suggestive of thoughts on the greatest themes of the time that its influence, though pensive, has been most fruitful" ([n.d.], *Letters*, 6:95–96). For his part, Channing wrote Fuller "I have felt all along that I was the one to be aided in our intercourse" (Frothingham, *Channing*, 181). Later, Fuller grouped Channing with Emerson as having "in different ways the celestial fire," adding that though they "may have faults," there was "no base alloy" (9 March 1849, *Letters*, 5:201).

Channing edited, along with Emerson and James Freeman Clarke, *Memoirs of Margaret Fuller Ossoli* and, in fact, was the driving force behind it and had the major editorial hand in its composition. The work gave him a new appreciation of Fuller, and he said of his editorial task, "I never knew or loved this glorious friend, it seems to me, till now!" (Frothingham, *Channing*, 441). The section below, describing Fuller's last hours, is based on interviews Channing had conducted with people at the scene of the shipwreck.

On Thursday, July 15th, at noon, the Elizabeth was off the Jersey coast, somewhere between Cape May and Barnegat; and, as the weather was thick, with a fresh breeze blowing from the east of south, the officer in command, desirous to secure a good offing, stood east-north-east. His purpose was, when daylight showed the highlands of Neversink, to take a pilot, and run before the wind past Sandy Hook. So confident, indeed, was he of safety, that he promised his passengers to land them early in the morning at New York. With this hope, their trunks were packed, the preparations made to greet their friends, the last good-night was spoken, and with grateful hearts Margaret and Ossoli put Nino to rest, for the last time, as they thought, on ship-board,—for the last time, as it was to be, on earth!

By nine o'clock, the breeze rose to a gale, which every hour increased in violence, till at midnight it became a hurricane. Yet, as the Elizabeth was new and strong, and as the commander, trusting to an occasional cast of the lead, assured them that they were not nearing the Jersey coast,—which alone he dreaded,—the passengers remained in their state-rooms, and caught such uneasy sleep as the howling storm and tossing ship permitted. Utterly unconscious they were, even then, amidst perils, whence only by promptest energy was it possible to escape. Though under close-reefed sails, their vessel was making way far more swiftly than any one on board had dreamed of; and for hours, with the combined force of currents and the tempest, had been driving headlong towards the sand-bars of Long Island. About four o'clock, on Friday morning, July 16th, she struck,—first draggingly, then hard and harder,—on Fire Island beach.

The main and mizzen masts were at once cut away; but the heavy marble in her hold had broken through her bottom, and she bilged. Her bow held fast, her stern swung round, she careened inland, her broadside was bared to the shock of the billows, and the waves made a clear breach over her with every swell. The doom of the poor Elizabeth was sealed now, and no human power could save her. She lay at the mercy of the maddened ocean.

At the first jar, the passengers, knowing but too well its fatal import, sprang from their berths. Then came the cry of "Cut away," followed by the crash of falling timbers, and the thunder of the seas, as they broke across the deck. In a moment more, the cabin skylight was dashed in pieces by the breakers, and the spray, pouring down like a cataract, put out the lights, while the cabin door was wrenched from its fastenings, and the waves swept in and out. One scream, one only, was heard from Margaret's state-room; and Sumner and Mrs. Hasty, meeting in the cabin, clasped hands, with these few but touching words: "We must die." "Let us die calmly, then." "I hope so, Mrs. Hasty." It was in the gray dusk, and amid the awful tumult, that the companions in misfortune met. The side of the cabin to the leeward had already settled under water; and furniture, trunks, and fragments of the skylight were floating to and fro; while the inclined position of the floor made it difficult to stand; and every sea, as it broke over the bulwarks, splashed in through the open roof. The windward cabin-walls, however, still yielded partial shelter, and against it, seated side by side, half leaning backwards, with feet braced upon the long table, they awaited what next should come. At first, Nino, alarmed at the uproar, the darkness, and the rushing water, while shivering with the wet, cried passionately; but soon his mother, wrapping him in such garments as were at hand and folding him to her bosom, sang him to sleep. Celeste too was in an agony of terror, till Ossoli, with soothing words and a long and fervent prayer, restored her to self-control and trust. When calmly they rested, side by side, exchanging kindly partings and sending messages to friends, if any should survive to be their bearer. Meanwhile, the boats having been swamped or carried away, and the carpenter's tools washed overboard, the crew had retreated to the top-gallant forecastle; but, as the passengers saw and heard nothing of them, they supposed that the officers and crew had deserted the ship, and that they were left alone. Thus passed three hours.

At length, about seven, as there were signs that the cabin would soon break up, and any death seemed preferable to that of being crushed among the ruins, Mrs. Hasty made her way to the door, and, looking out at intervals between the seas as they swept across the vessel amidships, saw some one standing by the foremast. His face was toward the shore. She screamed and beckoned, but her voice was lost amid the roar of the wind and breakers, and her gestures were unnoticed. Soon, however, Davis, the mate, through the door of the forecastle caught sight of her, and, at once comprehending the danger, summoned the men to go to the rescue. At first none dared to risk with him the perilous attempt; but, cool and resolute, he set forth by himself, and now holding to the bulwarks, now stooping as the waves combed over, he succeeded in reaching the cabin. Two sailors, emboldened by his example, followed. Preparations were instantly made

to conduct the passengers to the forecastle, which, as being more strongly
built and lying further up the sands, was the least exposed part of the ship.
Mrs. Hasty volunteered to go the first. With one hand clasped by Davis,
while with the other each grasped the rail, they started, a sailor moving
close behind. But hardly had they taken three steps, when a sea broke loose
her hold, and swept her into the hatch-way. "Let me go," she cried, "your
life is important to all on board." But cheerily, and with a smile,[1] he answered, "Not quite yet;" and, seizing in his teeth her long hair, as it floated
past him, he caught with both hands at some near support, and, aided by
the seaman, set her once again upon her feet. A few moments more of struggle brought them safely through. In turn, each of the passengers was helped
thus laboriously across the deck, though, as the broken rail and cordage
had at one place fallen in the way, the passage was dangerous and difficult
in the extreme. Angelino was borne in a canvas bag, slung round the neck
of a sailor. Within the forecastle, which was comparatively dry and sheltered, they now seated themselves, and, wrapped in the loose overcoats of
the seamen, regained some warmth. Three times more, however, the mate
made his way to the cabin; once, to save her late husband's watch, for Mrs.
Hasty; again for some doubloons, money-drafts, and rings in Margaret's
desk; and, finally, to procure a bottle of wine and a drum of figs for their
refreshment. It was after his last return, that Margaret said to Mrs. Hasty,
"There still remains what, if I live, will be of more value to me than anything," referring, probably, to her manuscript on Italy; but it seemed too
selfish to ask their brave preserver to run the risk again.

There was opportunity now to learn their situation, and to discuss the
chances of escape. At the distance of only a few hundred yards, appeared
the shore,—a lonely waste of sand-hills, so far as could be seen through
the spray and driving rain. But men had been early observed, gazing at the
wreck, and, later, a wagon had been drawn upon the beach. There was no
sign of a life-boat, however, or of any attempt at rescue; and, about nine
o'clock, it was determined that some one should try to land by swimming,
and, if possible, get help. Though it seemed almost sure death to trust one's
self to the surf, a sailor, with a life-preserver, jumped over-board, and,
notwithstanding a current drifting him to leeward, was seen to reach the
shore. A second, with the aid of a spar, followed in safety; and Sumner,
encouraged by their success, sprang over also; but, either struck by some
piece of the wreck, or unable to combat with the waves, he sank. Another

hour or more passed by; but though persons were busy gathering into carts whatever spoil was stranded, no life-boat yet appeared; and, after much deliberation, the plan was proposed,—and, as it was then understood, agreed to,—that the passengers should attempt to land, each seated upon a plank, and grasping handles of rope, while a sailor swam behind. Here, too, Mrs. Hasty was the first to venture, under the guard of Davis. Once and again, during their passage, the plank was rolled wholly over, and once and again was righted, with its bearer, by the dauntless steersman; and when, at length, tossed by the surf upon the sands, the half-drowned woman still holding, as in a death-struggle, to the ropes, was about to be swept back by the undertow, he caught her in his arms, and, with the assistance of a bystander, placed her high upon the beach. Thus twice in one day had he perilled his own life to save that of the widow of his captain, and even over that dismal tragedy his devotedness casts one gleam of light.

Now came Margaret's turn. But she steadily refused to be separated from Ossoli and Angelo. On a raft with them, she would have boldly encountered the surf, but alone she would not go. Probably, she had appeared to assent to the plan for escaping upon planks, with the view of inducing Mrs. Hasty to trust herself to the care of the best man on board; very possibly, also, she had never learned the result of their attempt, as, seated within the forecastle, she could not see the beach. She knew, too, that if a life-boat could be sent, Davis was one who would neglect no effort to expedite its coming. While she was yet declining all persuasions, word was given from the deck, that the life-boat had finally appeared. For a moment, the news lighted up again the flickering fire of hope. They might yet be saved,—be saved together! Alas! to the experienced eyes of the sailors it too soon became evident that there was no attempt to launch or man her. The last chance of aid from shore, then, was gone utterly. They must rely on their own strength, or perish. And if ever they were to escape, the time had come; for, at noon, the storm had somewhat lulled; but already the tide had turned, and it was plain that the wreck could not hold together through another flood. In this emergency, the commanding officer, who until now had remained at his post, once more appealed to Margaret to try to escape,—urging that the ship would inevitably break up soon; that it was mere suicide to remain longer; that he did not feel free to sacrifice the lives of the crew, or to throw away his own; finally, that he would himself take Angelo, and that sailors should go with Celeste, Ossoli, and herself. But, as before, Margaret decisively declared that she would not be parted from her husband or her child. The order was then given to "save themselves," and all but four of the crew jumped over, several of whom, together with the commander, reached shore alive, though severely bruised and wounded by the drifting fragments. There is a sad consolation in believing that, if Margaret judged it to be impossible that the *three* should escape, she in all probability was right. It required a most rare combination of courage, promptness, and persistency, to do what Davis had done for Mrs. Hasty. We may not conjecture the crowd of thoughts which influenced the lovers, the parents, in this awful crisis; but doubtless one wish was ever uppermost,—that, God willing, the last hour might come for ALL, if it must come for *one*.

It was now past three o'clock, and as, with the rising tide, the gale swelled once more to its former violence, the remnants of the barque fast yielded to the resistless waves. The cabin went by the board, the after-parts broke up, and the stern settled out of sight. Soon, too, the forecastle was filled with water, and the helpless little band were driven to the deck, where they clustered round the foremast. Presently, even this frail support was loosened from the hull, and rose and fell with every billow. It was plain to all that the final moment drew swiftly nigh. Of the four seamen who still stood by the passengers, three were as efficient as any among the crew of the Elizabeth. These were the steward, carpenter, and cook. The fourth was an old sailor, who, broken down by hardships and sickness, was going home to die. These men were once again persuading Margaret, Ossoli and Celeste to try the planks, which they held ready in the lee of the ship, and the steward, by whom Nino was so much beloved, had just taken the little fellow in his arms, with the pledge that he would save him or die, when a sea struck the forecastle, and the foremast fell, carrying with it the deck, and all upon it. The steward and Angelino were washed upon the beach, both dead, though warm, some twenty minutes after. The cook and carpenter were thrown far upon the foremast, and saved themselves by swimming. Celeste and Ossoli were caught for a moment by the rigging, but the next wave swallowed them up. Margaret sank at once. When last seen, she had been seated at the foot of the foremast, still clad in her white night-dress, with her hair fallen loose upon her shoulders. It was over,—that twelve hours' communion, face to face, with Death! It was over! and the prayer was granted, "that Ossoli, Angelo, and I, may go together, and that the anguish may be brief!"

Memoirs of Margaret Fuller Ossoli, ed. William Henry Channing, James Freeman Clarke, and Ralph Waldo Emerson, 2 vols. (Boston: Phillips, Sampson, 1852), 2: 341–49.

Note

1. Mrs. Hasty's own words while describing the incident. [Note in *Memoirs*]

[Epistolary Comments on Fuller in 1850, 1851, and 1852]

MARY MOODY EMERSON

Mary Moody Emerson (1774-1863) was Ralph Waldo Emerson's paternal aunt. Her life spanned the eve of the American Revolution to the middle of the Civil War, and she never lost the Calvinist beliefs of her youth. After the death of Emerson's father in 1811, she took it upon herself to help instill in each of the four Emerson boys a sense of their history, value, and duties as Emersons. After Waldo's brother William decided against the ministry, Mary engaged in a correspondence with Waldo trying (unsuccessfully) to keep him from turning from her faith toward Unitarianism and, as the Transcendentalist period approached, worse.

Fuller described an 1841 visit from Mary, during which "the best I have got from her is to understand as I suppose W[aldo] better," this way: "Knowing such a person who so perpetually defaces the high by such strange mingling of the low, I can better conceive how the daily bread of life should seem to [Waldo] gossip, and the natural relations sheaths from which the flower must burst and never remember them. It is certainly not pleasant to hear of God and Miss Biddeford in a breath." Still, Fuller continued, "some sparkles show where the gems might in better days be more easily disengaged from the rubbish. She is still valuable as a disturbing force to the lazy. But, to me, this hasty attempt at skimming from the deeps of theosophy, is as unpleasant as the rude vanity of reformers" ([ca. 20?] October 1841, *Letters*, 2:246). Waldo was more positive; he copied out four volumes full of extracts from her letters and diaries, often using them in his own writings, and wrote a memorial sketch, "Mary Moody Emerson" (*Lectures and Biographical Sketches* [1884]). Mary's letters to her nephew are about his editing of *Memoirs of Margaret Fuller Ossoli*.

Mary Moody Emerson to Ralph Waldo Emerson, 16 August 1850

I hope you will succeed in do[ing] justice to your lamented friend and give energy to its readers. I think if she had survived only her husband—and been impressed with that kind of grief which gives a zest of immortality to certain minds we read about, her expression etc. etc. I may as well confess—that in taking an interest in her fate I do not love to remember her want of beauty. She looked very sensible but as if contending with ill health and duties. Had I been favored with one sparkle of her fine wit—one argument for her dissent, from her fine mind, what a treasure to memory. She laid all the day and eve. on sofa and catechised me who told my literal "traditions" like any old bobin woman. . . .

Mary Moody Emerson to Lidian Jackson Emerson, 2 December 1851

. . . *What* was the mystery. No *record of her faith in immortality*! Had she been xian [that is, Christian]! What a spirit! And thro' the future what a bright and burning one who could be so generous. *And her truth*. Oh what an eternity awaits. And we forget all if with her powers and influence as like the waves which so soon ceased the feeble agitations which interred her remains. . . .

Mary Moody Emerson to Martha Bartlett, 25 February[?] 1852

. . . I have hastened to finish the painfull task of following so monsterous a temperment as Margaret's that you might have it. You will find classical information to reward the reading undoubtedly. And when the hopefull sport of her *best* and *real* existence occurs it invites a hope. But the highest exstacies of imajanation [that is, imagination] reach not the xian demands, and and they did not save her from her natural feverishness. Her opinion of our divine Saviour prevented any advance to the Infinite but thro instinct, paganism and being unhappily steeped in Goetheism. RWE has done justly by her and the publick I believe. And every good disposition and xian taught person will rejoice in their comparitive ignorance and hermit obscurity. The last line of the 23d page begins a sentence which redeems many a sad sympathy with the noble minded deceased and honors the biographer.[1] So somewhere in this first vol. the Editor and perhaps the extraordinary subject, allows that there "may lie fallow some of the best thoughts." It were pitiable to our future hopes if every thing were to be expended on this passing whirling stage, where theatricals abound and are suceeded continually. When reading her eulogists I could but regret the loss of so unique a mind. But I think her old age would have been very dark, if reason had continued. . . .

The Selected Letters of Mary Moody Emerson, ed. Nancy Craig Simmons (Athens: University of Georgia Press, 1993), 523, 537, 551–52. Mary Moody Emerson's idiosyncratic spellings have been retained.

Note

1. The sentence referred to is "So gratuitous, indeed, appeared her hypercriticism, that I [W. H. Channing] could not refrain from remonstrance, and to one of my appeals she thus replied: 'If a horror for the mania of little great men, so prevalent in this country,—if aversion to the sentimental exaggerations to which so many minds are prone,—if finding that most men praise, as well as blame, too readily, and that overpraise desecrates the lips and makes the breath unworthy to blow the coal of devotion,—if rejection of the ——s and ——s, from a sense that the priestess must reserve her pæans for Apollo,—if untiring effort to form my mind to justice and revere only the superlatively good, that my praise might be praise; if this be to offend, then have I offended' " (*Memoirs,* 2:23–24).

[Epistolary Comments on Fuller in 1851]

William Ellery Channing the Younger

William Ellery Channing the Younger ("Ellery") (1818–1901), nephew of the well-known Unitarian preacher William Ellery Channing and cousin of William Henry Channing, became a poet and longtime resident of Concord. He married Fuller's sister Ellen (1820–1856) in 1841, and they eventually had five children. Fuller had reservations about the match from the start, writing Emerson that the engagement "disturbs my mind" because "the connexion has been so precipitately formed that I feel overshadowed by it as by a deep tragedy that I foresee, but, as in a dream, cannot lift my hand to prevent" (8, 16 September 1841, *Letters*, 2:230, 232). Early on, she thought his ideas as "spiritual" as Alcott's, but with a "far finer sense of beauty without priggishness or cant," but, as she got to know him better, she found him of "hobgoblin nature and full of indirections," saying, "he reminded one of a great genius with a little wretched boy trotting beside him" (Capper, *Private Years*, 320; October 1842, [March?] 1843, Emerson, *Journals*, 8:289, 352). Still, Fuller tried to help the couple by printing his poems in the *Dial*, letting them stay with her in Cambridge one winter while he looked for employment, trying unsuccessfully to convince the Hawthornes to allow the Channings to board at the Old Manse with them, and, later, convincing Horace Greeley to hire Channing for the *Tribune* (from which he was eventually fired). The marriage was an unhappy one because Ellen was temperamental and sickly, and Ellery was away from home a good deal and generally cared little about how Ellen or anyone else viewed his actions, which lacked both fiscal and family responsibility. Fuller thought better of his poetry, calling it original but marred by his unfinished and obscure style in her essay on "American Literature" in *Papers on Literature and Art* (2:132–33).

No doubt Fuller's continual attempts to help her sister and brother-in-law were viewed as meddling by Channing, coloring his view of her. Moreover, he considered her "artificial," "disciplined," and "too ideal," telling her, "You will always be wanting to grow forward, now I like to grow backward too" (Myerson, "Fuller's 1842 Journal," 329).

William Ellery Channing the Younger to Marcus Spring, Concord, 5 June 1851

I think I said once in a letter which I wrote perhaps last winter, that in a solid year, a life of Margaret Fuller might be looked for. This may still be possible, but I regard it as doubtful.

At least two persons are now engaged with this difficult task, William H Channing and R W Emerson. The difficulty is in the great mass of materials, the character of the person, and the almost impossibility of embracing this whole in any one or two views. It has been represented throughout by William Channing. I believe, that each person had best sit down and write his view of Margaret Fuller. Yet some of her foremost friends decline this— to some it may be impossible. Not every one can write at all, not many upon subjects which are vital.

What should we say of Margaret Fuller's relation to Jane King, Eliz Hoar, Mrs Ripley and a *host* of others who are *not* ciphers, and of that other *host* unknown to society, unknown even to the biographers. Margaret Fuller was a private, more than a public person, and it is this "alarming" fact at least to a biographer, that forms one of the most formidable obstacles of this great and daring work.

By some secret magnetism, she drew from most of those who surrounded her the cherished secret, which now runs like a vein of fire through all the meshes of each one's correspondence. To each she answered in some one part, was an answer to some one question, and accomplished some one desire. Like a lyre of many strings she softly tuned for each the old, familiar lament, now warbling softly the youthful spring songs of joy, now like the wind among boughs at winter mournfully sighing.

Not only was she a mirror, but a reduplicating mirror. Every feature of those she loved she enlarged, and saw them in high and heroic aspects as part of a noble destiny which she also came courageously to perform.

With all this peculiar private side, which fairly took captive of each whole person, she was born a literary woman, and with a clearness, firmness, and a certain cold, dignified manliness which was her wont, how fairly she draws the portraits of a De Vigny, Beranger, Goethe, Canova and Beethoven. With Genius she largely and mysteriously shared the deep secret, nor less acutely portrays the world-renowned sorrow than the private grief. Master of many languages, an indefatigable writer, of many experiences, is it not a formidable task to sum up all this glittering wealth, to melt it, and while warm convert it to one handsome ring.

She must then be her own biographer, and like all private persons suffer in the description. But the task is one of so great difficulty, that even in the hands of that man Emerson, who has such industry, patience, and reverence we cannot say when it will be finished.

Francis B. Dedmond, "The Selected Letters of William Ellery Channing the Younger (Part Two)," in *Studies in the American Renaissance 1990,* ed. Joel Myerson (Charlottesville: University Press of Virginia, 1990), 184–85.

[Journal Comments on Fuller in 1851 and 1852]

CAROLINE HEALEY DALL

Here, Dall describes one of Bronson Alcott's Conversations. Unlike Fuller's Conversations, where she did hold forth herself a good deal but still involved the group in a socratic dialogue, Alcott generally monologued until a brave participant interrupted him. Perhaps Alcott was more willing to share the stage here because so many audience members knew Fuller personally. Dall's second journal entry recalls her reaction to reading *Memoirs of Margaret Fuller Ossoli*. Here, as elsewhere in her writings, it is clear how much Dall identifies herself and her trials with Fuller's own life and actions.

[3 FEBRUARY 1851] In the evening I went to Mr Alcott's with quite a large party. As a discussion of "Margaret Fuller" or of "Woman" it was entirely a failure but it was a fine talk. Mr. [Thomas Wentworth] Higginson of Newburyport, Ralph Emerson, and Miss Hunt were there in addition to the usual company. There were some facts stated about the severity of her early training, the wonderful character of her mind. Mr. Alcott said she was no New England woman—she might as well have been born in Greece or Rome. Greece and Rome were wherever she was. He spoke of the great ability of the letters to the Tribune. Anna Parsons spoke of the great power of love in her, to which Mr List objected the cutting severity of remark to which those who attended her conversations were exposed. He attributed this to her self-love.

I objected to this expression. I did not think it right to assume a reason for it. I had heard her speak to others when the tears came to my eyes, and my throat swelled at the bitterness of her words. But she had been long an invalid, suffered intensely, and it seemed to me that half of her irritation was physical whenever it occurred. Mr Alcott thought there was no doubt she was born under Scorpio, but she knew it, and strove to conquer it—She had confessed to having been a very unamiable child. Ednah [Dow Cheney] said that she had attended her last three winters' conversations, that in them all, but one instance of such severity, and for that she immediately and amply apologized. I said I felt that she would become capable of that, but she was not when I knew her. General conversation occurred on the subject of woman. Higginson spoke of Margaret's great intellectual activity. I spoke of her want of serenity, said what I had hoped from the influence of marriage and motherhood on her—Mr Alcott believed that she became nobler after it. The news of her marriage was a surprise to her friends but they were soon resigned to it. She was always more feminine, than he had expected to find her. At moments—she was the ideal Woman. Mr Emerson had with him a daguerreotype taken from a picture, made after her marriage, which answered all my questions.[1] The love and serenity in it were—beautiful. It is an admirable likeness and yet I have never seen her look so. . . .

I wish Mr Emerson had said what he thought of Margaret. I want to *know* that she had warmth and geniality. Perhaps however he thought our (frivolous conversation) filagree hardly fit to set a jewel in. The gentle men seemed unwilling to talk about Margaret.

Mrs [Abigail] Alcott came and thanked me for the help I had given Mr. A. He had felt it deeply—I had done what no one but Margaret Fuller had ever before done. My eyes filled with tears—for in truth Margaret's death was a private grief to me, and there is no American woman that stands near her. Others followed Mrs Alcott's example after the conversation was over. Mr Alcott said that Margaret could carry a title well. It belonged to her, she was born a queen—Victoria wherever she went.

The failure of this conversation was owing in part to the fact, that gentlemen seemed unwilling to criticize a woman—and women could not do her justice alone. . . .

[20 March 1852] In Margaret Fuller's Autobiography [that is, the *Memoirs*] I see my own life renewed. . . . Neither of us appears to have had natural childhood. Her father and mine were alike impatient, and we were both injured, by the imperative demand for clearness and precision in our statements, before it was possible that we should have clearness and precision in our thoughts. . . .

Margaret felt as I did, her own want of external grace. It always puzzled me that she should not have a sweeter voice. I never could see why a cultured nature, should not give volume, depth and intonation to that. . . .

I was delighted to find that Margaret had an interest in that wretched class of women—who have been so earnest a subject of thought with me for years. I thought her too deeply absorbed in intellectual growth—to think much upon this subject—nor do I suppose that she had ever had much intercourse with the wretched creatures in their habitual position, before she went to Sing Sing. These pages have been written out of my full heart—there remains to be spoken of, Margaret's romantic marriage. The parallel between our lives—follows even here. We both met our husbands—first in a church—we both refused the first offer—and we both in a period of sorrow and isolation learned to lean upon the heart, that we intellectually knew to be unsuited to us. What is said of Ossoli—well suits my husband. He is capable of the sacred love—the love passing that of woman. He cannot speculate about love—or anything. The spirit and the affections are his domain, and he cannot feel an interest in intellectual gymnastics. His appreciation of his wife is the best proof to those who know her, and not him, that he is worthy to possess her. But I feel that Margaret was happy to die, before the mist dissolved. The true union must be not only a union of heart and flesh—but of mind. We must think together until we have outgrown the rude discipline of earth, until we are great enough to spare each other the subservience of perpetual sympathy. We are not yet. Those who have tried the experiment know well that it is so, and the agony of a married life which does not answer its purpose is a thousand times worse than the loneliness of maidenhood. While we have hope to sustain us, we can endure anything, but when we felt that the matter is settled for this life, and that whatever may open to us in another, the heart must ache, through long long years, the spring of life is broken—and we need an infinite faith in the Love of God to live. And yet, if we could be married only thus, neither Margaret nor I would have it otherwise, for marriage is needed by both to develop our womanhood—and give us wide charity for others—true cognizance of our duty towards them. In her own words— "I neither rejoice nor grieve—I acted out my character," but what a testimony are they to the emptiness of a relation which should make the whole heart to "sing for joy."[2] . . .

Selected Journals of Caroline Healey Dall, Volume I: 1838–1855, ed. Helen R. Deese (Boston: Massachusetts Historical Society, 2006), 331, 359, 363, 368. Additional comments on Fuller may be found in Dall's *Daughter of Boston: The Extraordinary Diary of a Nineteenth-Century Woman*, ed. Helen R. Deese (Boston: Beacon Press, 2005).

Notes

1. Such a picture is unknown today. Either Dall was mistaken about when it was taken or it has been lost. [Deese's note]

2. See *Memoirs*, 2:277.

From *Memoirs of Margaret Fuller Ossoli* (1852)

WILLIAM HENRY CHANNING

> In this section of *Memoirs*, Channing describes his recollections of Fuller,
> beginning in the early 1830s, showing that, like so many others, his initial
> impressions were not positive, for he felt that, at first, "her vivacity, deci-
> sive tone, downrightness, and contempt of conventional standards, contin-
> ued to repel," an impression reinforced by "an imperial—shall it be said
> imperious?—air."

IT WAS WHILE Margaret was residing at Jamaica Plain, in the summer of
1839, that we first really met as friends, though for several years previous
we had been upon terms of kindest mutual regard. And, as the best way of
showing how her wonderful character opened upon me, the growth of our
acquaintance shall be briefly traced.

The earliest recollection of Margaret is as a schoolmate of my sisters,
in Boston. At that period she was considered a prodigy of talent and accomplishment; but a sad feeling prevailed, that she had been overtasked by
her father, who wished to train her like a boy, and that she was paying the
penalty for undue application, in nearsightedness, awkward manners, ex-
travagant tendencies of thought, and a pedantic style of talk, that made her
a butt for the ridicule of frivolous companions. Some seasons later, I call to
mind seeing, at the "Commencements" and "Exhibitions" of Harvard University, a girl, plain in appearance, but of dashing air, who was invariably
the centre of a listening group, and kept their merry interest alive by sparkles of wit and incessant small-talk. The bystanders called her familiarly,
"Margaret," "Margaret Fuller;" for, though young, she was already noted
for conversational gifts, and had the rare skill of attracting to her society,
not spirited collegians only, but men mature in culture and of established
reputation. It was impossible not to admire her fluency and fun; yet, though
curiosity was piqued as to this entertaining personage, I never sought an
introduction, but, on the contrary, rather shunned encounter with one so
armed from head to foot in saucy sprightliness.

About 1830, however, we often met in the social circles of Cambridge, and I began to observe her more nearly. At first, her vivacity, decisive tone, downrightness, and contempt of conventional standards, continued to repel. She appeared too *intense* in expression, action, emphasis, to be pleasing, and wanting in that *retenue* which we associate with delicate dignity. Occasionally, also, words flashed from her of such scathing satire, that prudence counselled the keeping at safe distance from a body so surcharged with electricity. Then, again, there was an imperial—shall it be said imperious?—air, exacting deference to her judgments and loyalty to her behests, that prompted pride to retaliatory measures. She paid slight heed, moreover, to the trim palings of etiquette, but swept through the garden-beds and into the doorway of one's confidence so cavalierly, that a reserved person felt inclined to lock himself up in his sanctum. Finally, to the cooly-scanning eye, her friendships wore a look of such romantic exaggeration, that she seemed to walk enveloped in a shining fog of sentimentalism. In brief, it must candidly be confessed, that I then suspected her of affecting the part of a Yankee Corinna.

But soon I was charmed, unaware, with the sagacity of her sallies, the profound thoughts carelessly dropped by her on transient topics, the breadth and richness of culture manifested in her allusions or quotations, her easy comprehension of new views, her just discrimination, and, above all, her *truthfulness*. "Truth at all cost," was plainly her ruling maxim. This it was that made her criticism so trenchant, her contempt of pretence so quick and stern, her speech so naked in frankness, her gaze so searching, her whole attitude so alert. Her estimates of men, books, manners, events, art, duty, destiny, were moulded after a grand ideal; and she was a severe judge from the very loftiness of her standard. Her stately deportment, border though it might on arrogance, but expressed high-heartedness. Her independence, even if haughty and rash, was the natural action of a self-centred will, that waited only fit occasion to prove itself heroic. Her earnestness to read the hidden history of others was the gauge of her own emotion. The enthusiasm that made her speech so affluent, when measured by the average scale, was the unconscious overflow of a poetic temperament. And the ardor of her friends' affection proved the faithfulness of her love. Thus gradually the mist melted away, till I caught a glimpse of her real self. We were one evening talking of American literature,—she contrasting its boyish crudity, half boastful, half timid, with the tempered, manly equipoise of

thorough-bred European writers, and I asserting that in its mingled practicality and aspiration might be read bright auguries; when, betrayed by
sympathy, she laid bare her secret hope of what Woman might be and do,
as an author, in our Republic. The sketch was an outline only, and dashed
off with a few swift strokes, but therein appeared her own portrait, and we
were strangers no more.

It was through the medium of others, however, that at this time I best
learned to appreciate Margaret's nobleness of nature and principle. My
most intimate friend in the Theological School, James Freeman Clarke, was
her constant companion in exploring the rich gardens of German literature;
and from his descriptions I formed a vivid image of her industry, compre-
hensiveness, buoyancy, patience, and came to honor her intelligent interest
in high problems of science, her aspirations after spiritual greatness, her
fine æsthetic taste, her religiousness. By power to quicken other minds, she
showed how living was her own. Yet more near were we brought by common attraction toward a youthful visitor in our circle, the untouched freshness of whose beauty was but the transparent garb of a serene, confiding,
and harmonious soul, and whose polished grace, at once modest and naïve,
sportive and sweet, fulfilled the charm of innate goodness of heart. Susceptible in temperament, anticipating with ardent fancy the lot of a lovely
and refined woman, and morbidly exaggerating her own slight personal defects, Margaret seemed to long, as it were, to transfuse with her force this
nymph-like form, and to fill her to glowing with her own lyric fire. No drop
of envy tainted the sisterly love, with which she sought by genial sympathy
thus to live in another's experience, to be her guardian-angel, to shield her
from contact with the unworthy, to rouse each generous impulse, to invigo-
rate thought by truth incarnate in beauty, and with unfelt ministry to weave
bright threads in her web of fate. Thus more and more Margaret became an
object of respectful interest, in whose honor, magnanimity and strength I
learned implicitly to trust.

Separation, however, hindered our growing acquaintance, as we both left
Cambridge, and, with the exception of a few chance meetings in Boston and
a ramble or two in the glens and on the beaches of Rhode Island, held no
further intercourse till the summer of 1839, when, as has been already said,
the friendship, long before rooted, grew up and leafed and bloomed. . . .

It was quite a study to watch the phases through which Margaret passed,
in one of these assemblies. There was something in the air and step with

which she chose her place in the company, betokening an instinctive sense, that, in intellect, she was of blood royal and needed to ask no favors. And then she slowly gathered her attention to take in the significance of the scene. Near-sighted and habitually using an eye-glass, she rapidly scanned the forms and faces, pausing intently where the expression of particular heads or groups suggested thought, and ending her survey with some apt home-thrust to her next neighbors, as if to establish full *rapport,* and so to become a medium for the circulating life. Only when thus in magnetic relations with all present, by a clear impress of their state and place, did she seem prepared to rise to a higher stage of communion. Then she listened, with ear finely vibrating to every tone, with all capacities responsive in sympathy, with a swift and ductile power of appreciation, that made her feel to the quick the varying moods of different speakers, and yet the while with coolest self-possession. Now and then a slight smile, flickering over her countenance, as lightning plays on the surface of a cloud, marked the inward process whereby she was harmonizing in equilibrium opposing thoughts. And, as occasion offered, a felicitous quotation, pungent apothegm, or symbolic epithet, dropped unawares in undertone, showed how swiftly scattered rays were brought in her mind to a focus.

When her turn came, by a graceful transition she resumed the subject where preceding speakers had left it, and, briefly summing up their results, proceeded to unfold her own view. Her opening was deliberate, like the progress of some massive force gaining its momentum; but as she felt her way, and moving in a congenial element, the sweep of her speech became grand. The style of her eloquence was sententious, free from prettiness, direct, vigorous, charged with vitality. Articulateness, just emphasis and varied accent, brought out most delicate shades and brilliant points of meaning, while a rhythmical collocation of words gave a finished form to every thought. She was affluent in historic illustration and literary allusion, as well as in novel hints. She knew how to concentrate into racy phrases the essential truth gathered from wide research, and distilled with patient toil; and by skilful treatment she could make green again the wastes of common-place. Her statements, however rapid, showed breadth of comprehension, ready memory, impartial judgment, nice analysis of differences, power of penetrating through surfaces to realities, fixed regard to central laws and habitual communion with the Life of life. Critics, indeed, might have been tempted to sneer at a certain oracular grandiloquence, that bore away her soberness in moments of elation; though even the most captious must presently have smiled at the humor of her descriptive touches, her dexterous exposure of folly and pretension, the swift stroke of her bright wit, her shrewd discernment, promptitude, and presence of mind. The reverential, too, might have been pained at the sternness wherewith popular men, measures, and established customs, were tried and found guilty, at her tribunal; but even while blaming her aspirations as rash, revolutionary and impractical, no honest conservative could fail to recognize the sincerity of her aim. And every deep observer of character would have found the explanation of what seemed vehement or too high-strung, in the longing of a spirited woman to break every trammel that checked her growth or fettered her movement.

In conversations like these, one saw that the richness of Margaret's genius resulted from a rare combination of opposite qualities. To her might have been well applied the words first used as describing George Sand: "Thou large-brained Woman, and large-hearted Man." She blended in closest union and swift interplay feminine receptiveness with masculine energy. She was at once impressible and creative, impulsive and deliberate, pliant in sympathy yet firmly self-centred, confidingly responsive while commanding in originality. By the vivid intensity of her conceptions, she brought out in those around their own consciousness, and, by the glowing vigor of her intellect, roused into action their torpid powers. On the other hand, she reproduced a truth, whose germ had just been imbibed from others, moulded after her own image and quickened by her own life, with marvellous rapidity. And the presence of congenial minds so stimulated the prolific power of her imagination, that she was herself astonished at the fresh beauty of her new-born thoughts. "There is a mortifying sense," she writes,

> of having played the Mirabeau after a talk with a circle of intelligent persons. They come with a store of acquired knowledge and reflection, on the subject in debate, about which I may know little, and have reflected less; yet, by mere apprehensiveness and prompt intuition, I may appear their superior. Spontaneously I appropriate all their material, and turn it to my own ends, as if it was my inheritance from a long train of ancestors. Rays of truth flash out at the moment, and they are startled by the light thrown over their familiar domain. Still

they are gainers, for I give them new impulse, and they go on their way rejoicing in the bright glimpses they have caught. I should despise myself, if I purposely appeared thus brilliant, but I am inspired as by a power higher than my own.

All friends will bear witness to the strict fidelity of this sketch. There were seasons when she seemed borne irresistibly on to the verge of prophecy, and fully embodied one's notion of a sibyl.

Admirable as Margaret appeared in public, I was yet more affected by this peculiar mingling of impressibility and power to influence, when brought within her private sphere. I know not how otherwise to describe her subtle charm, than by saying that she was at once a clairvoyante and a magnetizer [that is, hypnotist]. She read another's bosom-secret, and she imparted of her own force. She interpreted the cipher in the talisman of one's destiny, that he had tried in vain to spell alone; by sympathy she brought out the invisible characters traced by experience on his heart; and in the mirror of her conscience he might see the image of his very self, as dwarfed in actual appearance, or developed after the divine ideal. Her sincerity was terrible. In her frank exposure no foible was spared, though by her very reproof she roused dormant courage and self-confidence. And so unerring seemed her insight, that her companion felt as if standing bare before a disembodied spirit, and communicated without reserve thoughts and emotions, which, even to himself, he had scarcely named.

This penetration it was that caused Margaret to be so dreaded, in general society, by superficial observers. They, who came nigh enough to test the quality of her spirit, could not but perceive how impersonal was her justice; but, contrasted with the dead flat of conventional tolerance, her candor certainly looked rugged and sharp. The frivolous were annoyed at her contempt of their childishness, the ostentatious piqued at her insensibility to their show, and the decent scared lest they should be stripped of their shams; partisans were vexed by her spurning their leaders; and professional sneerers,—civil in public to those whom in private they slandered,—could not pardon the severe truth whereby she drew the sting from their spite. Indeed, how could so undisguised a censor but shock the prejudices of the moderate, and wound the sensibilities of the diffident; how but enrage the worshippers of new demi-gods in literature, art and fashion, whose pet shrines she demolished; how but cut to the quick, alike by silence or by speech, the self-love of the vain, whose claims she ignored? So gratuitous, indeed, appeared her hypercriticism, that I could not refrain from remonstrance, and to one of my appeals she thus replied:

> If a horror for the mania of little great men, so prevalent in this country,—if aversion to the sentimental exaggerations to which so many minds are prone,— if finding that most men praise, as well as blame, too readily, and that overpraise desecrates the lips and makes the breath unworthy to blow the coal of devotion,—if rejection of the —s and —s from a sense that the priestess must reserve her pæans for Apollo,—if untiring effort to form my mind to justice and revere only the superlatively good, that my praise might be praise; if this be to offend, then have I offended. . . .

Such Egoism as this, though lacking the angel grace of unconsciousness, has a stoical grandeur that commands respect. Indeed, in all that Margaret spoke, wrote, or did, no cynic could detect the taint of meanness. Her elation came not from opium fumes of vanity, inhaled in close chambers of conceit, but from the stimulus of sunshine, fresh breezes, and swift movement upon the winged steed of poesy. Her existence was bright with romantic interest to herself. There was an amplitude and elevation in her aim, which were worthy, as she felt, of human honor and of heavenly aid; and she was buoyed up by a courageous good-will, amidst all evils, that she knew would have been recognized as heroic in the chivalric times, when "every morning brought a noble chance." Neither was her self-regard of an engrossing temper. On the contrary, the sense of personal dignity taught her the worth of the lowliest human being, and her intense desire for harmonious conditions quickened a boundless compassion for the squalid, downcast, and drudging multitude. She aspired to live in majestic fulness of benignant and joyful activity, leaving a track of light with every footstep; and, like the radiant Iduna, bearing to man the golden apples of immortality, she would have made each meeting with her fellows rich with some boon that should never fade, but brighten in bloom forever.

This characteristic self-esteem determined the quality of Margaret's influence, which was singularly penetrating, and most beneficent where most deeply and continuously felt. Chance acquaintance with her, like a breath from the tropics, might have prematurely burst the buds of feeling in sensitive hearts, leaving after blight and barrenness. Natures, small in compass and of fragile substance, might have been distorted and shattered by attempts to mould themselves on her grand model. And in her seem-

ing unchartered impulses,—whose latent law was honorable integrity,—
eccentric spirits might have found encouragement for capricious license.
Her morbid subjectivity, too, might, by contagion, have affected others
with undue self-consciousness. And, finally, even intimate friends might
have been tempted, by her flattering love, to exaggerate their own importance, until they recognized that her regard for them was but one niche
in a Pantheon at whose every shrine she offered incense. But these ill effects were superficial accidents. The peculiarity of her power was to make
all who were in concert with her feel the miracle of existence. She lived
herself with such concentrated force in the moments, that she was always
effulgent with thought and affection,—with conscience, courage, resource,
decision, a penetrating and forecasting wisdom. Hence, to associates, her
presence seemed to touch even common scenes and drudging cares with
splendor, as when, through the scud of a rain-storm, sunbeams break
from serene blue openings, crowning familiar things with sudden glory.
By manifold sympathies, yet central unity, she seemed in herself to be a
goodly company, and her words and deeds imparted the virtue of a collec-
tive life. So tender was her affection, that, like a guardian genius, she made
her friends' souls her own, and identified herself with their fortunes; and
yet, so pure and high withal was her justice, that, in her recognition of their
past success and present claims, there came a summons for fresh endeavor
after the perfect. The very thought of her roused manliness to emulate the
vigorous freedom, with which one was assured, that wherever placed she
was that instant acting; and the mere mention of her name was an inspiration of magnanimity, and faithfulness, and truth.

> Sincere has been their striving; great their love,

"is a sufficient apology for any life," wrote Margaret; and how preëminently
were these words descriptive of herself. Hers was indeed

> The equal temper of heroic hearts,
> Made weak by time and fate, but strong in will,
> To strive, to seek, to find, and not to yield.

Memoirs of Margaret Fuller Ossoli, ed. William Henry Channing, James Freeman Clarke, and Ralph Waldo Emerson, 2 vols. (Boston: Phillips, Sampson, 1852), 2:5–9, 19–23, 112–14.

From *Memoirs of Margaret Fuller Ossoli* (1852)

FREDERIC HENRY HEDGE

Frederic Henry Hedge (1805–1890), Harvard College and Harvard Divinity School graduate, wrote an article on Coleridge in the March 1833 *Christian Examiner* that is acknowledged as one of the first documents in the Transcendentalist controversy. His removal to Bangor, Maine, in 1835 restricted his involvement with the movement and its participants, although the Transcendental Club was originally called the 'Hedge Club' because it first met during his trips back to Boston from Maine.

Hedge knew Fuller from her earliest days in Cambridge (his father was a professor at Harvard). Because he had actually studied in Germany from 1818 to 1822, his knowledge of German literature and culture was impressive, and it attracted Fuller as she herself began her study of Germany. She called him "Germanicus," and in 1830 described a meeting with him: "I never can feel more perfect enjoyment from any one's conversation. I return satisfied on many points and shall feel the pleasurable effects of the conversation for weeks. I feel as if I had taken into my mind his new metaphysicks, experience new beautiful things he has seen and known, and new beautiful imaginings." Indeed, Hedge's wife jokingly observed "that Henry and Margaret thought themselves such high geniuses that nobody could get up to or comprehend them" (22 February 1824, 23 January 1830, *Letters*, 1:135, 6:163). Although Hedge disappointed Fuller by not contributing as much to the *Dial* as she had hoped he would, still, in 1848, she called him "one of the most cultivated and refined minds of my country" (8 March 1848, *Letters*, 5:54). Hedge recognized that Fuller was disappointed that he failed to "take a more pronounced position with regard to the vexed questions of the time," and Julia Ward Howe, a mutual acquaintance, believed that Fuller "probably considered him timid where he felt her to be rash" (*Reminiscences*, 296, 300).

Hedge's negative physical descriptions of Fuller (she had "no pretensions to beauty then, or at any time") continued to be cited by writers on her for a century and a half, much to Fuller's detriment. Nevertheless, Hedge recognized the brilliance of her speech, which, "though finished and true as the most deliberate rhetoric of the pen, had always an air of spontaneity which

made it seem the grace of the moment," an effect that "made finished sentences as natural to her as blundering and hesitation are to most of us."

MY ACQUAINTANCE WITH Margaret commenced in the year 1823, at Cambridge, my native place and hers. I was then a member of Harvard College, in which my father held one of the offices of instruction, and I used
frequently to meet her in the social circles of which the families connected
with the college formed the nucleus. Her father, at this time, represented
the county of Middlesex in the Congress of the United States.

Margaret was then about thirteen,—a child in years, but so precocious
in her mental and physical developments, that she passed for eighteen or
twenty. Agreeably to this estimate, she had her place in society, as a lady
full-grown.

When I recall her personal appearance, as it was then and for ten or
twelve years subsequent to this, I have the idea of a blooming girl of a florid
complexion and vigorous health, with a tendency to robustness, of which
she was painfully conscious, and which, with little regard to hygienic principles, she endeavored to suppress or conceal, thereby preparing for herself
much future suffering. With no pretensions to beauty then, or at any time,
her face was one that attracted, that awakened a lively interest, that made
one desirous of a nearer acquaintance. It was a face that fascinated, without satisfying. Never seen in repose, never allowing a steady perusal of its
features, it baffled every attempt to judge the character by physiognomical
induction. You saw the evidence of a mighty force, but what direction that
force would assume,—whether it would determine itself to social triumphs,
or to triumphs of art,—it was impossible to divine. Her moral tendencies,
her sentiments, her true and prevailing character, did not appear in the
lines of her face. She seemed equal to anything, but might not choose to put
forth her strength. You felt that a great possibility lay behind that brow, but
you felt, also, that the talent that was in her might miscarry through indif-
ference or caprice.

I said she had no pretensions to beauty. Yet she was not plain. She escaped the reproach of positive plainness, by her blond and abundant hair,
by her excellent teeth, by her sparkling, dancing, busy eyes, which, though
usually half closed from near-sightedness, shot piercing glances at those

with whom she conversed, and, most of all, by the very peculiar and graceful carriage of her head and neck, which all who knew her will remember as
the most characteristic trait in her personal appearance.

In conversation she had already, at that early age, begun to distinguish
herself, and made much the same impression in society that she did in after
years, with the exception, that, as she advanced in life, she learned to control that tendency to sarcasm,—that disposition to 'quiz,'—which was then
somewhat excessive. It frightened shy young people from her presence, and
made her, for a while, notoriously unpopular with the ladies of her circle.

This propensity seems to have been aggravated by unpleasant encounters in her school-girl experience. She was a pupil of Dr. Park, of Boston,
whose seminary for young ladies was then at the height of a well-earned
reputation, and whose faithful and successful endeavors in this department
have done much to raise the standard of female education among us. Here
the inexperienced country girl was exposed to petty persecutions from the
dashing misses of the city, who pleased themselves with giggling criticisms
not inaudible, nor meant to be inaudible to their subject, on whatsoever
in dress and manner fell short of the city mark. Then it was first revealed
to her young heart, and laid up for future reflection, how large a place in
woman's world is given to fashion and frivolity. Her mind reacted on these
attacks with indiscriminate sarcasms. She made herself formidable by her
wit, and, of course, unpopular. A root of bitterness sprung up in her which
years of moral culture were needed to eradicate.

Partly to evade the temporary unpopularity into which she had fallen,
and partly to pursue her studies secure from those social avocations which
were found unavoidable in the vicinity of Cambridge and Boston, in 1824 or
5 she was sent to Groton, where she remained two years in quiet seclusion.

On her return to Cambridge, in 1826, I renewed my acquaintance, and
an intimacy was then formed, which continued until her death. The next
seven years, which were spent in Cambridge, were years of steady growth,
with little variety of incident, and little that was noteworthy of outward experience, but with great intensity of the inner life. It was with her, as with
most young women, and with most young men, too, between the ages of
sixteen and twenty-five, a period of preponderating sentimentality, a period of romance and of dreams, of yearning and of passion. She pursued at
this time, I think, no systematic study, but she read with the heart, and was
learning more from social experience than from books.

[129]

I remember noting at this time a trait which continued to be a prominent one through life,—I mean, a passionate love for the beautiful, which comprehended all the kingdoms of nature and art. I have never known one who seemed to derive such satisfaction from the contemplation of lovely forms.

Her intercourse with girls of her own age and standing was frank and excellent. Personal attractions, and the homage which they received, awakened in her no jealousy. She envied not their success, though vividly aware of the worth of beauty, and inclined to exaggerate her own deficiencies in that kind. On the contrary, she loved to draw these fair girls to herself, and to make them her guests, and was never so happy as when surrounded, in company, with such a bevy. This attraction was mutual, as, according to Goethe, every attraction is. Where she felt an interest, she awakened an interest. Without flattery or art, by the truth and nobleness of her nature, she won the confidence, and made herself the friend and intimate, of a large number of young ladies,—the belles of their day,—with most of whom she remained in correspondence during the greater part of her life.

In our evening re-unions she was always conspicuous by the brilliancy of her wit, which needed but little provocation to break forth in exuberant sallies, that drew around her a knot of listeners, and made her the central attraction of the hour. Rarely did she enter a company in which she was not a prominent object.

I have spoken of her conversational talent. It continued to develop itself in these years, and was certainly her most decided gift. One could form no adequate idea of her ability without hearing her converse. She did many things well, but nothing so well as she talked. It is the opinion of all her friends, that her writings do her very imperfect justice. For some reason or other, she could never deliver herself in print as she did with her lips. She required the stimulus of attentive ears, and answering eyes, to bring out all her power. She must have her auditory about her.

Her conversation, as it was then, I have seldom heard equalled. It was not so much attractive as commanding. Though remarkably fluent and select, it was neither fluency, nor choice diction, nor wit, nor sentiment, that gave it its peculiar power, but accuracy of statement, keen discrimination, and a certain weight of judgment, which contrasted strongly and charmingly with the youth and sex of the speaker. I do not remember that the vulgar charge of talking 'like a book' was ever fastened upon her, although, by her precision, she might seem to have incurred it. The fact was, her speech, though finished and true as the most deliberate rhetoric of the pen, had always an air of spontaneity which made it seem the grace of the moment,—the result of some organic provision that made finished sentences as natural to her as blundering and hesitation are to most of us. With a little more imagination, she would have made an excellent improvisatrice.

Here let me say a word respecting the character of Margaret's mind. It was what in woman is generally called a masculine mind; that is, its action was determined by ideas rather than by sentiments. And yet, with this masculine trait, she combined a woman's appreciation of the beautiful in sentiment and the beautiful in action. Her intellect was rather solid than graceful, yet no one was more alive to grace. She was no artist,—she would never have written an epic, or romance, or drama,—yet no one knew better the qualities which go to the making of these; and though catholic as to kind, no one was more rigorously exacting as to quality. Nothing short of the best in each kind would content her.

She wanted imagination, and she wanted productiveness. She wrote with difficulty. Without external pressure, perhaps, she would never have written at all. She was dogmatic, and not creative. Her strength was in characterization and in criticism. Her *critique* on Goethe, in the second volume of the Dial, is, in my estimation, one of the best things she has written. And, as far as it goes, it is one of the best criticisms extant of Goethe.

What I especially admired in her was her intellectual sincerity. Her judgments took no bribe from her sex or her sphere, nor from custom nor tradition, nor caprice. She valued truth supremely, both for herself and others. The question with her was not what should be believed, or what ought to be true, but what *is* true. Her yes and no were never conventional; and she often amazed people by a cool and unexpected dissent from the common-places of popular acceptation. . . .

Memoirs of Margaret Fuller Ossoli, ed. William Henry Channing, James Freeman Clarke, and Ralph Waldo Emerson, 2 vols. (Boston: Phillips, Sampson, 1852), 1:90–96. Clarke introduced these passages with "Somewhat older than Margaret, and having enjoyed an education at a German university, his conversation was full of interest and excitement to her. He opened to her a whole world of thoughts and speculations which gave movement to her mind in a congenial direction."

From *Memoirs of Margaret Fuller Ossoli* (1852)

JAMES FREEMAN CLARKE

James Freeman Clarke (1810–1888), Harvard College and Divinity School graduate, helped edit the *Western Messenger* (1836–1839), was a member of the Transcendental Club, and contributed to the *Dial*. He began his own congregation, the Church of the Disciples, in Boston in 1841, which caused controversy because its rules empowered the parishoners, not the clergy. He was, along with Emerson and William Henry Channing, a coeditor of *Memoirs of Margaret Fuller Ossoli*.

Clarke was much attracted to German literature and philosophy, a passion he shared with Fuller, and the two often studied together. He was one of her closest friends in the 1830s, and the two maintained a frequent correspondence about contemporary events and their readings, especially when he was in the Ohio Valley during 1833–1840 preaching and editing the *Messenger*. He initially approached her as a mentor and guide ("I feel grateful for the high intellectual culture and excitement of which you have been to me the source"), and Fuller often looked at him as her pupil as well as fellow student, praising his mind, "wholly practical in its tendency," quite "a strong mind, an aspiring mind, an active, and becoming a clear mind, but its cry is for 'action, action, action'" (18 September 1834, Clarke, *Letters to Fuller*, 79; diary entry, 25 November 1838, Clarke, *Autobiography*, 313). By 1839, though, they had drifted apart as Clarke grew up and saw Fuller more clearly, saying she had "less theoretic respect for humanity" than did Emerson, her "complex and various nature draws her in many directions," and her "beautiful and keen discriminating mind" causes her to be "exclusive in her tastes and aristocratic in her principles" (Capper, *Private Years*, 314). Clarke compared Fuller to himself as he would, respectively, grasshoppers to "father longlegs," for the former "collect themselves together and their whole body goes at once to a definite point, by a spring," while the latter "thrust out a leg, then another, and then a third as far as they will go and let their body come after as it can." For Clarke, grasshoppers are "apt to be special pleaders, one-sided arguers, but coherent and comprehensive"; father longlegs are "fair and candid in debate, caring for truth and not at all for consequences, but very prone to contradict themselves every other word" (Bolster, *Clarke*, 67–68). Despite all this, Clarke was from the beginning captivated by Fuller, as his recollections show.

. . . INEXHAUSTIBLE IN POWER of insight, and with a good-will "broad as ether," she could enter into the needs, and sympathize with the various excellences, of the greatest variety of characters. One thing only she demanded of all her friends,—that they should have some "extraordinary generous seeking,"[1] that they should not be satisfied with the common routine of life,—that they should aspire to something higher, better, holier, than they had now attained. Where this element of aspiration existed, she demanded no originality of intellect, no greatness of soul. If these were found, well; but she could love, tenderly and truly, where they were not. But for a worldly character, however gifted, she felt and expressed something very like contempt. At this period, she had no patience with self-satisfied mediocrity. She afterwards learned patience and unlearned contempt; but at the time of which I write, she seemed, and was to the multitude, a haughty and supercilious person,—while to those whom she loved, she was all the more gentle, tender and true.

Margaret possessed, in a greater degree than any person I ever knew, the power of so magnetizing others, when she wished, by the power of her mind, that they would lay open to her all the secrets of their nature. She had an infinite curiosity to know individuals,—not the vulgar curiosity which seeks to find out the circumstances of their outward lives, but that which longs to understand the inward springs of thought and action in their souls. This desire and power both rested on a profound conviction of her mind in the individuality of every human being. A human being, according to her faith, was not the result of the presence and stamp of outward circumstances, but an original *monad,* with a certain special faculty, capable of a certain fixed development, and having a profound personal unity, which the ages of eternity might develop, but could not exhaust. I know not if she would have stated her faith in these terms, but some such conviction appeared in her constant endeavor to see and understand the germinal principle, the special characteristic, of every person whom she deemed worthy of knowing at all. Therefore, while some persons study human nature in its universal laws, and become great philosophers, moralists and teachers of the race,—while others study mankind in action, and, seeing the motives and feelings by which masses are swayed, become eminent politicians, sagacious leaders, and eminent in all political affairs,—a few, like Margaret, study character, and acquire the power of exerting profoundest influence on individual souls. . . .

The insight which Margaret displayed in finding her friends, the magnetism by which she drew them toward herself, the catholic range of her intimacies, the influence which she exercised to develop the latent germ of every character, the constancy with which she clung to each when she had once given and received confidence, the delicate justice which kept every intimacy separate, and the process of transfiguration which took place when she met any one on this mountain of Friendship, giving a dazzling lustre to the details of common life,—all these should be at least touched upon and illustrated, to give any adequate view of her in these relations.

Such a prejudice against her had been created by her faults of manner, that the persons she might most wish to know often retired from her and avoided her. But she was "sagacious of her quarry," and never suffered herself to be repelled by this. She saw when any one belonged to her, and never rested till she came into possession of her property. I recollect a lady who thus fled from her for several years, yet, at last, became most nearly attached to her. This "wise sweet" friend, as Margaret characterized her in two words, a flower hidden in the solitude of deep woods, Margaret saw and appreciated from the first. . . .

Margaret's constancy to any genuine relation, once established, was surprising. If her friends' *aim* changed, so as to take them out of her sphere, she was saddened by it, and did not let them go without a struggle. But wherever they continued "true to the original standard," (as she loved to phrase it) her affectionate interest would follow them unimpaired through all the changes of life. The principle of this constancy she thus expresses in a letter to one of her brothers:—

> Great and even *fatal* errors (so far as this life is concerned) could not destroy my friendship for one in whom I am sure of the kernel of nobleness.

She never formed a friendship until she had seen and known this germ of good; and afterwards judged conduct by this. To this germ of good, to this highest law of each individual, she held them true. But never did she act like those who so often judge of their friend from some report of his conduct, as if they had never known him, and allow the inference from a single act to alter the opinion formed by an induction from years of intercourse. From all such weakness Margaret stood wholly free.

I have referred to the wide range of Margaret's friendships. Even at this period this variety was very apparent. She was the centre of a group very different from each other, and whose only affinity consisted in their all being polarized by the strong attraction of her mind,—all drawn toward herself. Some of her friends were young, gay and beautiful; some old, sick or studious. Some were children of the world, others pale scholars. Some were witty, others slightly dull. But all, in order to be Margaret's friends, must be capable of seeking something,—capable of some aspiration for the better. And how did she glorify life to all! all that was tame and common vanishing away in the picturesque light thrown over the most familiar things by her rapid fancy, her brilliant wit, her sharp insight, her creative imagination, by the inexhaustible resources of her knowledge, and the copious rhetoric which found words and images always apt and always ready. Even then she displayed almost the same marvellous gift of conversation which afterwards dazzled all who knew her,—with more perhaps of freedom, since she floated on the flood of our warm sympathies. Those who know Margaret only by her published writings know her least; her notes and letters contain more of her mind; but it was only in conversation that she was perfectly free and at home.

Margaret's constancy in friendship caused her to demand it in others, and thus she was sometimes exacting. But the pure Truth of her character caused her to express all such feelings with that freedom and simplicity that they became only as slight clouds on a serene sky, giving it a tenderer beauty, and casting picturesque shades over the landscape below. . . .

But among the young men who surrounded Margaret, a like variety prevailed. One was to her interesting, on account of his quick, active intellect, and his contempt for shows and pretences; for his inexhaustible wit, his exquisite taste, his infinitely varied stores of information, and the poetic view which he took of life, painting it with Rembrandt depths of shadow and bursts of light. Another she gladly went to for his compact, thoroughly considered views of God and the world,—for his culture, so much more deep and rich than any other we could find here,—for his conversation, opening in systematic form new fields of thought. Yet men of strong native talent, and rich character, she also liked well to know, however deficient in culture, knowledge, or power of utterance. Each was to her a study, and she never rested till she had found the bottom of every mind,—till she had satisfied herself of its capacity and currents,—measuring it with her sure line, as

> —All human wits
> Are measured, but a few.

It was by her singular gift of speech that she cast her spells and worked her wonders in this little circle. Full of thoughts and full of words; capable of poetic improvisation, had there not been a slight overweight of a tendency to the tangible and real; capable of clear, complete, philosophic statement, but for the strong tendency to life which melted down evermore in its lava-current the solid blocks of thought; she was yet, by these excesses, better fitted for the arena of conversation. Here she found none adequate for the equal encounter; when she laid her lance in rest, every champion must go down before it. How fluent her wit, which, for hour after hour, would furnish best entertainment, as she described scenes where she had lately been, or persons she had lately seen! Yet she readily changed from gay to grave, and loved better the serious talk which opened the depths of life. Describing a conversation in relation to Christianity, with a friend of strong mind, who told her he had found, in this religion, a home for his best and deepest thoughts, she says—"Ah! what a pleasure to meet with such a daring, yet realizing, mind as his!" But her catholic taste found satisfaction in intercourse with persons quite different from herself in opinions and tendencies. . . .

I am disposed to think, much as she excelled in general conversation, that her greatest mental efforts were made in intercourse with individuals. All her friends will unite in the testimony, that whatever they may have known of wit and eloquence in others, they have never seen one who, like her, by the conversation of an hour or two, could not merely entertain and inform, but make an epoch in one's life. We all dated back to this or that conversation with Margaret, in which we took a complete survey of great subjects, came to some clear view of a difficult question, saw our way open before us to a higher plane of life, and were led to some definite resolution or purpose which has had a bearing on all our subsequent career. For

Margaret's conversation turned, at such times, to life,—its destiny, its duty, its prospect. With comprehensive glance she would survey the past, and sum up, in a few brief words, its results; she would then turn to the future, and, by a natural order, sweep through its chances and alternatives,—passing ever into a more earnest tone, into a more serious view,—and then bring all to bear on the present, till its duties grew plain, and its opportunities attractive. Happy he who can lift conversation, without loss of its cheer, to the highest uses! Happy he who has such a gift as this, an original faculty thus accomplished by culture, by which he can make our common life rich, significant and fair,—can give to the hour a beauty and brilliancy which shall make it eminent long after, amid dreary years of level routine!

I recall many such conversations. I remember one summer's day, in which we rode together, on horseback, from Cambridge to Newton,—a day all of a piece, in which my eloquent companion helped me to understand my past life, and her own,—a day which left me in that calm repose which comes to us, when we clearly apprehend what we ought to do, and are ready to attempt it. I recall other mornings when, not having seen her for a week or two, I would walk with her for hours, beneath the lindens or in the garden, while we related to each other what we had read in our German studies. And I always left her astonished at the progress of her mind, at the amount of new thoughts she had garnered, and filled with a new sense of the worth of knowledge, and the value of life.

There were other conversations, in which, impelled by the strong instinct of utterance, she would state, in words of tragical pathos, her own needs and longings,—her demands on life,—the struggles of mind, and of heart,—her conflicts with self, with nature, with the limitations of circumstances, with insoluble problems, with an unattainable desire. She seemed to feel relief from the expression of these thoughts, though she gained no light from her companion. Many such conversations I remember, while she lived in Cambridge, and one such in Groton; but afterwards, when I met her, I found her mind risen above these struggles, and in a self-possessed state which needed no such outlet for its ferment. . . .

Memoirs of Margaret Fuller Ossoli, ed. William Henry Channing, James Freeman Clarke, and Ralph Waldo Emerson, 2 vols. (Boston: Phillips, Sampson, 1852), 1:64–66, 75, 77–79, 104–105, 107–109.

Note

1. These words of Goethe, which I have placed among the mottoes at the beginning of this chapter, were written by Margaret on the first page of a richly gilt and bound blank book, which she gave to me, in 1832, for a private journal. The words of Köerner are also translated by herself, and were given to me about the same time. [Clarke's note]

From *Memoirs of Margaret Fuller Ossoli* (1852)

Ralph Waldo Emerson

Ralph Waldo Emerson (1803–1882) had a vexed relationship with Fuller, so much so that it is one of the most discussed in American literature, even though its most intense period lasted only eight years, from about 1836 to 1844. After all, at her death he wrote, "I have lost in her my audience," a clear indication of the importance she had to him (July 1850, *Journals*, 11:258).

They were supposedly brought together by Elizabeth Palmer Peabody; however, when she requested the meeting, Emerson declined, asking, "What is there in her, anyway?" Peabody answered: "Why, Mr. Emerson, when first I called upon Margaret Fuller I felt, on leaving her, as if I had seen the universe!", at which Emerson turned to Lidian Emerson "in despair," saying, "we must have the young woman here if she can show us the universe!" (Wiggin, *My Garden of Memory*, 156). At the beginning, Emerson thought, "we shall never get far" because her "extreme plainness,—a trick of incessantly opening and shutting her eyelids,—the nasal tone of her voice,—all repelled." Soon, though, they were discussing German literature (she helped him improve his pronunciation), philosophy, continental writers, and all the events eventuating in Transcendentalism. Emerson praised her to his friends, even telling Hawthorne that she was "the greatest woman" of "ancient or modern times, and the one figure in the world worth considering" (8 April 1843, Hawthorne, *American Notebooks*, 371).

As Fuller was drawn closer to Emerson, though, she expected more from him. Their correspondence progressed from pleasant exchanges to discussions of how to edit the *Dial* to commenting on mutual friends to exchanging confidences; and as Fuller visited the Emersons in Concord more and more, they became close in ways that encouraged Fuller but concerned Emerson. Part of the problem was that Fuller seemed so opposite to him in many ways. According to Fuller, they agreed that "my god was love, his truth," or, as she put it in a letter to him, "You are intellect, I am life" (Myerson, "Fuller's 1842 Journal," 324; 13 July 1844, *Letters*, 3:209). For his part, he wrote in his journal that "A difference between you and me is that I like to hear of my faults and you do not like to hear of yours" (October 1841, Emerson, *Journals*,

8:108). He also described their conversations as "strange, cold-warm, attractive-repelling," and Fuller as one "whom I always admire, most severe when I nearest see, and sometimes love, yet whom I freeze, and who freezes me to silence, when we seem to promise to come nearest" (October 1841, Emerson, *Journals*, 8:109).

Matters came to a head during the summer and fall of 1840, when Emerson engaged in a three-way correspondence with Fuller and their mutual friend Caroline Sturgis about friendship (some of which was incorporated into Emerson's essay on "Friendship"). Fuller wanted a closer emotional tie than Emerson was willing to grant. In *Memoirs*, he probably referred to this period when he wrote, "I found she lived at a rate so much faster than mine, and which was violent compared with mine, I foreboded rash and painful crises." Fuller eventually pulled back, summing up the events in this fashion: "After the first excitement of intimacy with him,—when I was made so happy by his high tendency, absolute purity, the freedom and infinite graces of an intellect cultivated much beyond any I had known,—came with me the questioning season. I was greatly disappointed in my relation to him." To Fuller, Emerson seemed to lack "the living faith which enables one to discharge this holiest office of a friend," for he had "faith in the Universal, but not in the Individual Man; he met men, not as a brother, but as a critic." She had come to terms with this, though: "But I already see so well how these limitations have fitted him for his peculiar work, that I can no longer quarrel with them; while from his eyes looks out the angel that must sooner or later break every chain. Leave him in his cell affirming absolute truth; protesting against humanity, if so he appears to do; the calm observer of the courses of things" (25 August 1842, *Letters*, 3:91, where Emerson is identified as the subject of this letter). Or, as she wrote in her journal, "it is deeply tragic on the one side, my relation to him, but on the other, how noble, how dear! . . . Let me keep both sides duly balanced in my mind" (1 August 1844, Berg and Perry, "Fuller's 1844 Journal," 107–108). For his part, Emerson wrote Fuller, "I ought never to have suffered you to lead me into any conversation or writing on our relation" (24 October 1840, *Letters*, 2:352).

While reading Fuller's letters and journals as he compiled materials for the *Memoirs*, Emerson declared, "So much wit, ready and rapid learning, appreciation, so much probity, constancy and aspiration, when shall we see again? Then what capacity for friendship!" (17–18 November 1850, *Letters*, 8:266).

> As late as 1866, he believed that Fuller "with her radiant genius and fiery heart was perhaps the real centre that drew so many and so various individuals to a seeming union" (*Journals*, 16:22).

I BECAME ACQUAINTED with Margaret in 1835. Perhaps it was a year earlier that Henry Hedge, who had long been her friend, told me of her genius and studies, and loaned me her manuscript translation of Goethe's Tasso. I was afterwards still more interested in her, by the warm praises of Harriet Martineau, who had become acquainted with her at Cambridge, and who, finding Margaret's fancy for seeing me, took a generous interest in bringing us together. I remember, during a week in the winter of 1835-6, in which Miss Martineau was my guest, she returned again and again to the topic of Margaret's excelling genius and conversation, and enjoined it on me to seek her acquaintance: which I willingly promised. I am not sure that it was not in Miss Martineau's company, a little earlier, that I first saw her. And I find a memorandum, in her own journal, of a visit, made by my brother Charles and myself, to Miss Martineau, at Mrs. Farrar's. It was not, however, till the next July, after a little diplomatizing in billets by the ladies, that her first visit to our house was arranged, and she came to spend a fortnight with my wife. I still remember the first half-hour of Margaret's conversation. She was then twenty-six years old. She had a face and frame that would indicate fulness and tenacity of life. She was rather under the middle height; her complexion was fair, with strong fair hair. She was then, as always, carefully and becomingly dressed, and of ladylike self-possession. For the rest, her appearance had nothing prepossessing. Her extreme plainness,—a trick of incessantly opening and shutting her eyelids,—the nasal tone of her voice,—all repelled; and I said to myself, we shall never get far. It is to be said, that Margaret made a disagreeable first impression on most persons, including those who became afterwards her best friends, to such an extreme that they did not wish to be in the same room with her. This was partly the effect of her manners, which expressed an overweening sense of power, and slight esteem of others, and partly the prejudice of her fame. She had a dangerous reputation for satire, in addition to her great scholarship. The men thought she carried too many guns, and the women did not like one who despised them. I believe I fancied her too much interested in personal history; and her talk was a comedy in which dramatic justice was done to everybody's foibles. I remember that she made me laugh more than I liked; for I was, at that time, an eager scholar of ethics, and had tasted the sweets of solitude and stoicism, and I found something profane in the hours of amusing gossip into which she drew me, and, when I returned to my library, had much to think of the crackling of thorns under a pot. Margaret, who had stuffed me out as a philosopher, in her own fancy, was too intent on establishing a good footing between us, to omit any art of winning. She studied my tastes, piqued and amused me, challenged frankness by frankness, and did not conceal the good opinion of me she brought with her, nor her wish to please. She was curious to know my opinions and experiences. Of course, it was impossible long to hold out against such urgent assault. She had an incredible variety of anecdotes, and the readiest wit to give an absurd turn to whatever passed; and the eyes, which were so plain at first, soon swam with fun and drolleries, and the very tides of joy and superabundant life.

This rumor was much spread abroad, that she was sneering, scoffing, critical, disdainful of humble people, and of all but the intellectual. I had heard it whenever she was named. It was a superficial judgment. Her satire was only the pastime and necessity of her talent, the play of superabundant animal spirits. And it will be seen, in the sequel, that her mind presently disclosed many moods and powers, in successive platforms or terraces, each above each, that quite effaced this first impression. . . .

She had large experiences. . . . She had drawn at Cambridge, numbers of lively young men about her. She had had a circle of young women who were devoted to her, and who described her as "a wonder of intellect, who had yet no religion." She had drawn to her every superior young man or young woman she had met, and whole romances of life and love had been confided, counselled, thought, and lived through, in her cognizance and sympathy.

These histories are rapid, so that she had already beheld many times the youth, meridian, and old age of passion. She had, besides, selected, from so many, a few eminent companions, and already felt that she was not likely to see anything more beautiful than her beauties, anything more powerful and generous than her youths. She had found out her own secret by early comparison, and knew what power to draw confidence, what necessity to lead in every circle, belonged of right to her. Her powers were maturing, and nobler sentiments were subliming the first heats and rude experiments. She had outward calmness and dignity. She had come to the ambition to be filled with all nobleness. . . .

She wore this circle of friends, when I first knew her, as a necklace of diamonds about her neck. They were so much to each other, that Margaret seemed to represent them all, and, to know her, was to acquire a place with them. The confidences given her were their best, and she held them to them. She was an active, inspiring companion and correspondent, and all the art, the thought, and the nobleness in New England, seemed, at that moment, related to her, and she to it. She was everywhere a welcome guest. The houses of her friends in town and country were open to her, and every hospitable attention eagerly offered. Her arrival was a holiday, and so was her abode. She stayed a few days, often a week, more seldom a month, and all tasks that could be suspended were put aside to catch the favorable hour, in walking, riding, or boating, to talk with this joyful guest, who brought wit, anecdotes, love-stories, tragedies, oracles with her, and, with her broad web of relations to so many fine friends, seemed like the queen of some parliament of love, who carried the key to all confidences, and to whom every question had been finally referred.

Persons were her game, specially, if marked by fortune, or character, or success;—to such was she sent. She addressed them with a hardihood,—almost a haughty assurance,—queen-like. Indeed, they fell in her way, where the access might have seemed difficult, by wonderful casualties; and the inveterate recluse, the coyest maid, the waywardest poet, made no resistance, but yielded at discretion, as if they had been waiting for her, all doors to this imperious dame. She disarmed the suspicion of recluse scholars by the absence of bookishness. The ease with which she entered into conversation made them forget all they had heard of her; and she was infinitely less interested in literature than in life. They saw she valued earnest persons, and Dante, Petrarch, and Goethe, because they thought as she did, and gratified her with high portraits, which she was everywhere seeking. She drew her companions to surprising confessions. She was the wedding-guest, to whom the long-pent story must be told; and they were not less struck, on reflection, at the suddenness of the friendship which had established, in one day new and permanent covenants. She extorted the secret of life, which cannot be told without setting heart and mind in a glow;

and thus had the best of those she saw. Whatever romance, whatever virtue, whatever impressive experience,—this came to her; and she lived in a superior circle; for they suppressed all their common-place in her presence.

She was perfectly true to this confidence. She never confounded relations, but kept a hundred fine threads in her hand, without crossing or entangling any. An entire intimacy, which seemed to make both sharers of the whole horizon of each others' and of all truth, did not yet make her false to any other friend; gave no title to the history that an equal trust of another friend had put in her keeping. In this reticence was no prudery and no effort. For, so rich her mind, that she never was tempted to treachery, by the desire of entertaining. The day was never long enough to exhaust her opulent memory; and I, who knew her intimately for ten years,—from July, 1836, till August, 1846, when she sailed for Europe,—never saw her without surprise at her new powers.

Of the conversations above alluded to, the substance was whatever was suggested by her passionate wish for equal companions, to the end of making life altogether noble. With the firmest tact she led the discourse into the midst of their daily living and working, recognizing the good-will and sincerity which each man has in his aims, and treating so playfully and intellectually all the points, that one seemed to see his life *en beau,* and was flattered by beholding what he had found so tedious in its workday weeds, shining in glorious costume. Each of his friends passed before him in the new light; hope seemed to spring under his feet, and life was worth living. The auditor jumped for joy, and thirsted for unlimited draughts. What! is this the dame, who, I heard, was sneering and critical? this the blue-stocking, of whom I stood in terror and dislike? this wondrous woman, full of counsel, full of tenderness, before whom every mean thing is ashamed, and hides itself; this new Corinne, more variously gifted, wise, sportive, eloquent, who seems to have learned all languages, Heaven knows when or how,—I should think she was born to them,—magnificent, prophetic, reading my life at her will, and puzzling me with riddles like this, "Yours is an example of a destiny springing from character;" and, again, "I see your destiny hovering before you, but it always escapes from you."

The test of this eloquence was its range. It told on children, and on old people; on men of the world, and on sainted maids. She could hold them all by her honeyed tongue. A lady of the best eminence, whom Margaret occasionally visited, in one of our cities of spindles, speaking one day of her neighbors, said, "I stand in a certain awe of the moneyed men, the manufacturers, and so on, knowing that they will have small interest in Plato, or in Biot; but I saw them approach Margaret, with perfect security, for she could give them bread that they could eat." Some persons are thrown off their balance when in society; others are thrown on to balance; the excitement of company, and the observation of other characters, correct their biases. Margaret always appeared to unexpected advantage in conversation with a large circle. She had more sanity than any other; whilst, in private, her vision was often through colored lenses.

Her talents were so various, and her conversation so rich and entertaining, that one might talk with her many times, by the parlor fire, before he discovered the strength which served as foundation to so much accomplishment and eloquence. But, concealed under flowers and music, was the broadest good sense, very well able to dispose of all this pile of native and foreign ornaments, and quite able to work without them. She could always rally on this, in every circumstance, and in every company, and find herself on a firm footing of equality with any party whatever, and make herself useful, and, if need be, formidable. . . .

Margaret had, with certain limitations, or, must we say, *strictures,* these larger lungs, inhaling this universal element, and could speak to Jew and Greek, free and bond, to each in his own tongue. The Concord stage-coachman distinguished her by his respect, and the chambermaid was pretty sure to confide to her, on the second day, her homely romance.

I regret that it is not in my power to give any true report of Margaret's conversation. She soon became an established friend and frequent inmate of our house, and continued, thenceforward, for years, to come, once in three or four months, to spend a week or a fortnight with us. She adopted all the people and all the interests she found here. Your people shall be my people, and yonder darling boy I shall cherish as my own. Her ready sympathies endeared her to my wife and my mother, each of whom highly esteemed her good sense and sincerity. She suited each, and all. Yet, she was not a person to be suspected of complaisance, and her attachments, one might say, were chemical.

She had so many tasks of her own, that she was a very easy guest to entertain, as she could be left to herself, day after day, without apology. According to our usual habit, we seldom met in the forenoon. After dinner, we read something together, or walked, or rode. In the evening, she came to the library, and many and many a conversation was there held, whose details, if they could be preserved, would justify all encomiums. They interested me in every manner;—talent, memory, wit, stern introspection, poetic play, religion, the finest personal feeling, the aspects of the future, each followed each in full activity, and left me, I remember, enriched and sometimes astonished by the gifts of my guest. Her topics were numerous, but the cardinal points of poetry, love, and religion, were never far off. She was a student of art, and, though untravelled, knew, much better than most persons who had been abroad, the conventional reputation of each of the masters. She was familiar with all the field of elegant criticism in literature. Among the problems of the day, these two attracted her chiefly, Mythology and Demonology; then, also, French Socialism, especially as it concerned woman; the whole prolific family of reforms, and, of course, the genius and career of each remarkable person. . . .

It was soon evident that there was somewhat a little pagan about her; that she had some faith more or less distinct in a fate, and in a guardian genius; that her fancy, or her pride, had played with her religion. She had a taste for gems, ciphers, talismans, omens, coincidences, and birth-days. She had a special love for the planet Jupiter, and a belief that the month of September was inauspicious to her. She never forgot that her name, Margarita, signified a pearl. "When I first met with the name Leila," she said, "I knew, from the very look and sound, it was mine; I knew that it meant night,—night, which brings out stars, as sorrow brings out truths." Sortilege [divination by throwing lots] she valued. She tried *sortes biblicae* [a divinary consultation of the Bible], and her hits were memorable. I think each new book which interested her, she was disposed to put to this test, and know if it had somewhat personal to say to her. As happens to such persons, these guesses were justified by the event. She chose carbuncle for her own stone, and when a dear friend was to give her a gem, this was the one selected. She valued what she had somewhere read, that carbuncles are male and female. The female casts out light, the male has his within himself. "Mine," she said, "is the male." And she was wont to put on her carbuncle, a bracelet, or some selected gem, to write letters to certain friends. One of her friends she coupled with the onyx, another in a decided way with the amethyst. She learned that the ancients esteemed this gem a talisman to dispel intoxication, to give good thoughts and understanding "The Greek meaning is *antidote against drunkenness*." . . .

Coincidences, good and bad, *contretemps,* seals, ciphers, mottoes, omens, anniversaries, names, dreams, are all of a certain importance to her. Her letters are often dated on some marked anniversary of her own, or of her correspondent's calendar. . . . In this spirit, she soon surrounded herself with a little mythology of her own. She had a series of anniversaries, which she kept. Her seal-ring of the flying Mercury had its legend. She chose the *Sistrum* for her emblem, and had it carefully drawn with a view to its being engraved on a gem. . . .

I said that Margaret had a broad good sense, which brought her near to all people. I am to say that she had also a strong temperament, which is that counter force which makes individuality, by driving all the powers in the direction of the ruling thought or feeling, and, when it is allowed full sway, isolating them. These two tendencies were always invading each other, and now one and now the other carried the day. This alternation perplexes the biographer, as it did the observer. We contradict on the second page what we affirm on the first: and I remember how often I was compelled to correct my impressions of her character when living; for after I had settled it once for all that she wanted this or that perception, at our next interview she would say with emphasis the very word.

I think, in her case, there was something abnormal in those obscure habits and necessities which we denote by the word Temperament. In the first days of our acquaintance, I felt her to be a foreigner,—that, with her, one would always be sensible of some barrier, as if in making up a friendship with a cultivated Spaniard or Turk. She had a strong constitution, and of course its reactions were strong; and this is the reason why in all her life she has so much to say of her *fate.* She was in jubilant spirits in the morning, and ended the day with nervous headache, whose spasms, my wife told me, produced total prostration. She had great energy of speech and action, and seemed formed for high emergencies.

Her life concentrated itself on certain happy days, happy hours, happy moments. The rest was a void. She had read that a man of letters must lose many days, to work well in one. Much more must a Sappho or a sibyl. The capacity of pleasure was balanced by the capacity of pain. "If I had wist [that is, wit]"!—she writes, "I am a worse self-tormentor than Rousseau, and all my riches are fuel to the fire. My beautiful lore, like the tropic clime, hatches scorpions to sting me. There is a verse, which Annie of Lochroyan sings about her ring, that torments my memory, 'tis so true of myself."

When I found she lived at a rate so much faster than mine, and which was violent compared with mine, I foreboded rash and painful crises, and had a feeling as if a voice cried, *Stand from under!*—as if, a little further on, this destiny was threatened with jars and reverses, which no friendship could avert or console. This feeling partly wore off, on better acquaintance, but remained latent; and I had always an impression that her energy was too much a force of blood, and therefore never felt the security for her peace which belongs to more purely intellectual natures. She seemed more vulnerable. For the same reason, she remained inscrutable to me; her strength was not my strength,—her powers were a surprise. She passed into new states of great advance, but I understood these no better. It were long to tell her peculiarities. Her childhood was full of presentiments. She was then a somnambulist. She was subject to attacks of delirium, and, later, perceived that she had spectral illusions. When she was twelve, she had a determination of blood to the head. "My parents," she said, "were much mortified to see the fineness of my complexion destroyed. My own vanity was for a time severely wounded; but I recovered, and made up my mind to be bright and ugly."

She was all her lifetime the victim of disease and pain. She read and wrote in bed, and believed that she could understand anything better when she was ill. Pain acted like a girdle, to give tension to her powers. A lady, who was with her one day during a terrible attack of nervous headache, which made Margaret totally helpless, assured me that Margaret was yet in the finest vein of humor, and kept those who were assisting her in a strange, painful excitement, between laughing and crying, by perpetual brilliant sallies. There were other peculiarities of habit and power. When she turned her head on one side, she alleged she had second sight, like St. Francis. These traits or predispositions made her a willing listener to all the uncertain science of mesmerism and its goblin brood, which have been rife in recent years.

She had a feeling that she ought to have been a man, and said of herself, "A man's ambition with a woman's heart, is an evil lot." In some verses which she wrote "To the Moon," occur these lines:—

> But if I steadfast gaze upon thy face,
> A human secret, like my own, I trace;
> For, through the woman's smile looks the male eye.

[148]

And she found something of true portraiture in a disagreeable novel of Balzac's, *"Le Livre Mystique,"* in which an equivocal figure exerts alternately a masculine and a feminine influence on the characters of the plot. . . .

She had, indeed, a rude strength, which, if it could have been supported by an equal health, would have given her the efficiency of the strongest men. As it was, she had great power of work. The account of her reading in Groton is at a rate like Gibbon's, and, later, that of her writing, considered with the fact that writing was not grateful to her, is incredible. She often proposed to her friends, in the progress of intimacy, to write every day. "I think less than a daily offering of thought and feeling would not content me, so much seems to pass unspoken." In Italy, she tells Madame Arconati, that she has "more than a hundred correspondents;" and it was her habit there to devote one day of every week to those distant friends. The facility with which she assumed stints of literary labor, which veteran feeders of the press would shrink from,—assumed and performed,—when her friends were to be served, I have often observed with wonder, and with fear, when I considered the near extremes of ill-health, and the manner in which her life heaped itself in high and happy moments, which were avenged by lassitude and pain.

"As each task comes," she said, "I borrow a readiness from its aspect, as I always do brightness from the face of a friend. Yet, as soon as the hour is past, I sink."

I think most of her friends will remember to have felt, at one time or another, some uneasiness, as if this athletic soul craved a larger atmosphere than it found; as if she were ill-timed and mis-mated, and felt in herself a tide of life, which compared with the slow circulation of others as a torrent with a rill. She found no full expression of it but in music. Beethoven's Symphony was the only right thing the city of the Puritans had for her. . . .

Margaret at first astonished and repelled us by a complacency that seemed the most assured since the days of Scaliger. She spoke, in the quietest manner, of the girls she had formed, the young men who owed everything to her, the fine companions she had long ago exhausted. In the coolest way, she said to her friends, "I now know all the people worth knowing in America, and I find no intellect comparable to my own." In vain, on one occasion, I professed my reverence for a youth of genius, and my curiosity in his future,—"O no, she was intimate with his mind," and I "spoiled him, by overrating him." Meantime, we knew that she neither had seen, nor would see, his subtle superiorities.

I have heard, that from the beginning of her life, she idealized herself as a sovereign. She told —— she early saw herself to be intellectually superior to those around her, and that for years she dwelt upon the idea, until she believed that she was not her parents' child, but an European princess confided to their care. She remembered, that, when a little girl, she was walking one day under the apple trees with such an air and step, that her father pointed her out to her sister, saying, *Incedit regina.* . . .

It is certain that Margaret occasionally let slip, with all the innocence imaginable, some phrase betraying the presence of a rather mountainous ME, in a way to surprise those who knew her good sense. She could say, as if she were stating a scientific fact, in enumerating the merits of somebody, "He appreciates *me*." There was something of hereditary organization in this, and something of unfavorable circumstance in the fact, that she had in early life no companion, and few afterwards, in her finer studies; but there was also an ebullient sense of power, which she felt to be in her, which as yet had found no right channels. I remember she once said to me, what I heard as a mere statement of fact, and nowise as unbecoming, that "no man gave such invitation to her mind as to tempt her to a full expression; that she felt a power to enrich her thought with such wealth and variety of embellishment as would, no doubt, be tedious to such as she conversed with."

Her impatience she expressed as she could. "I feel within myself," she said, "an immense force, but I cannot bring it out. It may sound like a joke, but I do feel something corresponding to that tale of the Destinies falling in love with Hermes." . . .

I have inquired diligently of those who saw her often, and in different companies, concerning her habitual tone, and something like this is the report:—In conversation, Margaret seldom, except as a special grace, admitted others upon an equal ground with herself. She was exceedingly tender, when she pleased to be, and most cherishing in her influence; but to elicit this tenderness, it was necessary to submit first to her personally. When a person was overwhelmed by her, and answered not a word, except, "Margaret, be merciful to me, a sinner," then her love and tenderness would come like a seraph's, and often an acknowledgment that she had been too harsh, and even a craving for pardon, with a humility,—which, perhaps, she had caught from the other. But her instinct was not humility,—that was always an afterthought.

This arrogant tone of her conversation, if it came to be the subject of comment, of course, she defended, and with such broad good nature, and on grounds of simple truth, as were not easy to set aside. She quoted from Manzoni's *Carmagnola,* the lines:—

> Tolga il ciel che alcuno
> Piu altamente di me pensi ch'io stesso.

"God forbid that any one should conceive more highly of me than I myself." Meantime, the tone of her journals is humble, tearful, religious, and rises easily into prayer.

I am obliged to an ingenious correspondent for the substance of the following account of this idiosyncrasy:—

> Margaret was one of the few persons who looked upon life as an art, and every person not merely as an artist, but as a work of art. She looked upon herself as a living statue, which should always stand on a polished pedestal, with right accessories, and under the most fitting lights. She would have been glad to have everybody so live and act. She was annoyed when they did not, and when they did not regard her from the point of view which alone did justice to her. No one could be more lenient in her judgments of those whom she saw to be living in this light. Their faults were to be held as "the disproportions of the ungrown giant." But the faults of persons who were unjustified by this ideal, were odious. Unhappily, her constitutional self-esteem sometimes blinded the eyes that should have seen that an idea lay at the bottom of some lives which she did not quite so readily comprehend as beauty; that truth had other manifestations than those which engaged her natural sympathies; that sometimes the soul illuminated only the smallest arc—of a circle so large that it was lost in the clouds of another world. . . .

But qualities of this kind can only be truly described by the impression they make on the bystander; and it is certain that her friends excused in her, because she had a right to it, a tone which they would have reckoned intolerable in any other. . . .

I fear the remark already made on that susceptibility to details in art and nature which precluded the exercise of Margaret's sound catholic judgment, must be extended to more than her connoisseurship. She *had* a sound judgment, on which, in conversation, she could fall back, and anticipate and speak the best sense of the largest company. But, left to herself, and in her correspondence, she was much the victim of Lord Bacon's *idols of the cave,* or self-deceived by her own phantasms. I have looked over volumes of her letters to me and others. They are full of probity, talent, wit, friendship, charity, and high aspiration. They are tainted with a mysticism, which to me appears so much an affair of constitution, that it claims no more respect than the charity or patriotism of a man who has dined well, and feels better for it. One sometimes talks with a genial *bon vivant,* who looks as if the omelet and turtle have got into his eyes. In our noble Margaret, her personal feeling colors all her judgment of persons, of books, of pictures, and even of the laws of the world. This is easily felt in ordinary women, and a large deduction is civilly made on the spot by whosoever replies to their remark. But when the speaker has such brilliant talent and literature as Margaret, she gives so many fine names to these merely sensuous and subjective phantasms, that the hearer is long imposed upon, and thinks so precise and glittering nomenclature cannot be of mere *muscae volitantes,* phoenixes of the fancy, but must be of some real ornithology, hitherto unknown to him. This mere feeling exaggerates a host of trifles into a dazzling mythology. But when one goes to sift it, and find if there be a real meaning, it eludes search. Whole sheets of warm, florid writing are here, in which the eye is caught by "sapphire," "heliotrope," "dragon," "aloes," "Magna Dea," "limboes," "Stars," and "purgatory," but can connect all this, or any part of it, with no universal experience.

In short, Margaret often loses herself in sentimentalism. That dangerous vertigo nature in her case adopted, and was to make respectable. As it sometimes happens that a grandiose style, like that of the Alexandrian Platonists, or like Macpherson's Ossian, is more stimulating to the imagination of nations, than the true Plato, or than the simple poet, so here was a head so creative of new colors, of wonderful gleams,—so iridescent, that it piqued curiosity, and stimulated thought, and communicated mental activity to all who approached her; though her perceptions were not to be compared to her fancy, and she made numerous mistakes. Her integrity was perfect, and she was led and followed by love, and was really bent on truth, but too indulgent to the meteors of her fancy. . . .

Even in trifles, one might find with her the advantage and the electricity of a little honesty. I have had from an eye-witness a note of a little scene that passed in Boston, at the Academy of Music. A party had gone early, and taken an excellent place to hear one of Beethoven's symphonies. Just behind them were soon seated a young lady and two gentlemen, who made an incessant buzzing, in spite of bitter looks cast on them by the whole neighborhood, and destroyed all the musical comfort. After all was over, Margaret leaned across one seat, and catching the eye of this girl, who was pretty and well-dressed, said, in her blandest, gentlest voice, "May I speak with you one moment?" "Certainly," said the young lady, with a fluttered, pleased look, bending forward. "I only wish to say," said Margaret, "that I trust, that, in the whole course of your life, you will not suffer so great a degree of annoyance as you have inflicted on a large party of lovers of music this evening." This was said with the sweetest air, as if to a little child, and it was as good as a play to see the change of countenance which the young lady exhibited, who had no replication to make to so Christian a blessing.

On graver occasions, the same habit was only more stimulated; and I cannot remember certain passages which called it into play, without new regrets at the costly loss which our community sustains in the loss of this brave and eloquent soul.

People do not speak the truth, not for the want of not knowing and preferring it, but because they have not the organ to speak it adequately. It requires a clear sight, and, still more, a high spirit, to deal with falsehood in the decisive way. I have known several honest persons who valued truth as much as Peter and John, but, when they tried to speak it, *they* grew red and black in the face instead of Ananias, until, after a few attempts, they decided that aggressive truth was not their vocation, and confined themselves thenceforward to silent honesty, except on rare occasions, when either an extreme outrage, or a happier inspiration, loosened their tongue. But a soul is now and then incarnated, whom indulgent nature has not afflicted with any cramp or frost, but who can speak the right word at the right moment, qualify the selfish and hypocritical act with its real name, and, without any loss of serenity, hold up the offence to the purest daylight. Such a truth-speaker is worth more than the best police, and more than the laws or governors; for these do not always know their own side, but will back the crime for want of this very truth-speaker to expose them. That is the theory of the newspaper,—to supersede official by intellectual influence. But, though the apostles establish the journal, it usually happens that, by some strange oversight, Ananias slips into the editor's chair. If, then, we could be provided with a fair proportion of truth-speakers, we could very materially and usefully contract the legislative and the executive functions. Still, the main sphere for this nobleness is private society, where so many mischiefs go unwhipped, being out of the cognizance of law, and supposed to be nobody's business. And society is, at all times, suffering for want of judges and headsmen, who will mark and lop these malefactors.

Margaret suffered no vice to insult her presence, but called the offender to instant account, when the law of right or of beauty was violated. She needed not, of course, to go out of her way to find the offender, and she never did, but she had the courage and the skill to cut heads off which were not worn with honor in her presence. Others might abet a crime by silence, if they pleased; she chose to clear herself of all complicity, by calling the act by its name.

It was curious to see the mysterious provocation which the mere presence of insight exerts in its neighborhood. Like moths about a lamp, her victims voluntarily came to judgment: conscious persons, encumbered with egotism; vain persons, bent on concealing some mean vice; arrogant reformers, with some halting of their own; the compromisers, who wished to reconcile right and wrong;—all came and held out their palms to the wise woman, to read their fortunes, and they were truly told. Many anecdotes have come to my ear, which show how useful the glare of her lamp proved in private circles, and what dramatic situations it created. But these cannot be told. The valor for dragging the accused spirits among his acquaintance to the stake is not in the heart of the present writer. The reader must be content to learn that she knew how, without loss of temper, to speak with unmistakable plainness to any party, when she felt that the truth or the right was injured. For the same reason, I omit one or two letters, most honorable both to her mind and heart, in which she felt constrained to give the frankest utterance to her displeasure. . . .

Memoirs of Margaret Fuller Ossoli, ed. William Henry Channing, James Freeman Clarke, and Ralph Waldo Emerson, 2 vols. (Boston: Phillips, Sampson, 1852), 1:201–205, 213–21, 227–29, 231–32, 234–39, 279–80, 304–307.

[Epistolary Comments on Fuller in 1852]

SARAH HELEN WHITMAN

Sarah Helen Power Whitman (1803–1878) was a poet who spent all but five years of her life in Providence, Rhode Island. She married attorney John Winslow Whitman (1798–1833) in 1828, moving with him to Boston but returning to Providence upon his death. Whitman is primarily remembered today as the woman to whom Poe became briefly engaged after the death of his wife, Virginia; one of his "To Helen" poems was written for her. She later published *Edgar Poe and His Critics* (1860) and supplied Poe's English biographer, John H. Ingram, with much information for his work.

Whitman corresponded with Fuller about art, literature, and current events, including local gossip. The two moved in the same social circles in Providence, and Whitman joined a private class in German that Fuller was teaching. Writing to Emerson in 1839, Fuller mentioned receiving a letter from Whitman, "which I think so good that I would send it to you if there were not so many compliments that it would make you quite faint and ill" (3 June 1839, *Letters*, 2:69).

Sarah Helen Whitman to William Ellery Channing the Younger, [1852]

I too read it [*Memoirs*] with deep interest and profound attention, hoping at last to know Margaret and do her justice—but in vain I sought to solve the problem of a nature so complex—when she speaks of the loneliness of her life, her sorrows and conflicts (as on Thanksgiving day and other periods of depressing and desolating sadness) and of the divine consolation and the heaven-born courage that compensated and crowned those periods of gloom, I felt for her a tender sympathy mingled with adoration and respect. When I saw her patient and pitying love for her little brother born on her birthday—her love for the little E[ugene]. and the little boy, and for her own little boy whose presence was to fill the heaven with joy—redeem her own heart forever from its loneliness, I was ready to forget all her faults, but old memories still come back to obscure this fair impression, yet on the whole I think I know her better and admire her more than I did before

I read the book. Some passages called up a train of associations which it was pleasant to revive on page 191 of Vol. I. She speaks of a Christ by Raphael which brought Christianity more home to her heart than ever did sermons. I remember the walk we took together one golden afternoon in the autumn of 1838. I spoke to her of those engravings which belonged to a friend of mine then recently returned from Italy, and she made an appointment to see them at my house—I was to borrow them for her. She brought James Freeman Clarke with her, and I read to her while she looked at them, the description of an old French writer of the last century. I remember her amusing remarks about the deity in the square velvet cap and her delight at the free out-of-door bare-footed life of the ladies in the picture of Apollo and the Muses. The owner of these pictures, Mr. Dorrance, afterwards went with Margaret, Ellen and me to one of my favorite spots in the woods—a place for mid-summer night's dream—sheltered and shadowy and full of nooks and banks and long dim vistas. On our way, Margaret sat down in what seemed to me a bleak place to look at a wide open landscape that had no attraction for my eye. I thought "if she is enchanted here, what will she think of my glen." But to my regret she could see nothing but dead leaves and damp earth where I saw so much beauty. Each of us was blind to what most charmed the other. If I should meet her in that world to which she had ascended we should I doubt not exchange friendly greetings, but our homes would lie far apart in remote quarters in the spiritual kingdom. . . .

John Grier Varner, "Sarah Helen Whitman: Seeress of Providence" (Ph.D. dissertation, University of Virginia, 1940), 169–70.

[Epistolary and Other Comments on Fuller in 1856, 1882, and 1884]

George William Curtis

George William Curtis to Daniel Ricketson, 23 April 1856

She was always kind and very full of fun with me,—and when I last saw her in Florence, there was a quiet tenderness in her manner which I recall with great satisfaction. She was very unprepossessing personally. Her hair was scant and sandy. Her skin dry and soft. Her features were large and the eyes not lovely. The expression, owing largely to illness, was a kind of sniffing conceit and scornfulness. She has some affliction of the spine which threw

[157]

her head forward in an unfortunate manner. She knew so much more than all the women and most of the men she met that she could not disguise her superiority, from a consciousness already full of self-esteem. Then she had a passionate love of beauty, grace and personal fascination,—and she seemed stung with secret disappointment that she could not make all she had take the place of all she had not. I never knew anyone more truly loyal to loveliness of every kind.

She dressed always simply, but dowdily and never handsomely. But here again she recognized and admired in others all kinds of beautiful dressing and ornament.

When I saw her after she was married, she was very sweet and gentle, and indeed she is altogether very beautiful in my memory, and I cannot long think of her without tears. No one who knew her well—and her friends were among the noblest and truest of human beings—but had a kind of passionate regard for her. . . .

Ossoli I saw a few times. He was a young, modest Italian, and, as he spoke no English, very silent. He was evidently entirely absorbed in her— and it was very touching to mark their mutual tenderness. . . .

"Editor's Easy Chair," *Harper's New Monthly Magazine,* March 1882

We have recently seen a description of a visit made during the present winter to [the site of Brook Farm], and the visitor remarks, with emotion: "Most interesting of all to us was Margaret Fuller's cottage, still standing on the crest of a little hill, in the midst of a copse of cedars. It is cruciform in shape, covered with wide wooden clapboards, and is now the dwelling of the superintendent of the estate and his family. Our guide remarked, *sotto voce,* that Miss Fuller received a thousand dollars for it in the distribution of the property." But then it was not Margaret Fuller's cottage, and she was never a Brook Farmer, and if she received any sums of money "in the distribution of the property," it was a free gift. Neither was Mr. Emerson ever at the farm as a resident or an associate. Concord was a Mecca for Brook Farmers, as it has long been for Cambridge students of a certain taste and sympathy, but Brook Farm, although curious and interesting to Mr. Emerson, seldom drew him personally within its borders. Miss Fuller made occasional visits, often remaining some days, and she was always most warmly welcomed.

Those who think of this accomplished woman as a mere *bas bleu* [intellectual woman], a pedant, a solemn Minerva, should have heard the peals of laughter which her profuse and racy humor drew from old and young. The Easy Chair remembers stepping into Noah Gerrish's West Roxbury omnibus one afternoon in Cornhill, in Boston, to drive out the nine miles to Brook Farm. The only other passenger was Miss Fuller, then freshly returned from her "summer on the lakes," and never was a long, jolting journey more lightened and shortened than by her witty and vivid sketches of life and character. Her quick and shrewd observation is shown in the book, but the book has none of the comedy of the *croquis* [sketches] of persons which her sparkling humor threw off, and which she too enjoyed with the utmost hilarity, joining heartily in the laughter, which was only increased by her sympathy with the amusement of her auditor.

Miss Fuller was not only a woman of remarkable literary cultivation, but her resources were always at command. Before the Brook Farm days, and when she was a teacher in the Green Street school in Providence, the Easy Chair—then a mere stool or cricket—has heard her tilting with the cleverest men, who were purposely testing her acquirements, leaving them vanquished upon the field. There was undoubtedly in her manner a consciousness of superiority, but this was heightened by a slight physical peculiarity which made it seem very much greater, and which sometimes gave the impression of disdainful self-complacency. She had the natural contempt and impatience which every high-spirited and intellectual and cultivated woman feels for the masculine assumption of superiority because of sex. In the mouths and in the minds of such women the word "mannish" is just as impatient an adjective as "womanish" in the mouths and minds of many men. "That is just like a woman," a man exclaims, petulantly, serenely unconscious that his own conduct also stings a sensible woman into the same protest, "That is just like a man." Hawthorne's Zenobia was his conception of a beautiful and graceful Margaret Fuller, little foreseeing, however, that the catastrophe of his story would have its counterpart in the melancholy death of the noble woman whom he admired. . . .

"Editor's Easy Chair," *Harper's New Monthly Magazine,* March 1884

It is the fate of the most scholarly accomplished American woman to be known only by the tradition of her personal friends and their memoirs of her, and not in any adequate manner by her own works, for the literary remains of Margaret Fuller give no satisfactory impression of the woman herself. Mrs. [Julia Ward] Howe has just written a brief and admirable biography which will serve to remind the present generation of readers of one of the most striking figures in the American intellectual life of forty years ago.

Unfortunately the current and false impression of Miss Fuller as a typical blue-stocking, an unfeminine and arrogant Amazon, and pretentious *précieuse,* is perpetuated in Lowell's "Fable for Critics," where Miss Fuller appears as Minerva; and a certain self-conscious tone and want of simplicity and fluency in her writing does not remove this impression. In fact, however, probably those who knew and liked her most read her writings least. The richness, profusion, wit, and wisdom of her conversation, her keen and delicate observation, her delightful, rollicking, and abounding humor, her lofty character, integrity, and unselfishness, her broad and accurate knowledge and critical insight, made her so charming a companion, so lofty, true, and stimulating a friend, that her formal literary work seems to her friends meagre and unsatisfactory.

She was nobly unselfish, but so intent upon turning every opportunity to the best account that she was often plainly impatient of pretense and shallowness, and grudged the golden hours to charlatans of every degree. But she was in no sense austere except in her devotion to duty. If Minerva was as fond of fun, could see as shrewdly the amusing aspect of things, and laugh as heartily and intelligently as Miss Fuller, then Minerva was a much less prim body than she is painted. Indeed, if Miss Fuller were able, although some very clever people are not able, to imagine accurately the kind of person that many excellent persons supposed her to be, nothing could have given her more intense amusement. "If I were the kind of man that you fancied me to be," wrote an author to a correspondent who confessed his former dislike, "I should have despised myself as heartily as you despised me."

Miss Fuller's "magnetism," as Mrs. Howe points out, opened the hearts of men and women; she received the most intimate confidences of the noblest persons, and she repaid them a thousandfold. Her influence was a moral tonic. She strengthened, refined, and stimulated those who knew her best, and without making the least demand upon them in return. She set for others as for herself the highest standards, and her perpetual impression was that of loftiness of life. Indeed, in the transcendental renaissance of forty and fifty years ago, women may well feel that they were fitly represented among the remarkable group of men by this remarkable woman. Her studies were as wide and deep as those of many of the leaders of the movement. Her humane sympathies and aspirations were not less, her character was as lofty, and her life as true.

Personally she was plain and not of a graceful carriage, although Dr. Hedge, who knew her as a girl, remembers her as not ungraceful. She dressed always neatly, and never oddly. Her manner was peculiar. Certain looks and movements seemed like mere tricks, and there was sometimes a peremptory tone in her address and a half haughtiness of bearing which was very disconcerting to those, whether man or women, who wished to be seen to scorn blue-stockings and men-women. Never was there so little of a man-woman as Margaret Fuller; and had she possessed the personal beauty which Hawthorne gave to his Zenobia, a character in many aspects plainly studied from Miss Fuller, she would have been universally irresistible.

It was the fortune of the Easy Chair to be one of the few who had known her—as a boy knows a woman—in her last days in New England as Margaret Fuller, to know her also in the last romantic, pathetic days in Italy as Madame Ossoli. In the sunny Piazza Santa Maria Novella in Florence, near the church to which Cimabue's Virgin was brought in proud and joyful procession, he saw her and her husband and child. She was then thirty-nine years old, her husband perhaps ten years younger, a tall, slight, dark, quiet, gentlemanly man, fondly devoted to her, and plainly proud, as well he might be, of his wife. There was a gentle deference in his manner toward her which was very touching, and on that long vanished summer morning the little happy household on the third floor would be a very beautiful picture in memory except for the feeling at the time that the future, depending chiefly upon that brave and steady but not strong woman, was necessarily doubtful, and for the tragedy which was so soon to obliterate it from the earth.

It is hard to think that a woman so admirable and remarkable must be only a name to her countrymen, and a name growing necessarily less and less significant. It is vain, indeed, to plead for a mere name against oblivion. But it is something to assure those who look at the name of Margaret Fuller with sympathy and curiosity and wistful wonder, that, although she left no adequate monument of her powers, she was a woman whom the best loved most, and who was a purifying and ennobling influence in every life with which she was associated. . . .

George William Curtis to Daniel Ricketson, 23 April 1856, Houghton Library, Harvard University (published in [George William Curtis], "Editor's Easy Chair," *Harper's New Monthly Magazine* 80 [March 1890]: 637-39); from [George William Curtis], "Editor's Easy Chair," *Harper's New Monthly Magazine* 64 (March 1882): 627-28, and 68 (March 1884): 640-41.

From "Margaret Fuller Ossoli" (1861)

HENRY GILES

Henry Giles (1809–1882), clergyman, lecturer, and magazine contributor, was born in Ireland. Brought up as a Roman Catholic, he became a Unitarian, later emigrating to America in 1840. He published *Human Life in Shakespeare* (1868). Giles's recollection of Fuller is during the 1842 visit of Charles Dickens to America, when he was wined and dined in Boston. Even though Giles was "young and strange in Boston society, and knew nothing of its celebrities," he found Fuller friendly to him, commenting that she "did not so much converse as 'think aloud.'"

IN CLOSING OUR brief narrative of these impressive events [of her life], we have only one remark to make on the pathetic consistency of fate which belonged to all that concerned this very extraordinary woman. The word *"fragmentary"* seems best to characterize all that related to her. Her early education was severe yet not harmonious. Her self-culture was earnest and deep, yet it does not appear to have been systematic or continuous. She had constant interruptions in all her pursuits and purposes; she was taxed and over-taxed with responsibility and toil. She had no time to mature, compact, or concentrate her powers. She had to think from hand to mouth and from day to day. Accordingly, her compositions are but broken and detached efforts. It is really painful to read her modest but longing desires for an income of six hundred dollars a year, that she might remain in Italy in order to perfect herself in the study of its art and literature, and to know that her wishes could not be gratified. The pain is increased when we consider that persons of both sexes, incomparably her inferiors, could gather as many thousands easily as the hundreds which she vainly coveted. Had she lived and taken to the rostrum as women are now doing—as they have a full right to do if so they choose—she might have had dollars to her heart's content, for Margaret was a born orator; and there is no Lyceum talker, big or little, male or female, white, black, or brown that she would not, with the genius of her surprising eloquence, have shot beyond as a rifle does a pop-gun. Her time was frittered, and worst of all, it was not, even as to money, profitably frittered. And her great heart, too, battling long amidst conflicting aspirations, was at last silenced, when it had found its highest action and its noblest rest. She coveted love with immeasurable desire; she met with love, she gave it the magnitude of her own massive and impassioned character; and before satiety, or deception, or the loss of glorious illusions came to disappoint her, she died and disappeared—died and disappeared amidst the roaring breakers and the tossing pieces of the sea-tour ship. The tragedy had an appropriate catastrophe. . . .

The first time the writer ever met Margaret is connected in his mind with memorable associations. It was nearly twenty years ago. Charles Dickens was on a visit to America. We were invited to a large party in Boston, of which he was the foremost guest—"the mould of form, the glass of fashion, and the observed of all observers." We had a word, or, it may be, a few words with the genial hero of the evening, and then we were introduced to Miss Fuller. She sat dreamily and quietly in a corner, with head half bent and drooping eyes. We took a chair near her. She simply permitted it. We said a few ordinary words. She quietly replied. Her mood was cool; her tones were low; her phrases were formal; and, to say the least, her influence on us was not exciting or encouraging. And yet it was, in some unexplainable way, attractive. At that time we were young and strange in Boston society, and knew nothing of its celebrities. We were, therefore, entirely ignorant of Miss Fuller's local and literary distinction. But we were not long ignorant that we were in the presence of one whose "mind her kingdom was." From word to word she grew warmer and warmer, until her whole spirit seemed to burn and to shine. Still her manner was quiet, her voice subdued. She did not so much converse as "think aloud." It was more monologue than dialogue—for we were all but silent. "Things old and new" were brought out easily from a wonderfully rich treasury, and the old things and the new were made with a subtle enchantment to fit each other. The results of reading in all great literatures and philosophies melted in, naturally and unpedantically, with the news of the day or the suggestion of the moment. There was no loudness, no impetuosity, no obtrusive urgency, no aggressive emphasis; but there was what seemed to us almost a miracle of utterance in such a play of thought, fancy, feeling, learning, and imagination as we had never heard before—as we never hope to hear again. Yet we had heard fine talkers. We had, ourselves, in a small way, obtained

[164]

some credit for that sort of exercise. But this was of such surpassing power as not only to humble our vanity but to dispel the glory of our memories. It was at first strange and startling, but before it ended it was a delight as well as a marvel: it was the most complete union of surprise and pleasure that our experience can recall.

Shortly after this we were, on a Sunday evening, in a friend's drawing-room conversing quietly with the lady of the house. Miss Fuller came in unexpectedly. She had been to hear Father Taylor, the famous sailor-preacher of Boston. She began at once to describe the sermon, and went on for half an hour in a continued strain of rapture. If the preacher were as eloquent as his reporter was, it is a pity that the sermon is lost to the world. But though there were only three of us, we had not from her the slightest recognition. We were neither wounded nor offended, but attributed the seeming neglect to absence of mind or peculiarity of character. Occasionally, once or twice, *we* met her in the society of New York. We did not converse with her, but observed that, without sacrificing any of her mental or moral independence, she appeared to cultivate more and more the spirit of patience and of conciliation. The last time we met her was in one of the New York streets. She stopped us of her own accord, and was gracious and gentle exceedingly. She told us she was going to Europe; and knowing that we had some relations with England, inquired, in the kindest manner, in what way she could there do us service. Never again did we see her with the seeing of the eye, though much we heard of her with the hearing of the ear.

The general idea of Margaret Fuller, so far as we could learn it from her friends or critics, has been that of a person distinguished by surprising *intellectuality*. This, we confess, has not been our idea. We admit that Margaret Fuller had a fine intellect; for without vigor of intellect there can be no impressive power of any kind. But as compared with the higher order of minds—and this is the only comparison which would be just to a thinker of her rank—her pre-eminence is not in the intellect. We think *that* belongs to her *moral* nature. In saying this we consider that we award her superlative praise. At all events, in saying it we express our honest opinion and conviction.

She had a profound consciousness of the moral life in all its worth and its reality. This consciousness was not a mere ethical apprehension of right and wrong, and a formal admission of the claims of duty. It was in her a spiritual conviction, was inseparable from her faith in the infinite and the immortal, and was as deep as her own deep nature. This characteristic appeared very early in the terrible remorse which she experienced for the commission of a childish fault. The bitterness of her repentance showed the depth of her moral feeling; and the permanent change which followed her contrition proved that it was radical and thorough. That moral inspiration— nourished by mystical philosophy and religious sentiment—was the force which worked the most deeply in her character we have decisive evidence, alike in her conduct and in her writings. . . .

We can not have written thus far without leaving the impression on our readers that we hold Margaret Fuller Ossoli's intellect in considerable esteem. A narrow or feeble intellect could not have belonged to one who had so large and strong a moral nature. The human faculties are never with one another so out of measure. The faculty which we peculiarly call intellect is in vital harmony with the faculties which we call emotions and the will; and as the quality and direction of the faculties determine the good or evil of character, the energy and reach of them determine its compass, grade, and order. Extraordinary character is not the associate of ordinary intellect. But in the aggregate of faculties which we term "the mental" as distinguished from "the moral," we include fancy and imagination as well as intellect. Margaret had a bold and vigorous intellect, in which the element of memory seems to have been of uncommon force; in quickness, fullness, variety, and retentiveness. This was a faithful and ready servant of her mind in its thinking; but it was a more zealous, earnest, and willing servant of her mind in its imagining and fancying. In Margaret's mind the tendency was more to color and combine than to discriminate and analyze. She did not want imagination, but we consider that fancy and memory dominated among her mental qualities. Her mind was, therefore, not analytic but analogical. Neither was it inductive. In a word, it was not *logical.* It was deficient in that sustained and consecutive meditation which discerns or discovers those hidden or unobvious relations that bind facts into systems or ideas into laws, and that connect the links of chains vastly extended in scientific or speculative reasoning. It may be objected, however, that to do this belongs only to highest order of masculine thinkers. We admit it; but we class Margaret with the highest order of female minds: and this defect, if defect it is, does no intellectual discredit to her, since she shares it not only with women in general, but with women of genius. Exceptions there are—but exceptions, as it has been always said, prove the rule; and the rule will stand until facts disprove it. If such a result would be to the gain of woman—if in the attainment of it she would not lose more of her own real superiority—we would be among the first to hail her victory. Upon such conditions we wish her good-speed, and may she go on to conquer. But as yet the ratiocinative process has not been strikingly observable in the productions of women, and least of all in the productions of those who claim it most. It is not distinctive in the writings of Madame Ossoli, although she, we believe, has been cited as an instance of it. But this, we repeat, is no impeachment of her general mental power, since the deficiency of one quality may be more than compensated by a surplus of better qualities. Reasoning is not truth or knowledge; neither is it the only method by which nature or genius arrives at truth or knowledge; and logic is often but the instrument of sophistry and craft. If, therefore, there is not in Madame Ossoli's writings much of syllogistic sequence, there is no want of genuine mental and moral revelation. She was most lovingly susceptible to all the higher influences of outward nature, of social life, and to all that was individual or original, whether in character or genius. Æsthetic sensibility was a prevailing element in her temperament. She loved the beautiful with passion; her craving after it was almost morbid. But it seemed to act most powerfully on her as it was through art shaped to her through the plastic imagination. She was not, therefore, a good observer of mere external objects or phenomena. She was too subjective to be so; too much tempted to live within herself, and to wander among the richly garnished chambers of her own memory, and brood over her own suggestive ideas. She was, on this account, not a poet, a critic, or a describer of the worlds of objects or of life— as entirely separated from the *human*. Nature does impress her divinely, and gives her an inward rapture; but this comes from a sense of its spiritual influence, and from a sense of its infinite mystery and grandeur. . . .

From "Margaret Fuller Ossoli," *Harper's New Monthly Magazine* 23 (July 1861): 220–29.

[Anniversary Celebration of Fuller's Sixtieth Birthday] (1870)

AMOS BRONSON ALCOTT AND FREDERIC HENRY HEDGE

> It was a sign of renewal of interest in Fuller that the anniversary of her sixtieth birthday would be celebrated in Boston, if only by the New England Women's Club rather than a group with a broader membership base. Unfortunately, Alcott was ill and could not speak, though his comments on the gathering are still of interest. Hedge's comments continue in the negative, decidedly noncelebratory vein of his section of the *Memoirs*.

Amos Bronson Alcott

[23 MAY 1870] P.M. At the Celebration of Marg. Fuller's 60th Birthday held at the rooms of the Woman's Club. The company is worthy of the occasion. [James Freeman] Clarke, [Frederic Henry] Hedge, [William Henry] Channing, [Christopher Pearse] Cranch, Mr and Mrs [Rebecca] Spring, Miss [Elizabeth Palmer] Peabody, [Thomas Wentworth] Higginson, Mrs [Ednah Dow] Cheney, Mrs [Julia Ward] Howe, bear eloquent testimony to her exalted character and genius. Emerson is unable to be present, having a lecture to give in Cambridge, and I am too hoarse and ill-conditioned to speak fitly.

I know not whether I may call her friend or acquaintance. Though an assistant in my school, we were seldom there at the same hours, and saw one another less often than I wished. But my instinct served me in place of more intimate acquaintance. If I might characterize her in a word, I should say, she was a *diviner*, one of the Sibylline souls who read instinctively the mysteries of life and thought, and translate these in shining symbols to those competent to apprehend them. Her conversation gave a far better measure of her remarkable powers than her writings, wherein she seemed constrained and ill at ease. I saw her oftenest at the sittings of the Transcendental Club, where she was sure to say extraordinary things surprising to all who heard her: and where she was oftener the leader, while at the same time, one of the most eager listeners in that eager circle. She drew all towards her by her potent and fascinating magnetism. Her scorn was majestic, her satire consuming, her wit the subtlest of any I have known. She had the intellect of a man inspired by the heart of a woman, combining in harmonious marriage, the masculine and feminine in her genius. We have had no woman approaching so near our conception of the ideal woman as herself.

It was my misfortune to have met her not always under the best circumstances, and to have fallen under a cloud after she left my school, so that I have not escaped the feeling that she never quite fathomed my secret—wise as she was, and seeking subjects for her divination. But better than most—more truly than any, unless it were Emerson and [William Ellery] Channing [the Younger], she comprehended my drift and purposes, and bore testimony to these, when many of my former friends were staggered at my course, and those who knew me not took sides against me.—It was a fate disastrous not to her alone, but to her country whose shores she so nearly touched, that she sank in sight to disappear forever.

Frederic Henry Hedge

. . . it seemed that nature intended her for beauty but missed the aim by giving her an undue proportion of brain, which induced premature consciousness and prevented the repose necessary for beautiful development—as when the mold is too much shaken, the statue comes out awry. In those days it was hard for Margaret to forgive nature or herself for this want of beauty. She would have given all the powers of her mind for the pink and white prettiness of some other girls. This made her bitter and sarcastic.

Amos Bronson Alcott, "Journal for 1870," 287–90, Houghton Library, Harvard University. Hedge's comments are in an unidentified newspaper clipping pasted in Alcott's "Autobiographical Collections, 1868–1871," 138, Houghton Library, Harvard University.

From *Harriet Martineau's Autobiography* (1877)

HARRIET MARTINEAU

Harriet Martineau (1802–1876), British author and reformer, was the sister of influential Unitarian minister James Martineau and friends with the Wordsworths and Carlyles. She visited America in 1834–1836, reporting on her travels in *Society in America* (1837) and *A Retrospect of Western Travel* (1838), the former describing her meeting with Emerson and other notable Bostonians. Fuller got on famously with Martineau when they met in Cambridge in 1836. Martineau helped Fuller to meet Emerson when, as the latter's houseguest, she praised Fuller's "excelling genius and conversation, and enjoined it on [him] to seek her acquaintance" (*Memoirs*, 1:201). Martineau encouraged Fuller in writing her biography of Goethe, and Fuller saw Martineau "a great deal" over "many happy hours" and "love[d] her more than ever," concluding, "I trust we shall now be dear friends forever" (30 January, 29 January 1836, *Letters*, 1:243, 6:277). Fuller even planned (unsuccessfully) a trip to Britain with friends, planning to stay with Martineau in London "and see the best literary society" (*Letters*, 1:243). All did not continue well, however, and when Martineau sent Fuller an inscribed copy of *Society in America*, the recipient's response was not pleasing to the author. Fuller started with ambivalence, saying that frequently she "felt pleasure and admiration, but more frequently disappointment, sometimes positive distaste," and then launched into a criticism of the work: "A want of soundness, of habits of patient investigation, of completeness, of arrangement, are felt throughout the book; and, for all its fine descriptions of scenery, breadth of reasoning, and generous daring, I cannot be happy in it, because it is not worthy of my friend, and I think a few months given to ripen it, to balance, compare, and mellow," would have made it better. Fuller went on to complain of Martineau's shabby treatment of Bronson Alcott and her strident abolitionism ([ca. November 1837], *Letters*, 1:307–10). Still, Fuller made her one of the first persons she visited after arriving in Britain in 1846 (reported briefly in *Dispatches from Europe*, 58).

While Martineau liked Fuller personally and called *Woman in the Nineteenth Century* "Beautiful!" (*Letters to Wedgwood*, 85), she felt a disparity between the drawing-room discussions of reform that Fuller led in her

Conversations and the real world attempts that Martineau herself endorsed, as well as her belief that Fuller was reaching only the elite classes rather than the middle classes for whom Martineau wrote. Fuller, too, recognized their differences over educational matters, writing, "I am not without my dreams and hopes as to the education of women," which she wished to "prove at last my vocation," though they are "not at all of the Martineau class" (9 December 1838, *Letters*, 1:354).

... THE DIFFERENCE between us was that while she was living and moving in an ideal world, talking in private and discoursing in public about the most fanciful and shallow conceits which the transcendentalists of Boston took for philosophy, she looked down upon persons who acted instead of talking finely, and devoted their fortunes, their peace, their repose, and their very lives to the preservation of the principles of the republic. While Margaret Fuller and her adult pupils sat "gorgeously dressed," talking about Mars and Venus, Plato and Goethe, and fancying themselves the elect of the earth in intellect and refinement, the liberties of the republic were running out as fast as they could go, at a breach which another sort of elect persons were devoting themselves to repair: and my complaint against the "gorgeous" pedants was that they regarded their preservers as hewers of wood and drawers of water, and their work as a less vital one than the pedantic orations which were spoiling a set of well-meaning women in a pitiable way. All that is settled now. It was over years before Margaret died. I mention it now to show, by an example already made public by Margaret herself, what the difference was between me and her, and those who followed her lead. This difference grew up mainly after my return from America. We were there intimate friends; and I am disposed to consider that period the best of her life, except the short one which intervened between her finding her real self and her death. She told me what danger she had been in from the training her father had given her, and the encouragement to pedantry and rudeness which she derived from the circumstances of her youth. She told me that she was at nineteen the most intolerable girl that ever took a seat in a drawing-room. Her admirable candor, the philosophical way in which she took herself in hand, her genuine heart, her practical insight, and, no doubt, the natural influence of her attachment to myself, endeared her to me, while her powers, and her confidence in the use of them, led me to expect great things from her. . . .

How it might have been with her if she had come to Europe in 1836, I have often speculated. As it was, her life in Boston was little short of destructive. I need but refer to the memoir of her. In the most pedantic age of society in her own country, and in its most pedantic city, she who was just beginning to rise out of pedantic habits of thought and speech relapsed most grievously. She was not only completely spoiled in conversation and manners: she made false estimates of the objects and interests of human life. She was not content with pursuing, and inducing others to pursue, a metaphysical idealism destructive of all genuine feeling and sound activity: she mocked at objects and efforts of a higher order than her own, and despised those who, like myself, could not adopt her scale of valuation. All this might have been spared, a world of mischief saved, and a world of good effected, if she had found her heart a dozen years sooner, and in America instead of Italy. It is the most grievous loss I have almost ever known in private history—the deferring of Margaret Fuller's married life so long. . . .

Harriet Martineau's Autobiography, ed. Maria Weston Chapman, 2 vols. (Boston: James R. Osgood, 1877), 2:381–83.

[Margaret Fuller] (1884)

SARAH FREEMAN CLARKE

Sarah (Ann) Freeman Clarke (1808–1896), James Freeman Clarke's older sister, was one of Fuller's most devoted friends. When they first met in 1833, they began their acquaintance "by expressing our certainty that we should never get along together; and, that being conceded, we did get along most swimmingly" (25 October, Clarke, "Letters of a Sister"). Perhaps this is why she reacted positively to Fuller's directness, noting that though "she spoke rudely searching words, and told you startling truths" that "broke down your little shams and defenses, you felt exhilarated by the compliment of being found out, and even that she had cared to find you out." Clarke attended Fuller's Conversations, and remembered that at the first meeting the ladies in attendance "all and each declared that they should not speak a word." As a result, on the first day Fuller "took the conversation into her own hands and explained to them her wishes and intentions in so animated a manner that they turned about and declared that it would be base in the extreme not to be willing to do all they could, while she so generously did her part" (17 November 1839, Clarke, "Letters of a Sister"). Fuller accompanied Clarke, her brother James, and a few friends on a trip lasting from May to September 1843, visiting Illinois, Michigan, and Wisconsin. This journey formed the basis for Fuller's *Summer on the Lakes,* for which Clarke provided the illustrations. Fuller also obtained a poem from her for the *Dial.* Clarke contributed this reminiscence to Thomas Wentworth Higginson's *Margaret Fuller Ossoli,* an authoritative work in the "American Men of Letters" series.

IN LOOKING FOR the causes of the great influence possessed by Margaret Fuller over her pupils, companions, and friends, I find something in the fact of her unusual truth-speaking power. She not only did not speak lies after our foolish social customs, but she met you fairly. She broke her lance upon your shield. Encountering her glance, something like an electric shock was felt. Her eye pierced through your disguises. Your outworks fell before her first assault, and you were at her mercy. And then began the delight of true intercourse. Though she spoke rudely searching words, and told you startling truths, though she broke down your little shams and defenses, you felt exhilarated by the compliment of being found out, and even that she had cared to find you out. I think this was what attracted or bound us to her. We expected good from such a new condition of our relations, and good usually came of it.

No woman ever had more true lovers among those of her own sex, and as many men she also numbered among her friends. She had an immense appetite for social intercourse. When she met a new person she met him courageously, sincerely, and intimately. She did not study him to see beforehand how he might bear the shock of truth, but offered her best of direct speech at once. Some could not or would not hear it, and turned away; but often came back for more, and some of these became her fast friends.

Many of us recoiled from her at first; we feared her too powerful dominion over us, but as she was powerful, so she was tender; as she was exacting, she was generous. She demanded our best, and she gave us her best. To be with her was the most powerful stimulus, intellectual and moral. It was like the sun shining upon plants and causing buds to open into flowers. This was her gift, and she could no more help exercising it than the sun can help shining. This gift, acting with a powerful understanding and a generous imagination, you can perceive would make an educational force of great power. Few or none could escape on whom she chose to exercise it. . . .

From Thomas Wentworth Higginson, *Margaret Fuller Ossoli* (Boston: Houghton, Mifflin, 1884), 117–18.

[Journal Comments on Fuller in 1858] (1884)

NATHANIEL HAWTHORNE

Hawthorne's journal comments on Fuller and her husband, first published in his son Julian's *Nathaniel Hawthorne and His Wife* (1884), were considered scandalous when they appeared. Not only do they depict Ossoli as an illiterate fool ("her clownish husband") who could not distinguish between a left and a right foot, they express the worst side of Hawthorne's feelings about Fuller, from his considering her "a great humbug; of course with much talent, and much moral reality, or else she could not have been so great a humbug," to his final conclusion that "On the whole, I do not I know but I like her the better for it;—the better, because she proved herself a very woman, after all, and fell as the weakest of her sisters might." He also reports Mozier's comment that Fuller's book on the Roman Revolution had never existed. At least Julian omitted his father's statement that Fuller's interest in Ossoli could only be "purely sensual," which would have further upset contemporary sensibilities and sparked even more debate.

Joseph Mozier (1813–1870) was born in Burlington, Vermont, moving on to become a successful merchant in New York. In 1845, he moved to Florence to study sculpture, later establishing a studio in Rome. Known as a neoclassical artist, he produced works based on literature, myth, and generic themes such as "Pocahontas," "Esther," "Undine," "Truth," and "Silence." There is no evidence to suggest any rift between him and Fuller; indeed, they seem good friends. She had been nursed by Mozier and his wife, Isabella Hogg Mozier (1818–1889), when she became sick in Florence in 1847, and he had tried unsuccessfully to get her a contract for writing a series of "Letters from Florence" (31 October 1849, *Letters*, 5:278). When she first met Mozier, Fuller believed him "a man of fortune, who has taken to sculpture from love, and shows promise of much excellence"; later, she commented favorably on Mozier's sculptures in the *New-York Tribune* (see *Dispatches from Europe*, 268). Mozier's wife was, thought Fuller, "a very good and sweet woman," and she described Fuller as "a mild saint and ministering angel" (16 October 1847, *Letters*, 4:300; Capper, *Public Years*, 408). When finances forced Fuller to accept payment for teaching the Moziers' child Isabella, she regretted "very much" that she needed to do this in order "to eke out the bread and salt and coffee till April," because it would be "inadequate compensation" for his "active and steady interest" in her (30 November 1849, *Letters*, 5:285).

Julian's timing could not have been worse. The previous year Julia Ward Howe had published a favorable biography of Fuller that attempted to give a sense of her personality. When Thomas Wentworth Higginson's *Margaret Fuller Ossoli* appeared in 1884, it was widely praised for achieving its aim of stressing Fuller's "vigorous executive side" as an antidote to the *Memoirs*, which Higginson felt had left Fuller "a little too much in the clouds" (5). The publication of Hawthorne's remarks eclipsed interest in these two biographies, as such friends of Fuller's as James Freeman Clarke, Sarah Freeman Clarke, Christopher Pearse Cranch and his wife, Fuller's nephew Frederick, and William Wetmore and Emelyn Story came to her defense in print. Julian defended himself in a number of articles for, among other accomplishments, correctly assigning Fuller to "her place with the numberless other dismal friends who fill the limbo of human pretensions and failure" and pointing out her " 'I am holier than thou' attitude"; not surpisingly, a number of commentators noted that the more Julian argued, the more offensive he became (Hawthorne, "Hawthorne and Fuller," 4; Hawthorne, "Hawthorne and His Critics," 4).

[ROME, 3 APRIL 1858] . . . From [discussing Horatio] Greenough, Mr. [Joseph] Mozier passed to Margaret Fuller, whom he knew well, she having been an inmate of his during a part of her residence in Italy. His developements about poor Margaret were very curious. He says that Ossoli's family, though technically noble, is really of no rank whatever; the elder brother, with the title of Marquis, being at this very time a working bricklayer, and the sisters walking the streets without bonnets—that is, being in the station of peasant-girls, or the female populace of Rome. Ossoli himself, to the best of his belief, was Margaret's servant, or had something to do with the care of her apartments. He was the handsomest man whom Mr. Mozier ever saw, but entirely ignorant even of his own language, scarcely able to read at all, destitute of manners; in short, half an idiot, and without any pretensions to be a gentleman. At Margaret's request, Mr Mozier had taken him into his studio, with a view to ascertain whether he was capable of instruction in sculpture; but, after four months' labor, Ossoli produced a thing intended to be a copy of a human foot; but the "big toe" was on the wrong side. He could not possibly have had the least appreciation of Margaret; and the wonder is, what attraction she found in this boor, this hymen without the intellectual spark—she that had always shown such a cruel and bitter scorn of intellectual deficiency. As from her towards him, I do not understand what feeling there could have been, except it were purely sensual;[1] as from him towards her, there could hardly have been even this, for she had not the charm of womanhood. But she was a woman anxious to try all things, and fill up her experience in all directions; she had a strong and coarse nature, too, which she had done her utmost to refine, with infinite pains, but which of course could only be superficially changed. The solution of the riddle lies in this direction; nor does one's conscience revolt at the idea of thus solving it; for—at least, this is my own experience—Margaret has not left, in the hearts and minds of those who knew her, any deep witness for her integrity and purity. She was a great humbug; of course with much talent, and much moral reality, or else she could not have been so great a humbug. But she had stuck herself full of borrowed qualities, which she chose to provide herself with, but which had no root in her.

Mr. Mozier added, that Margaret had quite lost all power of literary production, before she left Rome, though occasionally the charm and power of her conversation would re-appear. To his certain knowledge, she had no important manuscripts with her when she sailed, (she having shown him all she had, with a view to his procuring their publication in America;) and the History of the Roman Revolution, about which there was so much lamentation, in the belief that it had been lost with her, never had existence. Thus there appears to have been a total collapse in poor Margaret, morally and intellectually; and tragic as her catastrophe was, Providence was, after all, kind in putting her, and her clownish husband, and their child, on board that fated ship. There never was such a tragedy as her whole story; the sadder and sterner, because so much of the ridiculous was mixed up with it, and because she could bear anything better than to be ridiculous. It was such an awful joke, that she should have resolved—in all sincerity, no doubt—to make herself the greatest, wisest, best woman of the age; and, to that end, she set to work on her strong, heavy, unpliable, and, in many respects, defective and evil nature, and adorned it with a mosaic of admirable qualities, such as she chose to possess; putting in here a splendid talent, and there a moral excellence, and polishing each separate piece, and the whole together, till it seemed to shine afar and dazzle all who saw it. She took credit to herself for having been her own Redeemer, if not her own Creator; and, indeed, she was far more a work of art than any of Mr. Mozier's statues. But she was not working on an inanimate substance, like marble or clay; there was something within her that she could not possibly come at, to re-create and refine it; and, by and by, this rude old potency bestirred itself, and undid all her labor in the twinkling of an eye. On the whole, I do not I know but I like her the better for it;—the better, because she proved herself a very woman, after all, and fell as the weakest of her sisters might. . . .

The French and Italian Notebooks, ed. Thomas Woodson (Columbus: Ohio State University Press, 1980), 155–57. When Julian Hawthorne published the extracts from his father's journal in *Nathaniel Hawthorne and His Wife,* he changed a number of words and the punctuation, though only one (see note one) seriously affecting the meaning (2:259–62).

Note

1. "except it were purely sensual" is not in *Hawthorne and His Wife.*

From *Reminiscences of Ednah Dow Cheney* (1902)

Ednah Dow Cheney

> Ednah Dow Littlehale Cheney (1824–1904), author and reformer, wrote the first biography of Louisa May Alcott. Growing up in a well-to-do Boston household, she interacted with many of the political and literary figures of the time, including Bronson Alcott and Emerson. Cheney was a participant in Fuller's Conversations, which led to her later interests in feminism and abolitionism (she was a supporter and friend of Harriet Jacobs). In 1853, she married painter Seth Cheney (1810–1856), by whom she had one child. Cheney later lectured on art at Alcott's Concord School of Philosophy.

HER NATURE WAS intense, sensitive, and passionate, and a hereditary tendency to self-consciousness and apparent self-conceit was so blended with loftiness of the soul and the highest ambition that she was constantly misunderstood by the crowd about her, who saw only the outward manner. She herself speaks of "my arrogance of youthful hope and pride." This tendency was fostered by her father's recognition of her unusual intellectual gifts, and the classic education which he gave her. Without wholesome correctives of a well-ordered school, her mind was intensely stimulated by her early study of the Greek and Roman authors, and her imagination created a world of heroic beings among whom she lived, and with whom she felt her own likeness and equality.

Lydia Maria Child described to a friend this little scene, which she herself witnessed, and which gives a picture of Margaret as a child.

She went to a dancing-school taught by a lively and rather irascible Frenchman. In some way she offended him so much that he ordered her to leave the room. Margaret tossed her head, and walked out with an air so commanding, that the master called out "Shtop, Miss Fullair! You sall not walk so superb, you tink you General *Wasington*."

She seemed indeed like Saul, a head taller than all her brethren, and while she was ever willing to lift others up to herself, it required long training to teach her the reverence of things below her.

One of her oldest and dearest friends says of her, "In my first acquaintance, I was much offended by the arrogant manner, as it seemed to me, that she wore, and wore as if it were habitual. It took time before I could begin to understand the capacity for love and sympathy which lay hidden under this unlovely aspect."

When a little child walking under the apple trees, her father pointed to her, saying "Incedit regina" (She walks like a queen).

W. H. Channing said, "Her stately deportment but expressed high-heartedness." . . .

In 1837 she engaged to teach in the Green Street School in Providence. When asked what salary she expected for teaching she replied, "What do you pay the governor of your State?" She exercised a great influence upon many of her scholars, for which they were profoundly grateful through life, but she never felt quite satisfied with her work. Probably her own rich, stimulating, but somewhat desultory education did not specially fit her for the daily drill and practical routine of a schoolroom, but she influenced her pupils by her high moral bearing. When any child asked a question which she was not prepared to answer, she never bluffed her, or said, "See what you can find out, and I will tell you to-morrow if you are right," but she replied, "I do not know, but I think we can find out. We will look it up together."

Her influence over children is well illustrated by an anecdote of a little girl, who had been accused of disobedience in touching a microscope, which was found broken. The child was shut up as a punishment, not for the fault alone, but for falsehood in denying it. When Miss Fuller came she took the weeping child on her knee, and said, "Now, my dear little girl, tell me all about it. Only remember that you must be careful, for I shall believe every word that you say." Thus encouraged, the child told the innocent story, and upon investigation was completely acquitted. This reminds me of an answer which I once heard her make, in one of her conversations, to a lady who asked, "But would you not tell a child that God does not love her when she is naughty?" "No," said Margaret, "it is not true."

She appears to have taught less than two years in Providence, and gladly left the profession to devote herself more entirely to literary work. Her summer vacation, of only three weeks, began on August 19th. As she had been rising at half-past four or five, and with the exception of two hours at noon, had worked or studied until six o'clock at night, and filled up the evening with exercise or calls, we cannot wonder that she was weary and wanted rest when she left Providence in 1838. But she accepts the discipline and experience of the years spent in teaching, and although she wishes for a different life, she believes "that if duty should again call her to this work, she could take it up, and produce better results both for herself and others." . . .

Reminiscences of Ednah Dow Cheney (Boston: Lee and Shepard, 1902), 195–96, 203–204.

[The "Margaret-ghost"] (1903)

HENRY JAMES

Henry James (1843–1916), novelist and critic, was early influenced by his father, Henry James, Sr. (1811–1882), a philosopher and Swedenborgian who
knew Fuller and wrote to her. He once described her to Emerson, a family
friend, as a "dear noble woman!" (Capper, *Public Years*, 132). His brother,
William (1842–1910), became one of America's foremost philosophers and
a founder of pragmatism. James remembers being a child when Washington
Irving brought his father the news of Fuller's death (Capper, *Public Years*,
514). Because James believed that Story had accomplished relatively little, his
biography was really more about Story's friends and life in Italy than about its
announced subject. William Story, incidentally, attended Fuller's Conversations and appeared in Caroline Healey Dall's *Margaret and Her Friends*.

. . . OUR KINDLY DIARIST [Mrs. Emelyn Story] "went home with Margaret
and sat with her in her quiet little upper chamber all the evening. W[illiam].
came for me, and we stayed until a late hour of the night." The unques-
tionably haunting Margaret-ghost, looking out from her quiet little upper
chamber at her lamentable doom, would perhaps be never so much to be
caught by us as on some such occasion as this. What comes up is the won-
derment of *why* she may, to any such degree, be felt as haunting; together
with other wonderments that brush us unless we give them the go-by. It is
not for this latter end that we are thus engaged at all; so that, making the
most of it, we ask ourselves how, possibly, in our own luminous age, she
would have affected us on the stage of the "world," or as a candidate, if so
we may put it, for the cosmopolite crown. It matters only for the amusement of evocation—since she left nothing behind her, her written utterance
being naught; but to what would she have corresponded, have "rhymed,"
under categories actually known to us? Would she, in other words, with
her appetite for ideas and her genius for conversation, have struck us but as
a somewhat formidable bore, one of the worst kind, a culture-seeker without a sense of proportion, or, on the contrary, have affected us as a really
attaching, a possibly picturesque New England Corinne?

[182]

Such speculations are, however, perhaps too idle; the *facts* of the appearance of this singular woman, who would, though conceit was imputed to her, doubtless have been surprised to know that talk may be still, after more than half a century, made about her—the facts have in themselves quite sufficient colour, and the fact in particular of her having achieved, so unaided and so ungraced, a sharp identity. This identity was that of the talker, the moral *improvisatrice,* or at least had been in her Boston days, when, young herself, she had been as a sparkling fountain to other thirsty young. In the Rome of many waters there were doubtless fountains that quenched, collectively, any individual gush; so that it would have been, naturally, for her plentiful life, her active courage and company, that the little set of friends with whom we are concerned valued her. She had bitten deeply into Rome, or, rather, *been,* like so many others, by the wolf of the Capitol, incurably bitten; she met the whole case with New England arts that show even yet, at our distance, as honest and touching; there might be ways for her of being vivid that were not as the ways of Boston. Otherwise what she would mainly prompt us to interest in might be precisely the beautiful moral complexion of the little circle of her interlocutors. That is ever half the interest of any celebrated thing—taking Margaret's mind for celebrated: the story it has to tell us of those for whom it flourished and whose measure and reflection it necessarily more or less gives. Let us hasten to add, without too many words, that Mme. Ossoli's circle represented, after all, a small stage, and that there were those on its edges to whom she was not pleasing. This was the case with Lowell and, discoverably, with Hawthorne; the legend of whose having had her in his eye for the figure of Zenobia, while writing "The Blithedale Romance," surely never held water. She inspired Mrs Browning, on the other hand, with sympathy and admiration, and the latter, writing of her in 1852, after the so lamentable end of her return-voyage, with her husband and child, to America—the wreck of the vessel, the loss of father, mother and small son in sight of shore—says that "her death shook me to the very roots of my heart. The comfort is," Mrs Browning then adds, "that she lost little in the world—the change could not be loss to her. She had suffered, and was likely to suffer still more." She had previously to this, in December 1849, spoken of her, in a letter to Miss Mitford, as having "taken us by surprise at Florence, retiring from the Roman world with a husband and child above a year old. Nobody had even suspected a word of this underplot, and her American friends stood in mute astonishment before this apparition of them here. The husband is a Roman marquis appearing amiable and gentlemanly, and having fought well, they say, at the siege, but with no pretension to cope with his wife on any ground appertaining to the intellect." The "underplot" was precisely another of the personal facts by which the lady could interest—the fact that is, that her marriage should be an underplot, and that her husband, much *decaduto* [recently dead], should make explanation difficult. These things, let alone the final catastrophe, in short, were not talk, but life, and life dealing with the somewhat angular Boston sibyl on its own free lines. All of which, the free lines overscoring the unlikely material, is doubtless partly why the Margaret-ghost, as I have ventured to call it, still unmistakably walks the old passages. . . .

Henry James, *William Wetmore Story and His Friends,* 2 vols. (Boston: Houghton, Mifflin, 1903), 1:127–31.

From *Alcott Memoirs* (1915)

Frederick L. H. Willis

Frederick Llewellyn Hovey Willis (1830–1914) was born in Cambridge, but his father suffered financial failure, and soon afterwards his parents died, leaving him to be raised by his grandparents. He became fast friends with the Alcott family, staying with them numerous times in Concord and Boston from 1844 on. After briefly attending the Harvard Divinity School, he moved to Rochester, New York, where he served as a physician and lecturer. He married Maria Love Whitcomb (1824–1904), a fellow spiritualist, in 1858, and they had one child.

OF GIFTED MARGARET FULLER I retain a most vivid impression. She often visited the Alcotts during my life with them. I remember one occasion when at tea in the Alcott's Concord home, Emerson, Thoreau, Hawthorne, and Margaret Fuller sat at the table with Mr. and Mrs. Alcott, Louisa, her three sisters, and myself. I have long since realized this was a golden hour in my life; that six of the eleven people about that kindly board were destined, each in their own particular literary sphere, to ultimate lofty status in American letters.

Margaret Fuller was a "beautifully plain" young woman. Physically she was a robust person, tall, and with a certain stateliness though inclined to corpulency. She was possessed of expressive gray eyes, a wealth of reddish brown hair, a colorless complexion, and magnificent teeth, which she showed constantly while speaking. Despite a queenly carriage to the head she had nothing of what is called "handsome" in its application to a woman. She had a habit of incessantly opening and closing her eyes, rather than "winking," and her voice was nasal in tone. But her whole face, notwithstanding her mannerisms, was stamped with individuality and her manner full of a studious dignity. Her genius found its best expression in conversation wherein she had a most extraordinary ability. Before she was thirty she was thoroughly conversant with French, German, Spanish, and Italian, as well as her native English, and was also an accomplished Greek, Latin, and

Hebrew scholar. She had Plato, Seneca, Epictetus, and Horace at her fingers' ends. She had a most keen regard for Mr. Alcott and discoursed much with him upon the writings and philosophy of these ancient masters.

I remember hearing her speak with Mr. Alcott of her experiences in teaching French and Latin in that philosopher's Boston school in 1837, and mentally recording I was only seven years old at that time. As a little boy and a recognized member of the family, Margaret Fuller has spoken to me perhaps forty times, simple words of greeting whose substance I do not remember save that upon one occasion she mentioned she was twenty-one years my senior and that her birthplace in Cambridge was within a stone's throw of the house in which I first saw the light upon January 29th, 1830. . . .

Alcott Memoirs (Boston: Richard G. Badger, 1915), 95–96.

[A Brother's Memories of Fuller] (1936)

RICHARD FREDERICK FULLER

Richard Frederick Fuller (1821–1869), Fuller's younger brother, was schooled in Concord for entry to Harvard College. With Margaret's encouragement, Richard approached Emerson for advice on how to prepare for school, and the older man took him under his wing. Richard stayed in Concord for five months, studying fourteen hours a day, except on those occasions when he walked with Henry David Thoreau or recited the classics under Elizabeth Hoar's instruction. The tutoring in Concord helped. Richard was admitted to Harvard College by President Josiah Quincy, and he was fifth in his class when he graduated in 1844. Later, he was a Boston lawyer who dabbled in verse and published a life of his brother, Arthur Buckminster Fuller, who died in the Civil War. Margaret once told Richard that he had "talent, nobleness, a good person, good health, good position, [and] good education" (1 January 1848, *Letters*, 5:39). No other member of the Fuller family left such extensive recollections of Margaret as did Richard.

... IN THE STUDY of history she would dwell upon what was excellent in distinguished characters, and try to incite us to emulation. I was deliberate in my judgment and not impressible. I remember discouraging her after one of her historical talks in which she urged us to be ambitious of attaining what was really valuable in life by remarking that I would never be ambitious. Caesar was ambitious, and I knew it was not right. She despaired at that time of enlightening my slow as well as obstinate understanding and left me to my obscure fate! Herself of great quickness and astonishing rapidity in the acquisition of knowledge, dullness on the part of her pupils wounded her sensibilities more, I really believe, than acts of unkindness could have done. I put her to the torture, but she controlled her nerves, and thus she really gained as well as imparted, for she received from us a discipline to her patience in return for the learning which she could only slowly impart. Arthur, though quick, was at this period of his life very active in the region of fancy, and air castles were more attractive to him than the solid structures of history, mathematics, etymology and grammar could be. So on the whole we were by no means superior scholars, and being the first Margaret taught she measured us principally by her own achievements. She could not conceal from us, even if she tried, that our progress was unpromising and unsatisfactory. She openly reproached me with mediocrity of understanding; and she found this, like a goad with a sluggish animal, more effectual than the inducements of ambition that she had held before me to lure me on. This "mediocrity" always troubled me, and I could not forget it till, years afterward, I induced her to reconsider and mitigate the sentence. When we recited we had certain nervous ways of twitching about which annoyed her inexpressibly. I laughingly remember a habit of incessant movement of the hands, as if catching at succor, in our recitations when we were drowning in the deep places of Virgil. It was absolutely impossible for us to think of our hands and keep them still while agonized with classical difficulties and trembling in dread of the doom of a bad recitation. Sometimes our bright answers in geography or history made her laugh outright. She preferred to laugh rather than weep, which was her only alternative. Some of these responses she recorded at the end of the geography textbook. . . .

During my last two years in college Margaret rented a house on Ellery street, Dana Hill, Cambridge, and Mother also made the house bright with her presence. Margaret's society was very valuable—or rather, it was invaluable—to me. Independently of the family tie which she never disregarded, the kindest friendship subsisted between us. This mode of speech implies that I was not solely the beneficiary; that I conferred as well as received. This was true. With all her intellect and all its rich stores she could not dwell on the isolated heights of the mind alone. Her heart was equally large, and craved friendship with a yearning which would not yield to intellectual ambition. She depended on the reciprocal sentiment of those she loved. She was at least once cruelly disappointed in friendship. I was the witness as well as the confidant of what she suffered. Her heart had gone out for years to some lady friends of beautiful artistic taste and rare culture. But this did not prevent them from being selfish in their intellectual beauty, and the scanty current ran icily through their shrunken hearts. Some signal illustration of this cold selfishness brought it into sudden light and shocked and repelled Margaret's friendship. Her heart had become so much knit to them that it was a long and cruel work to disengage her affection. She endured the trial with fortitude, but she told me she should make no such costly friendships; they could not satisfy her heart. Her large requirements demanded a better, even a heavenly, friend; and He afterwards vouchsafed her a heart's fullness even of earthly affection in a noble husband and a darling child.

The characteristic of Margaret just referred to made her seek my friendship quite as much, and in the beginning even more, than I did hers. Her distinction and consideration among those about her did not dazzle nor even attract my eye, for my disposition was obstinately opposed to following others in their admiration unless my own judgment led me to it. I overheard a conversation between her and a friend visiting the house in which the latter remarked that my manner did not indicate that regard for my sister which so many others felt. Margaret replied that I should do her justice in the sequel, and she added a favorable opinion of me which I well remember. A magnanimity like this, which dispensed its regard without exacting a return, was peculiarly winning. A friendship grew up of which I retain delightful memories. Margaret was confidential, and she led others to be so. In her society the heart spoke as it hardly did even in secret and solitary meditation, and the mind developed in consciousness fair surprises of thought. She could not bear the distances of conventualism, nor those walls which we build around ourselves insulating ourselves from God and man. I have never known other conversation like hers either in degree or kind. It was not merely that it was superior; it was of a different type from other discourse. The mind soared, the heart expanded, the cheek glowed, and the eye was filled with light. Invigorating mountain air may affect the body as her conversation did the soul. She did not so much display herself as ourselves in her inspiring discourse, while the influence of her mind fell on us like genial sunlight, quickened a conscious joy and life which in itself half forgets the luminary to which it is indebted. The thought in leaving her company was much less "How remarkable she is!" than "How remarkable I am!" I had no idea my mind had such powers, my tongue such eloquence, and my heart such ardor! But when afterwards in solitude, our thoughts were dispersed, disconnected, and ineffectual, or when conversation in ordinary life seemed like miserable degradation compared to hers, then we said to ourselves, "Margaret must have a magnetic power, and a certain elevation in discourse, more akin to a better world than to this." She had, to be sure, great eloquence and unrivalled words; but these powers were so much less than the effect she wrought with them that they attracted little comparative notice. They were too perfect to permit us to escape their influence sufficiently to be spectators and admirers of their working. Much as I am willing to concede to her power of discussion, developed by very great culture in many languages and varied schools of thought, I yet believe she had superadded a greater power than these—love of truth. It was the latter more than the former that wrought her wonders in conversation, and that makes her to be spoken of as remarkable beyond any talker in remembrance. She believed in the truth and was sincere. She spoke directly to the heart and the interior consciousness, with no devotion to the idolatries of custom either in thought or life. Every mind was thus enabled in her society to throw off the shackles of habit and the long prejudice of years and to rise for the time to the true godlike stature of man and breathe the better natal air of the soul. There was religion in this; for Margaret was eminently religious. Her life was in exalted and eternal things while she walked upon the earth, and she reached out a hand to lead us in discourse to that elevation where her thought habitually dwelt.

I had the help of Margaret's rare critical powers in all my studies. She pointed out the merits and demerits and the relative place of each writer in the great structure of literature. I was thoroughly satisfied with her reasoning and its results respecting books, and might have rested in her opinions with perfect confidence had she not habitually stimulated me to test them by my own thought. Since I have lost her society I have found her critical writings doubly precious, not only as furnishing a complete and impartial view of favorite authors and keeping their characters and works fresh in mind, but as recalling those genial hours when she introduced me to the classic friendship of great and good books. It is with pleasure and admiration of her kindness that I recall the sacrifices she made to put me in the path of the beautiful and good. Her literary efforts, especially the "Conversations" which she conducted in Boston, produced almost invariably torturing headaches in which her nervous agony was so great that she could not always refrain from screaming; yet she could not remit these efforts without giving up a home for Mother and me, and she bravely endured them. She would besides stint herself to give me tickets to concerts of Beethoven's Symphonies, which she regarded as very elevating. I accepted the tickets; nor can I think it too chivalrously generous in her to bestow, or unsuitable for me to receive at her hands an entertainment which could not but have a lasting influence on my character. She would sometimes give me a very favorite book, though depriving herself of it by the means; and there could have been no more expressive token of her sisterly regard. She did not bestow books that she had done with or found very dispensable; but only such as she loved as her own benefactors would she deign to give. I remember once when I was discussing a present I was proposing to make and declared my purpose to have it costly of its kind she expressed approbation, and said if the thing were done it should be done handsomely and well, though of course not out of proportion to the occasion or my circumstances. One book she gave me was Elizabeth Barrett's poems, which were very dear to her. She accompanied the gift by saying she was glad she could believe me worthy of the book. She knew I should read it and reverence it as her book, which she had well read, and now bestowed because not able to buy a new one. She particularly spoke at that time of the poem called "The Swan's Nest." How much I have loved Mrs. Browning's poetry since, not only for its benefit to me but for what it did for Margaret. She spoke to me of Mrs. Browning with love and reverence, and she seemed especially pleased when an author she admired was a woman.

She often pointed out to me intellectual and moral excellencies of her sex, and trained me to a respect for women as the equal of man which I have never lost. Books which she did not think it necessary to give she would place in my hands as tenant-in-common with her, and speak of leaving them to me when she should be no more. Thus she did with Shakspeare, a fine edition which her Providence scholars had presented to her, and Wordsworth, made precious by her marks of emphatic approbation. These books I now have. Shelley, Coleridge, and Keats she also sought to interest me in. The first in his beauty was too disordered for my approbation. I admired a good deal of Coleridge, though I thought him sometimes needlessly subtle and occasionally bordering on the garrulous. She had a lady relative of Keats as one of her pupils—a girl who possessed the splendid eyes of the poet, and resembled the likeness in the frontispiece of his poems. The moral element transfused Margaret's whole character. Brilliancy, success, achievement had yet one test which they must undergo before admission within the pale of her approbation: were they noble in their purpose, character and aim? Without a moral grandeur which conforms the human to the divine, many things and many people esteemed great among men were in her view pitiably small. All the energies of her life were bent to a high aim, and she wished others to form and follow out a noble purpose in life. Candor distinguished her intercourse; and the sincere words of truth were always to be expected from her undissembling lips. It was on this account that the self-deceived who avoided the searching of their hearts did not find themselves pleasantly or comfortably situated in Margaret's society. To her own family she was as frank as affectionate. She told me that I was selfish in the then state of my development; but she hoped and believed that bye and bye I should attain true disinterestedness. This reproach struck me with surprise; I did not think of being indignant at what she said. I endeavored to try my heart; but I found it hard to realize that the criticism was just. I have since acknowledged it to be so.

Margaret herself had indeed a disinterestedness which indeed made real the greatness of her character. When she was in Europe a person here whom I considered as troublesome and who had no claims upon her precious time wished me to request her to select some engravings for him. I communicated the message, at the same time writing that I hoped she would not trouble herself about it. In her answer she gently reproved me for want of interest in this person's project, and reminded me that "mankind is one." This maxim was her watchword and formed the key to her life. The grand interests of mankind were the theme of her constant study and thought. She was intimate with current events, made herself familiar with her own and past times and sought out the laws of man's development as a social being. She was an ardent patriot, and often sought to rouse me to a just appreciation of my privileges in this free, expansive country and my corresponding duties. But no narrower tie than universal brotherhood could limit her interest in the welfare of her race. There was and still is a band of generous hearts fired with the same noble sentiment. I cannot tell whether this common flame has been communicated from one to the other, or fallen like the fire of Pentecost directly from heaven. Dr. Channing's nobleness of devotion not only to the first and great commandment but to the second, which is like it, has seemed to me so strictly akin to hers that I cannot tell how much he may have influenced her. She often spoke of him. In his college life he had resided on Dana Hill, which was traversed by Ellery street, and Margaret pointed out to me the spot where in retirement "the great doctor," as she called him, had first settled in his mind that view of the noble capacity and possible destiny of every individual man which afterward prompted the efforts of his useful life. I had many pleasant walks with Margaret in Cambridge. A grove on the river side, where the Cambridge cemetery is now located, was a favorite resort with us. Here I shared the sisterly confidence of one who I knew was bound to the whole human family with that same kindred feeling and tender benevolence which rendered her useful to me. On this account regarding her as everybody's sister I have spoken of her here more warmly and fully than might otherwise have been prudent. What I say, however, can do very little justice to her merits. I have met no one in life who had her inspiring influence on me and on others. I do not expect the like again in the narrow and conventional limits of our social state.

With regard to Margaret's personal appearance I did not share the opinion which has been occasionally expressed, and which she herself intimated. Personal beauty had indeed been assigned to Ellen as more particularly her earthly gift. But so far as the form of the head, the face, and the eye speak the mould of the mind, Margaret, I thought, had a classic dignity and grace. Her head in particular was most symmetrically proportioned, and of the fair oval which expresses a balanced mind and heart. The language in her large eye, and the soul which animated her glance, were perhaps too dazzling for a common admiration, but I regarded them as proudly expressive of a might which seldom falls to the lot of woman.

Boy as I was, Margaret thought a good deal of my judgment in practical affairs. I smile to recall a difficulty which she had, in leaving Jamaica Plain, as to disposing of the furniture, and which I told her I would clear away. "Ah," she exclaimed, "if you can adjust this I shall always consult you in practical affairs!" I solved the difficulty, and she really did afterwards resort to me for advice. . . .

Richard F[rederick]. Fuller, *Recollections of Richard F. Fuller* (Boston: Privately printed, 1936), 30, 63–68, which incorporates material from his "The Younger Generation in 1840 from the Diary of a New England Boy," *Atlantic Monthly* 136 (August 1925): 222–24.

[Reminiscences of Margaret Fuller] (1974)

CAROLINE HEALEY DALL

When she was preparing *Margaret and Her Friends* (1895), Dall brought together a number of her journal entries on Fuller, to which she often added later reflections on their accuracy. In a sense, this is Dall's only attempt at a "biography" of the woman who influenced her so much. Indeed, when Dall published her *Transcendentalism in New England* in 1897, she concluded by saying, "I do not think I am mistaken in saying that what is meant by New England Transcendentalism perished with Margaret Fuller" (38).

[7 AUGUST 1859] . . . I knew Margaret only three years and *not* intimately as *she* would have said. But I was a close observer, and beside being a positive clairvoyante at moments, I was a keener judge than those who knew her better, because I was wholly independent of her personal magnetism. This was from the time that I was fifteen until I was eighteen, when she was a woman of from 28 to 31. Margaret did not like me, indeed my presence at her conversations irritated her, and my "clairvoyance," told me, at one time, that she was on the point of asking me to leave the class. Whether she ever spoke of this intention I do not know. Had I been her "guest," I would have put her out of pain, but I had paid a certain number of hard dollars for my place in it, and valued it too much as a means of culture, to give it up. If this was ungenerous, it was the only ungenerous movement of mine towards her, and if magnanimity were in my case a personal and not a constitutional trait, I should take some credit to myself for the love and honor I bear to Margaret. It has little to do with me. I was born "fully armed" in this respect!

I was disgusted and pained to see how men of ability bowed before her. Margaret and Theodore Parker alike required a sort of personal submission before new-comers could be admitted to a cordial understanding. I have always wondered that Theodore endured me in those early days. Margaret was true to the law of her being. *She* could not love that "upstart child." Yet I was neither an "upstart" or a "child," nor was it because I was self-conceited, because I set *any* value, *undue* or otherwise, on my mental or moral characteristics, that I would not bow.

In Shakspeare himself, I should have resented any *assumption* of superiority, but gladly would I have knelt to the humblest human creature in whom I perceived it. Many a pure-hearted child has bent the knee, that only stiffened before Margaret. And this, not because I was not willing to recognise her nobleness, but because I felt that the worthiest crown, we could either of us inherit, it depended on our own wills to wear. Before I could honor *her* above myself, she must have relinquished the love of power for its own sake, have stretched out generous sustaining tendrils to the feeble soul, have broken up her court, and entered into "society." If there was any thing in my natural temper, which sympathised with her faults, I only felt on that account, how necessary it was, that she should put them "under her heel." I honored her nobleness too much to yield to her folly.

I kept a close record of the "Conversations"—as I read them over after the lapse of nearly twenty years, I can fully forgive Margaret's irritation at the tone I kept. She saw nothing but my youth; would have believed nothing of my inner life, had I confessed it to her.

Often in my "clairvoyance" the sad oppressive gift, which it was God's will that I should have, I foresaw the words that she was about to utter, and might by taking them out of her mouth, have vexed her, and surprised others. I was never for a moment tempted to do this, and perhaps the fact that this sense of honor has never forsaken me, may explain how I have kept the secret of my "sensitiveness" and gone through life without suspicion. Once, I remember, just after Bode's Book on the Orphic Hymns came out, I quoted it in one of our talks. There were but two copies in America, Theodore Parker's and one which Everett had lent to Prof. Felton. I had seen Felton's copy, and had read the proofs of an article upon it, which came out afterward in the North American [Review].

After the conversation closed, she crossed the room, imperiously and tapping her foot hastily, asked;

"How did *you* come to get at such a thing as that first?"

She made some further enquiries rapidly, as if to confuse me, and show me, if not others, my own emptiness.

I was quite serene. Quietly watching her, I told her all I knew, that I had looked over the book with reference to this conversation, but had not read it, and probably should not.

She went away with a puzzled air, and I sighed, for if she had but looked into my heart, she would have found there a warmly glowing love.

To Margaret's estimate of me, to my self-assertion in her presence, I owe much of the misunderstanding and superficial condemnation which has made my public life, unnecessarily painful and severe. People whom I loved and honored, whom I would gladly have made my friends, saw the manner in which I met Margaret and were repelled by it.

They thought me self-conceited, when I obeyed an instinct of self *possession,* for I was never yet so enamored of any, as to lose my own centre—yet I have known what it was to love. I would gladly have had the love of these persons in this world, but I felt sure of being understood by them in another. I can see now, that there was a sort of rebuke, to older and wiser persons, in that cool manner, which hurt them, and made them unbelieving.

Yet I was never skeptical of *her* as Emerson was. I questioned nothing except *her* "divine right to rule." Learning and Genius might have ruled *through* her, and welcome, but every body knows, something else happened.

She was the least impressible person, I ever saw. Had it been otherwise, she must at times, have understood me. We generally *feel* the "virtue that goes out" of us, to use the scripture phrase, but I must have been deceived as to her *utter* insensibility. Much as I was conscious that I annoyed her, I supposed myself utterly without consequence in her eyes. I did not imagine she ever thought of me, except when I spoke, and that was very seldom. Since her death, however I have heard, yet not believed that she reproached Elizabeth Peabody several times for inviting me, to join the class, and to another friend, she spoke with a good deal of irritation about my presence.

I have often wished that she had written me a note asking me to stay away. I am sure she would have valued the reply I could have made, as much as any compliment she ever received, and her magnanimity would have profited by the occasion.

No direct insult to myself, could ever have vexed me, but her rude manner to persons much older, to Ida Russell's mother for instance, *kept* me, where I originally stood.

Margaret was at times, beautifully tender and considerate, but it was from the "height of her queenliness" that she was so. Her "possibilities" enthralled me, but never her actual self. Men would never have bowed to one of their own sex, however able, as they did to her. It was every way unfit.

My relation to Elizabeth Peabody, at this time was very singular. I saw a great deal of her, read portions of her Journal, and whenever she had any little bit of prose or poetry that was precious was sure to hear of it. Very long conversations, have I held with her, letting her run on for hours, with affectionate dogmatism, while I watched the play of her mind, delighted myself with its sparkle, and refreshed myself with its flow. As she felt inwardly that she had vexed Margaret, through her intended kindness to me, she felt bound to give me an occasional schooling.

And so she did! but of a sort very different from what the loving soul intended. Never once, was I tempted to speak to her freely of my thoughts and purposes, of my inmost being. Reserved myself, I dreaded her loquacity. The purpose will surely fail, which is prattled over, be it never so privately. But to *my* mind, hers presented an endless panorama of action and incident.

I have watched the rapids above Lake Erie, and the opening of the Gulf of the St Lawrence, with precisely the same feeling. Her benevolence was too aggressive for me to trust to it. She never began to lay plans for me, but I drew back;—feeling all the time that she was enthroned in her wide loving sympathy, far more securely than Margaret, in her exclusive individuality. Yet we could not have lived together, without a speedy difference that the world would have called, a quarrel. When she saw my judgment hold itself steady, without ever leaning toward hers, she called me pertinacious, while on the other hand, I was obliged to hold the helm, with all my strength, to escape the Maelströmn of her affectionate mistakes. To be loved as Elizabeth Peabody could love, by a person with an intellect like Margaret's would be a happiness this life will hardly offer.

Once Elizabeth asked me to put on spectacles. "It is because you are near-sighted that you make so many mistakes" said she "if you had only seen Emerson look at you, last night, I am sure you would never have said some things you did."

I could not help smiling inwardly. I had felt through eyes that never made mistakes, the full measure of Emerson's contempt, the night before, but I had not felt humiliated by it. I had asked a question which ought to have been inoffensive. He had a right to think it silly, but he had *no* right to feel as he did towards me, in consequence.

I hardly knew how to answer Elizabeth but at length I said;—"If I thought that putting on glasses, would give me any keener consciousness, of the estimate in which others hold me, I should refuse to do it, for that reason alone; I am already too sensitive in that way."

She looked so puzzled that I hastened to relieve her by adding:—"that it was useless to talk about it, for I suffered from a disease of the optic nerve, and blindness would be the probable result of their use!"

Another time I carried Margaret an exquisite bunch of flowers. I felt that I had annoyed her, and wished her to understand by my flowers, that I had not done so intentionally. Flowers were very costly twenty years ago. I do not know how Margaret received my flowers, but I am confident that she did not see what I meant. Her vivid imagination always refused to read their *natural* language. For her they spoke an idiom of which I had no notion.

Perhaps she *mis*understood them and me, for Elizabeth said the next day:—"You should not have given Margaret those flowers."—and in the next breath—"They were very magnificent, where did you get them?"

This question I did not answer. I had taken so much pains about them, that I was ashamed to confess it!

No bouquet ever cost me so much of time and money, if I except that I sent Sophia Hawthorne, the morning she was married.

It seems to me, that Theodore Parker hates Margaret, and I never can understand why, unless it be that in their *faults,* they resemble each other. Yet this is a strange solution of the feeling. I feel tenderly toward others when I see them victims to the same tyrant as myself, and from my knowledge of my own heart, am led to be generous in judging others, who seem to err from the same temptations. This, and not an intense subtle antagonism like theirs would seem to be the natural result of a moral or rather of an *im*moral sympathy!

Once, nine or ten years ago, I was complaining to Theodore, that I had not been able to perfect my copy of the Dial, that after endless seeking, I had been forced to bind up one volume incomplete.

"What was in the missing number?" he asked, but I did not remember.

"It was probably my essay on the Pharisees" he continued. "It had the largest sale of any single paper, and made a great stir, but you need not regret the loss, for you have that in another form, and there was *nothing else* (!) in that number."

This remark followed a very harsh criticism on Margaret, yet how Margaret-tish, it was! yet if Margaret had said the same thing, she would have tempered it by a half deprecating laugh, as if conscious of the audacity.

[198]

I should not have objected to the first half of the statement for I dare say, it was true, and the man who cannot see and tell, if need be, a simple truth about himself, as well as another, is either a coward or a hypocrite, but that "nothing else" was the cloven foot itself.

"Elizabeth Peabody cannot speak the truth if she tries," was his assertion one evening, which I translated—"She has sometime said something untrue about T. P. or one of his friends."

Theodore sent me a note, when he went away, in which he claims to appreciate the final scope and inner purpose of my life.

I thanked him for the note, but he was mistaken in thinking he had any notion of my life. My purposes are not scattered on the surface, like sea shore pebbles, to be gathered by every idle wanderer's hand. He never attended to me long enough at any one time in his life, to begin to understand me, yet he loved me, and treated me like an equal, which Margaret never did. I don't mean he ever *neglected* or wounded me. I have not the shadow of such a thought or feeling. I have only one friend, who ever took the pains which such an understanding of me would involve, and he thank Heavens! is no New Englander,—with caution on the one side of him, and acquisitiveness on the other. . . .

[21 August 1895] Yesterday I passed an hour with Mrs Spalding and she told me two new and interesting anecdotes of Margaret.

1. She said that Wm. C. Todd, who is recovering from a very severe illness, had lately made her a visit. He told her that when Margaret was about 14, he went out to Cambridge to discuss some matter of importance with her father. Margaret sat apart apparently occupied with a book open on her knee. At some moment, Mr Fuller said "Margaret what have you to say about this?" She lifted her eyes for a moment and gave him an answer, good, full of common sense, but such as many people might have given. "Is that the best that you can say?" returned her father. She started, laid down her book, and instantly recast her thought, giving the same idea but a most eloquent statement! Mr Todd was much impressed. He wondered at the marvellous training which had made the re-cast of thought possible, but the training would have effected nothing, if our Margaret had not been there.

2. Mrs [Horace] Greeley invited Mrs Spalding who was then Miss Tappan, to spend the winter with her while Margaret was there. Something prevented, but the next winter she went, Margaret had gone. One day, the old Irish cook came to her and said, "Miss Tappan did you ever see Miss

Fuller?" "No," answered Mrs Spalding. "Didn't you ever hear her talk?" "No." "Well, I pity ye, for she did talk most beautiful!" . . .

[November 1895] In revising my Journal for 1840 and 41, that nothing unsuitable might be preserved concerning the sad, sad years distinguished by my mother's mental alienation and consequent irritability and distrust;—when by carrying her cares, I could not pursue my own culture, nor satisfy my father's demands, I have found comments on my intercourse with Margaret Fuller and Elisabeth Peabody, part of which I should have been glad to add to the Preface of "Margaret and her Friends." I will put them here.

Mar 1, 1841. I met with Miss Fuller's class this evening at Mr Ripley's, and although I understand it was not a fair specimen of her power, I was delighted. I think I never enjoyed an evening so much. Mrs Ripley pleases me greatly, she has not forgotten the claims of her body in cultivating her mind. Of Miss Fuller, I have not yet formed an opinion. There was a want of coherence in her talk and a want of grammar, which last is a great trial to my ear. I did not come away as I expected to do, feeling that it would be forever impossible for me to accomplish as much as Miss Fuller. I found her more agreeable and more modest than I had been told. She talked exquisitely but like a woman.

Mar 8, 1841. Miss Fuller is lively and sarcastic in general conversation. She is of under size, delicately formed with rather sharp features and light hair. Her head is small, but thrown almost wholly in front of the ears. Her forehead is of good height. Her nose inclines to the Roman, and her mouth is thin and ungraceful. Her eyes are small and grey. But their flash is vivid and her laugh is almost childlike. Her manners are reserved, but those of one who has seen good society. We found it very difficult to appreciate Greek beauty in a Greek way,—sufficient proof Miss Fuller thought that no Greek genius could thrive in our time. "Let us suppose a man ever so gigantic, he must stand upon a pedestal of Boston instead of Athens, and seem a pigmy in comparison."

Mar 19, 1841. Miss Fuller was out of the vein tonight. The meeting has been put off because she has been unwell. Although we had Mr Hedge, talk was not as pleasant as usual. . . .

Mar 22, 1841. E. P. P. lent me her Journal, and her reports of Margaret's talks. The last are far better than mine, but not so exact. I am so new to the whole matter that I dare give nothing but the very words of the speakers, while she is so familiar with the subject and the talkers, that she follows the train of thought for each, but perhaps not always successfully. . . .

April 3, 1841. . . . Miss Fuller very bright tonight, thinks we cannot exhaust our subject in six talks as seems to have been proposed. She means to give 12. . . .

April 29, 1841. Enjoyed myself very much, although this was not a very profitable meeting. Miss Peabody told Margaret that Alexander Everett had come to her own reception the night before on purpose to meet Miss Fuller. Margaret said with characteristic emphasis that to him, she was no "*new show*." Elizabeth said she was glad to hear it, she had been afraid that he came from curiosity alone! Miss Fuller replied that he must recently have seen her mother in New Orleans, and had probably something to tell her on that account. "Perhaps" she added playfully, "he only came to ask after the Life of Göethe. He delivered an oration some years ago, of which he sent me a copy. In it he spoke of the fair authoress who was engaged in translating the work. I never thanked him by word or deed and it has lain upon my conscience ever since."

She spoke of the heliotrope as her favorite flower. . . .

May 6, 1841. Our last meeting. I succeeded in getting a beautiful bouquet for Margaret, but was not satisfied as I could find only two or three bits of her favorite flower. I was very sad, for I have no hope of living till another winter, and if I do, she may not. Never have I enjoyed anything as much as this "class."

Note 1895—Margaret took these flowers coldly, to my surprise, for I thought she would smile on them if not on me. It was of this costly treasure, for which I sacrificed many small pleasures, that E. P. P. said "it was impertinent for me to offer it." . . .

Portsmouth N. H. Friday Sept 18, 1846. Read . . . from papers on "Literature and Art" by S. M. Fuller, which I think are written with a great deal of discrimination and strength. What she says of Mad. de Staël, however is true of herself. She can discourse but she cannot converse, at least, she discourses best. To converse, a person must appreciate the minds of others, and so draw them out, and make use of them and send them away proud and happy. I do not think Margaret has an uncommon tact at doing this, but I have seen her do it in the best way. Her flow of language and power of association is very great. By the last I mean the capacity to perceive, recall and associate far divergent links, in the chain of thought. . . .

Boston. Feb. 1, 1865. I spent this day with Dr Hedge, talking over theological matters. He told me an anecdote of Margaret which I had never heard. He said no one not even Carlyle talked as well as she did. She was only thirteen when he first saw her and he was simply astonished. Afterward he became very intimate with her. She was at that time very corpulent, and greatly disgusted at it, and began to lace very tightly. Once when she was staying with them Mrs Hedge was obliged to call a stout Irishwoman from the kitchen to fasten Margaret's dress, it was so tight. No evil results were apparent while Margaret remained in this country but Dr Hedge said he could never forget the shock he received when he first saw her in Rome. A spinal disease had developed, and she looked like a humpback. She was married but he did not know it. When they parted, she seemed struggling with some pent-up secret. At last she threw her arms around his neck and burst into tears. A note followed him, in which she said she often thought she should not live to return. If *not* he must write a good verse to put on her tomb-stone. Dr Hedge said he would give 100$ for that note now, but it was with some letters that he wrote Clarke at the time the "Life" was written, and it was lost.

What did Hedge mean, by saying that this horrible habit showed no results. Her head aches, side aches, indigestions and irritability may all be traced to it. Why did not her father and mother find it out? It is very possible that Hedge saw her before the birth of her child in Rome and therefore has misunderstood a stoop that she assumed. No one else ever heard of the "hump."

From Joel Myerson, "Caroline Dall's Reminiscences of Margaret Fuller," *Harvard Library Bulletin* 22 (October 1974): 414–28.

Permissions

Interview with Caroline Dall on 27 April 1910, by Edith Fuller, Ms Am 1086, Box A, used by permission of the Houghton Library, Harvard University.

Joel Myerson, "Bronson Alcott's 'Journal for 1836,'" in *Studies in the American Renaissance 1978,* ed. Myerson (Boston: Twayne, 1978). Reprinted by permission of the editor.

Larry A. Carlson, "Bronson Alcott's 'Journal for 1837' (Part One)," in S*tudies in the American Renaissance 1981,* ed. Joel Myerson (Boston: Twayne, 1981). Reprinted by permission of the editor.

Larry A. Carlson, "Bronson Alcott's 'Journal for 1838' (Parts One–Two)," in *Studies in the American Renaissance 1993–94,* ed. Joel Myerson (Charlottesville: University Press of Virginia, 1993–1994). Reprinted by permission of the editor.

The Selected Letters of Lidian Jackson Emerson, ed. Delores Bird Carpenter (Columbia: University of Missouri Press, 1987), used by permission of the Ralph Waldo Emerson Memorial Association.

Daniel Shealy, "Margaret Fuller and Her 'Maiden': Evelina Metcalf's 1838 School Journal," in *Studies in the American Renaissance 1996,* ed. Joel Myerson (Charlottesville: University Press of Virginia, 1996). Reprinted by permission of the editor.

Frank Shuffelton, "Margaret Fuller at the Greene Street School: The Journal of Evelina Metcalf," in *Studies in the American Renaissance 1985,* ed. Joel Myerson (Charlottesville: University Press of Virginia, 1985). Reprinted by permission of the editor.

Laraine R. Fergenson, "Margaret Fuller as a Teacher in Providence: The School Journal of Ann Brown," in *Studies in the American Renaissance 1991,* ed. Joel Myerson (Charlottesville: University Press of Virginia, 1991). Reprinted by permission of the editor.

Edward A. Hoyt and Loriman S. Brigham, "Glimpses of Margaret Fuller: The Green Street School and Florence," *New England Quarterly* 29 (March 1956): 87–98. Reprinted by permission of the New England Quarterly, Inc., and the MIT Press.

Nancy Craig Simmons, "Margaret Fuller's Boston Conversations: The 1839–1840 Series," in *Studies in the American Renaissance 1994,* ed. Joel Myerson (Charlottesville: University Press of Virginia, 1994). Reprinted by permission of the editor.

Elizabeth Maxfield-Miller, "Elizabeth of Concord: Selected Letters of Elizabeth Sherman Hoar (1814–1878) to the Emersons, Family, and the Emerson Circle (Parts Two–Three)," in *Studies in the American Renaissance 1985–1986,* ed. Joel Myerson (Charlottesville: University Press of Virginia, 1985–1986). Reprinted by permission of the editor.

Nathaniel Hawthorne, *The Letters, 1813–1843,* ed. Thomas Woodson et al. (Columbus: Ohio State University Press, 1984). Reprinted by permission of the Ohio State University Press.

Nathaniel Hawthorne, *The American Notebooks,* ed. Claude M. Simpson (Columbus: Ohio State University Press, 1972). Reprinted by permission of the Ohio State University Press.

"Journals of Theodore Parker: July–December 1840," bMS 101. Reprinted by permission of the Andover-Harvard Theological Library, Harvard Divinity School, Harvard University.

Thomas Carlyle, *The Correspondence of Emerson and Carlyle,* ed. Joseph Slater (New York: Columbia University Press, 1964). Reprinted by permission of the Ralph Waldo Emerson Memorial Association.

Emelyn Story, "The Private Marriage," Ms Am 1450 (178). Printed courtesy of the Trustees of the Boston Public Library/Rare Books and Manuscripts Department.

The Selected Letters of Mary Moody Emerson, ed. Nancy Craig Simmons (Athens: University of Georgia Press, 1993). Reprinted by permission of the Ralph Waldo Emerson Memorial Association.

Francis B. Dedmond, "The Selected Letters of William Ellery Channing the Younger (Part Two)," in *Studies in the American Renaissance 1990,* ed. Joel Myerson (Charlottesville: University Press of Virginia, 1990). Reprinted by permission of the editor.

Selected Journals of Caroline Healey Dall, Volume I: 1838–1855, ed. Helen R. Deese (Boston: Massachusetts Historical Society, 2006). Reprinted by permission of the Massachusetts Historical Society.

Caroline Dall to T. W. Higginson (copy), 29 May 1908, Ms Am 1086, Box A. Reprinted by permission of the Houghton Library, Harvard University.

George William Curtis to Daniel Ricketson, 23 April 1856, bMS Am 1124 (110). Reprinted by permission of the Houghton Library, Harvard University.

Amos Bronson Alcott, "Journal for 1870," MS Am 1130.12 (40). Reprinted by permission of the Houghton Library, Harvard University.

Sarah Freeman Clarke, "Letters of a Sister," galley proof, bMS Am 1569.3 (12). Reprinted by permission of the Houghton Library, Harvard University.

Nathaniel Hawthorne, *The French and Italian Notebooks,* ed. Thomas Woodson (Columbus: Ohio State University Press, 1980). Reprinted by permission of the Ohio State University Press.

Joel Myerson, "Caroline Dall's Reminiscences of Margaret Fuller," *Harvard Library Bulletin* 22 (October 1974): 414–28. Reprinted by permission of the President and Fellows of Harvard College.

Works Cited

Berg, Martha L., and Alice de V. Perry. "'The Impulses of Human Nature': Margaret Fuller's Journal from June through October 1844." *Proceedings of the Massachusetts Historical Society* 102 (1990): 38–126.

Bolster, Arthur S., Jr. *James Freeman Clarke: Disciple to Advancing Truth.* Boston: Beacon Press, 1954.

Brockway, Beman. *Fifty Years in Journalism.* Watertown, NY: Daily Times Printing and Publishing, 1891.

Capper, Charles. *Margaret Fuller: An American Romantic Life.* Vol. 1, *The Private Years.* Vol. 2, *The Public Years.* New York: Oxford University Press, 1992, 2007.

Carlyle, Thomas. *The Collected Letters to Thomas and Jane Welsh Carlyle.* Edited by Clyde de L. Ryals and Kenneth J. Fielding. 33 vols. to date. Durham: Duke University Press, 1970– .

———. *New Letters of Thomas Carlyle.* Edited by Alexander Carlyle. 2 vols. London: John Lane, 1904.

Channing, William Henry, James Freeman Clarke, and Ralph Waldo Emerson, eds. *Memoirs of Margaret Fuller Ossoli.* 2 vols. Boston: Phillips, Sampson, 1852.

Clarke, James Freeman. *Autobiography, Diary and Correspondence.* Edited by Edward Everett Hale. Boston: Houghton, Mifflin, 1891.

———. *The Letters of James Freeman Clarke to Margaret Fuller.* Edited by John Wesley Thomas. Hamburg, Germany: Cram, de Gruyter, 1957.

Clarke, Sarah Freeman. "Letters of a Sister." Galley proofs, Houghton Library, Harvard University.

Dall, Caroline Healey. *Margaret and Her Friends.* Boston: Roberts Brothers, 1895.

———. *Selected Journals of Caroline Healey Dall, Volume I: 1838–1855.* Edited by Helen R. Deese. Boston: Massachusetts Historical Society, 2006.

———. *Transcendentalism in New England.* Boston: Roberts Brothers, 1897.

Emerson, Ralph Waldo. *The Journals and Miscellaneous Notebooks of Ralph*

Waldo Emerson. Edited by William H. Gilman, Ralph H. Orth, et al. 16 vols. Cambridge: Harvard University Press, 1960–1982.

———. *The Letters of Ralph Waldo Emerson*. Edited by Ralph L. Rusk and Eleanor M. Tilton. 10 vols. New York: Columbia University Press, 1939, 1990–1995.

Frothingham, Octavius Brooks. *Memoir of William Henry Channing*. Boston: Houghton, Mifflin, 1886.

Fuller, Margaret. *The Letters of Margaret Fuller*. Edited by Robert N. Hudspeth. 6 vols. Ithaca, NY: Cornell University Press, 1983–1994.

———. *Papers on Literature and Art*. 2 vols. New York: Wiley and Putnam, 1846.

———. *"These Sad But Glorious Days": Dispatches from Europe, 1846–1850*. Edited by Larry J. Reynolds and Susan Belasco Smith. New Haven: Yale University Press, 1992.

Grodzins, Dean. *American Heretic: Theodore Parker and Transcendentalism*. Chapel Hill: University of North Carolina Press, 2002.

Hawthorne, Julian. "Hawthorne and Margaret Fuller." *Boston Daily Evening Transcript*, 2 January 1885, 4.

———. "Mr. Hawthorne and His Critics." *Boston Daily Evening Transcript*, 5 February 1885, 4.

———. *Nathaniel Hawthorne and His Wife*. 2 vols. Boston: Houghton, Mifflin, 1884.

Hawthorne, Nathaniel. *The American Notebooks*. Edited by Claude M. Simpson. Columbus: Ohio State University Press, 1972.

Higginson, Thomas Wentworth. *Letters and Journals of Thomas Wentworth Higginson*. Edited by Mary Thacher Higginson. Boston: Houghton, Mifflin, 1921.

———. *Margaret Fuller Ossoli*. Boston: Houghton, Mifflin, 1884.

Howe, Julia Ward. *Reminiscences 1819–1899*. Boston: Houghton, Mifflin, 1899.

Jewsbury, Geraldine Endsor. *Selections from the Letters of Geraldine Endsor Jewsbury to Jane Welsh Carlyle*. Edited by Mrs. Alexander Ireland. London: Longmans, Green, 1892.

Linton, W. J. "The Italian Gratuitous School." *People's Journal* 2 (4 July 1846): 147–48.

Martineau, Harriet. *Harriet Martineau's Letters to Fanny Wedgwood*. Edited by Elisabeth Sanders Arbuckle. Stanford, CA: Stanford University Press, 1983.

Miller, John Carl, ed. *Poe's Helen Remembers*. Charlottesville: University Press of Virginia, 1979.

Myerson, Joel. "Margaret Fuller's 1842 Journal: At Concord with the Emersons." *Harvard Library Bulletin* 21 (July 1973): 320–40.

———. "Mrs. Dall Edits Miss Fuller: The Story of *Margaret and Her Friends.*" *Papers of the Bibliographical Society of America* 72 (2d Quarter 1978): 187–200.

[Putnam, George Palmer]. "Foreign Correspondence." *Literary World* 2 (18 September 1847): 155–56.

Thomas, Dwight, and David K. Jackson. *The Poe Log.* Boston: G. K. Hall, 1987.

Wiggin, Kate Douglas. *My Garden of Memory.* Boston: Houghton, Mifflin, 1923.

Yannella, Donald, and Kathleen Malone Yannella. "Evert A. Duyckinck's 'Diary: May 29–November 8, 1847.'" In *Studies in the American Renaissance 1978,* edited by Joel Myerson, 207–58. Boston: Twayne Publishers, 1978.

Index

WRITERS IN THEIR OWN TIME

Alcott in Her Own Time
Edited by Daniel Shealy

Emerson in His Own Time
Edited by Ronald A. Bosco and Joel Myerson

Fuller in Her Own Time
Edited by Joel Myerson

Hawthorne in His Own Time
Edited by Ronald A. Bosco and Jillmarie Murphy

Whitman in His Own Time
Edited by Joel Myerson